The Bruce Lee Library

Bruce Lee's Commentaries on
the Martial Way

Jeet Kune Do

Compiled and Edited by **John Little**

TUTTLE PUBLISHING
Tokyo • Rutland, Vermont • Singapore

The family of Bruce Lee wishes to acknowledge:

The dedication of John Little, whose passion for the art and philosophy of Bruce Lee has inspired this publication, and who has spent countless hours researching, studying, annotating, and organizing Bruce Lee's prolific writings, photos, memorabilia and gathering the recollections of friends and students.

And, Adrien Marshall, attorney for the estate of Bruce Lee for nearly thirty years, who, with caring attention to the best interests of his friend, Bruce Lee, has been instrumental in the publication of this series.

All photos appearing in this book are courtesy of the archive of Linda Lee Cadwell, the Estate of Bruce Lee, and Warner Brothers Films.

Published by Tuttle Publishing, an imprint of Periplus Editions (HK) Ltd., with editorial offices at 364 Innovation Drive, North Clarendon, Vermont 05759 U.S.A.

Library of Congress Catalog Card Number: 97061948

ISBN 978-0-8048-3132-1

Distributed by:

North America, Latin America & Europe
Tuttle Publishing
364 Innovation Drive
North Clarendon, VT. 05759-9436 U.S.A.
Tel: 1 (802) 773-8930
Fax: 1 (802) 773-6993
info@tuttlepublishing.com
www.tuttlepublishing.com

Japan
Tuttle Publishing
Yaekari Building, 3rd Floor
5-4-12 Osaki
Shinagawa-ku
Tokyo 141 0032
Tel: (81) 03 5437-0171
Fax: (81) 03 5437-0755
tuttle-sales@gol.com

Asia Pacific
Berkeley Books Pte. Ltd.
61 Tai Seng Avenue #02-12
Singapore 534167
Tel: (65) 6280-1330
Fax: (65) 6280-6290
inquiries@periplus.com.sg
www.periplus.com

Indonesia
PT Java Books Indonesia
Kawasan Industri Pulogadung
JI. Rawa Gelam IV No. 9
Jakarta 13930
Tel: (62) 21 4682-1088
Fax: (62) 20 461-0207
cs@javabooks.co.id

13 12 11 10 09   20 19 18 17 16
Text design—Vernon Press, Inc.
Cover design—Horuga Yakobusu
Printed in the United States of America

TUTTLE PUBLISHING® is a registered trademark of Tuttle Publishing, a division of Periplus Editions (HK) Ltd.

Martial art has a very, very deep meaning as far as my life is concerned because, as an actor, as a martial artist, as a human being, all these I have learned from martial art.
—Bruce Lee

This book is dedicated to every martial artist who has an inquiring, rational, and compassionate mind; to every person who can throw off the chains of comfortable habit and unwarranted assumption and move in a new direction that is guided by reason and observational evidence, no matter where that direction may lead; and to every person who tries a thing and immediately thinks How can I make this better?

By both word and deed, Bruce Lee taught us that a true "champion" is seldom—if ever—one who wins a tournament, but rather one who is able to look at people and not see members of a particular sect or nationality, but human beings; one who is unafraid to challenge the false beliefs of the herd; and one who has the additional courage necessary to lead others out of the caves into the light. It is to these "champions of the human spirit" and those still to come that we owe our enormous gratitude.

Contents

PART 4: THE TOOLS OF COMBAT—PART TWO: THE LOWER LIMBS

PART 5: ON TRAINING IN JEET KUNE DO

PART 6: BEYOND SYSTEM—THE ULTIMATE SOURCE OF JEET KUNE DO

Proceed with Caution!

By Linda Lee Cadwell

"Boy! This is it!" Bruce would frequently exclaim as he sat at his desk or propped up in bed, writing his descriptions of the absolute fighting system. "When I have finished writing down everything that goes into my Way of gung fu, that will be it!"

The story of how Bruce Lee came to transcribe the notes that appear in this volume is a testament to his intelligence and determination, to his powers of observation and irrepressible positive nature. Bruce wrote most of his *Commentaries on the Martial Way* after he sustained a severe back injury from improper weight training in 1970. The medical tests showed damage to the fourth sacral nerve and the doctor cautioned Bruce to forgo his martial arts training because the force of kicks and punches could cause further injury. Total rest was prescribed with the hope that Bruce would recuperate sufficiently to lead a "normal" lifestyle, not the active lifestyle of a martial artist. Bruce was disheartened, to say the least.

After a few days' confinement to bed, Bruce decided how he was going to turn this stumbling block into a stepping stone. If he could not physically train in his martial art, then he would *mentally* practice it. He asked me to go to a stationery store and buy several large, black, expandable binders. He filled each one with blank paper and jotted on the dividers notes of topics he intended to cover. For the next six months, Bruce exercised only his mind.

It was, however, literally impossible for this perpetually active man to assume a sedentary way of life. Determined to prove the doctors wrong in their dire predictions, carefully and gradually, Bruce retrained himself physically, from walking with assistance to eventually performing his full range of martial art motions. From 1971 to 1973 he completed four and one-half physically demanding films, and we are left today with not only the celluloid record of his determination, but with volumes of his journal-writing exercises compiled in his down-time.

With his time and attention increasingly turned to filmmaking, and then, with his early death at the age of thirty-two, Bruce's literary pursuits came to an end. But even before then, he was coming to the realization that attempting to encapsulate fighting in words was like trying to capture something on paper that is alive and constantly changing. He began to see that he was in danger of producing the exact opposite of what he was trying to describe: *By developing a formula for efficient combat he could solidify something that, by its very demand to be efficient, must remain fluid.*

Can something that flows like a river be turned into a river of concrete without losing its essential nature? This was Bruce's dilemma. This is the danger that Bruce perceived and the warning I feel I must issue before the reader embarks on the discoveries within these pages:

1. Memorizing and regurgitating Bruce Lee's words does not increase one's intelligence. However, *adapting his thoughts for one's own actions gives life to his words.*

2. One cannot learn to do martial art by reading the words in this book. However, *one's depth of understanding martial art can be enhanced.*

3. The notes within this volume should not be considered the bible of martial arts, *for there is no one way. There is only the way that works at a given moment in time.*

4. Do not think that this is it—the sum total of Bruce Lee's way of martial art. But, *do think of it as a set of clues to aid in your search for the voice of your own self-expression.*

5. Knowledge is not useful in a vacuum. However, *observing the practical application of knowledge on a moment-by-moment basis is to* experience *the essence of Bruce Lee's martial art.*

6. When you catch yourself quoting something that Bruce Lee said or wrote, *ask yourself if this has meaning for your life. Do you really* understand—*can you* apply—*what he meant?*

7. This is not a book about martial art. *This is a book, stripped of interpretation, that shows how a real human being thought. This is a book about savoring every moment. This is a book about living to the ripe, old age of thirty-two.*

For the reader who fails to heed these words of caution, I sincerely hope you enjoy reading the ideas about unarmed combat that were important to Bruce Lee. For the discriminating thinker, welcome to a world of insights that will change your life.

FOREWORD

By Ted Wong

It is tough to know how to begin this foreword. After all, how does one capsulize in a few brief paragraphs the magnitude of what was given to me by a man such as Bruce Lee? [He was my mentor, my sifu, my personal advisor, and, most importantly, my close friend.] He gave me confidence in myself, he taught me how to relate to other people, he taught me about life, the world, my place in it, the nature of relationships, health, fitness (both physical and mental), spirituality, and, of course, he gave hundreds of hours of his time teaching me his martial art of jeet kune do.

Simply acknowledging the magnitude of the debt I owe Bruce Lee makes me realize how one-sided our relationship was. He was the giver and I the willing recipient of his gifts. Yes, he obviously considered me more than simply a student and I was proud—extremely proud—to be considered his close friend. And though I learned much, if not all, that I know about martial art directly from Bruce Lee, having had the tremendous privilege of spending close to six years in private study with him, it is the post-workout conversations, the in-car discourses during drives to bookstores and to martial arts supply stores, the laughter we shared over dim sum in our favorite Chinese restaurants, the family get-togethers and just general day-to-day experiences with him that I count among my most precious and redeeming time spent with him. For it is in witnessing first-hand how a person leads their life that one gains insight into another person's character. And, based upon my observations (of which there were plenty), Bruce Lee's character was pure platinum.

If you were fortunate enough to be his friend, there was no one as loyal and devoted as Bruce Lee. If you were down, he'd be the first one to try to cheer you up; if you needed money and he had it, he'd give it to you; if you were up, he'd remember stories and jokes that would lift you up even higher. Many words come to mind when I think about Bruce, but the two that come to mind most frequently are "great company." I've never met a person who I've more enjoyed spending time with. Not only was it intellectually rewarding to spend time in his presence, it was an emotionally uplifting experience as well. My soul actually felt fortified at the end of a day spent with Bruce.

I was fortunate in being able to train and share life experiences with Bruce in Los Angeles, Oakland, and Hong Kong. I remember coming to visit him at this house in Bel Air after he had hurt his back in 1970 and he was forced to stay in bed for six months. However, during that time—and true to his philosophy of "turning a stumbling block into a stepping-stone"—Bruce didn't complain or lament this apparently cruel twist of fate. Instead, he began to write—and his writings filled volumes (seven of them, in fact). I marveled then (and again now that I think about it) how productive and artistic he was—even while injured. Lesser human beings would simply have given up, but then Bruce Lee was never a lesser human being. He was always a great human being; an inspiration and role model for not only individuals of Chinese ancestry such as myself, but for all individuals who value, as Bruce did, the potential of the human spirit for achievement and producing work of outstanding and enduring quality.

And while some of the combative beliefs, philosophy, and illustrations that Bruce committed to paper during this period of his convalescence became *The Tao of Jeet Kune Do*, (Ohara Publications, 1975), many of them did not. And it is these other writings that have filled this book, in combination with some incredible never-before-seen written and photographic material of Bruce's, that I believe have made this book, *Jeet Kune Do: Bruce Lee's Commentaries on the Martial Way*, the definitive presentation of Bruce Lee's way of martial art. Drawing from diverse and authentic source materials, with sections on combative techniques, training methodology, philosophy, motivational/inspirational beliefs, lesson plans, teaching/coaching strategies, as well as Bruce's own comments on the historical development of his art, this is a book that deserves to be read, re-read, studied, and poured over again and again not only by those who share a serious interest in the preservation and perpetuation of Bruce Lee's art of jeet kune do, but bt those who also seek to frame a more accurate picture of the true nature and character of Bruce Lee. This book accurately captures the essence of Bruce's personality and beliefs on such a wide range of subjects that it is the closest thing I've ever experienced to what it was actually like to train privately with Bruce Lee.

I'm delighted to note both the quantity and caliber of the material that has been gathered together in this book by my good friend and Bruce Lee historian, John Little. I met John back in 1993, and since then we have forged a close friendship with many training sessions and discussions together. We both share a common interest and goal in the art and philosophy of jeet kune do. With tireless energy, John has spent tremendous amounts of hours over the last four years of his life in putting together this book. He has made many personal sacrifices while enduring financial hardships. He has sifted through, read, and studied some six thousand pages of Bruce's notes and personal papers and has read, studied and interviewed many of Bruce's original students and friends with an eye toward finally putting together a multi-volume book series that will perfectly clarify Bruce Lee's "commentaries on the martial way."

I consider John Little to be one of the foremost individuals in terms of his knowledge of this subject matter, and his sincerity, respect, and loyalty for preserving and perpetuating Bruce's true teachings have given new insight into the art of jeet kune do. We are very fortunate to have John take up the task of editing Bruce's materials for future generations to learn about Bruce Lee and his art. More importantly, John wants to promote Bruce not just as a great martial artist, but also as a philosopher and a pointer of truth.

A huge debt of thanks is also owed Linda Lee Cadwell, Bruce's wife of nine years and the lady that Bruce once told me was "directly responsible" for his success. Linda has always remained loyal to Bruce and was not only the mother of their two children, Brandon and Shannon, but, in my opinion, she is also the spiritual mother of jeet kune do for, without her entering his life and being the yin to his yang, Bruce would have had to work a nine-to-five job and thereby been deprived of the time necessary to create such a beautiful art and to share it with the world.

Jeet kune do is a unique martial art in that it is the first martial art that is not based solely upon tradition. Granted, jeet kune do has specific and distinguishing techniques and a core curriculum that Bruce thought important enough to teach to all of his students. However, this is viewed more as a "launching pad" from which the individual practitioner initiates his own exciting journey of self-discovery and self-expression. In fact, to truly ascend to the higher aspects of this art, one really has to do it on one's own. What Bruce is offering us in the pages of this book and in the personal lessons he taught to those of us fortunate enough to have studied under him is a prescription for freedom—both in combat and in day-to-day life—and that prescription lies in the discovery that we already are free, we simply have to be willing to do the homework necessary to realize it.

When I hear people say "You shouldn't bother to train like Bruce Lee did, nor to follow his teachings, because you don't possess his attributes," I realize that they've missed the point as to what Bruce Lee was all about. He would frequently tell us that he wasn't anything "special," but rather that he was simply a very dedicated trainer. Bruce was so good because he made himself so good. He practiced all the time and then looked for ways to make his practicing even more efficient. If you only work out twenty minutes a day, or three days a week—I mean, if that's all you're willing to commit to your jeet kune do training—then, yes, it would be impossible for you to obtain attributes similar to Bruce's because he practiced long and hard for every inch of progress he made. Don't expect Bruce Lee–like results, unless you're willing to put in Bruce Lee–like hours to obtain them.

I know that the more I practice what Bruce taught me, the better I become at it—and the same is true for anybody who applies what they read in this book. I always looked up to Bruce Lee for his work ethic. And even now, if I find myself sitting around not wanting to train, my memory is jogged by an image of Bruce Lee, and how hard he worked, and I feel guilty for not having more faith in the potential of my ability.

Bruce always emphasized the need for us to experiment with what he was teaching us. Not experiment in the sense of a test-drive, wherein you try something out and if for some reason it "seems" like a bad fit, you discard it. Rather, Bruce wanted us to practice diligently on what he shared with us, not for hours or even days, but for years. He wanted us to practice on such things as the on-guard position, mobility or footwork, the lead punch, the cross, the hook, the finger jab, the side kick, the hook kick, and so on, until they became second-nature to us. This type of "experimentation" takes years, but it's well worth the time invested because you end up learning much about yourself and, by extension, you learn significant things about others as well. For one thing, you learn about the commonality we all share as human beings and how it is possible to achieve efficiency in things such as movement, force production, and combat. All you have to do is be willing to work at it.

This book is your road map to an exciting journey of self-knowledge. It has value in being a guidepost to help you in the process of your own personal development. And then, at the end of the journey, you can throw it away for you will have then learned the significance of one of Bruce's most significant statements:

> The medicine for my suffering I had within me from the very beginning.

Note: Ted Wong is considered one of the most knowledgeable men in the world regarding Bruce Lee's art of jeet kune do. Wong was Bruce Lee's private student from 1967 until Lee's death in 1973. Lee's daytimer diaries reveal that he and Wong got together on no less than 122 separate occasions. Wong received certification in jeet kune do directly from Bruce Lee himself.

PREFACE

Between the ages of twenty two and thirty two, martial arts legend Bruce Lee was a very prolific writer. To be sure, not all of his writings were in the form of essays or systematic presentations of themes and philosophical dissertations. However, it is worth observing that during this brief span of time, Lee wrote and self-published one book, prepared manuscripts for two additional books (that he later decided not to have published), authored several articles that were published on the theory and nature of unarmed combat, scripted no less than three screenplays, and penned seven volumes of writings containing his thoughts, ideas, opinions, and research into the science and art of unarmed combat. And then there were the notes! Whether on an airplane at 35,000 feet above the ground, in a car traveling down a bumpy dirt road in the Indian Desert, or in the privacy of his own study, when Lee wasn't training or reading, he was writing. And his mind was constantly active, triangulating new viewpoints on techniques, technique efficiency, and training methods to realize novel ways of improving each.

Lee also made extensive notes on Eastern philosophy and (believe it or not) Western psychotherapy (and the two disciplines are not so diverse as one might initially think), among other subjects. Bruce Lee held that "there is no such thing as an effective segment of a totality," and in keeping with this belief, he held that life itself was the totality, and all aspects of martial art, philosophy, physical fitness, nutritional science, reading, talking, teaching, learning, and so on, were simply facets that served to make up this totality. Further, from this viewpoint, Lee concluded that art was a bridge to higher learning; that is, the higher up the ladder of martial art mastery one climbed, the clearer the view became that art was simply a metaphor for life itself and that, as Blake once said, it was indeed possible to "see the world in a grain of sand," and for one who had truly mastered a martial art to be availed of a new and wonderful insight into the human condition. There were and are no opposites, only interconnected facets of the existence of which all of us are a part.

Lee once made the comment, "All knowledge ultimately means self-knowledge," and his writings reflect the depth of his search within. When he severely injured his lower back in 1970, the medical community made the conclusion that he would never be able to perform martial arts again. Lee, however, realized that with the correct application of his will he would not only be able to rehabilitate himself, but actually surpass his previous level of martial ability. And he did just that. While he may have been bedridden for six months, Lee, unable to train his body, began to train his mind as never before, reading voraciously and taking copious notes that would fill seven separate volumes on the art and science of combat. Many of those notes were gathered up and published collectively in the book *The Tao of Jeet Kune Do* (Ohara Publications, 1975) under the auspices of his widow, Linda Lee Cadwell. However, there was much material that was left out of that book. So much so, in fact, that it has filled the bulk of this book (along with his reading annotations, additional notes on combat, and excerpted interview materials). To obtain a more complete picture of the thought process and depth of Bruce Lee and the martial art and philosophy he created, I would strongly recommend that you read *The Tao of Jeet Kune Do* in addition to any other books that feature authentic writings of Bruce Lee. Don't bifurcate into an "either/or" situation; take in the whole picture. "But who was to be the ultimate arbiter of which information was more important?" some of you will ask. Holding to Bruce's philosophy of there not being any effective segments of a totality, it is my belief that while this book holds an important segment of the totality that was Bruce Lee, you can only obtain the full picture by doing your homework and broadening your research.

Still, within the pages of this book you will find many of Bruce Lee's never-before-published insights into the world of martial arts. There is much wisdom in these words, gleamed from written and recorded sources not available previously. These "commentaries on the martial way" (the subtitle of this book was actually taken from the title he gave to his seven volumes of personal writings) will serve to provide you with additional insights into the totality of the man's soul, his thoughts on martial art, on the creation of his own martial art and philosophy of jeet kune do, as well as many of his personal, private, and public lesson plans that he implemented for the correct teaching of his art during his lifetime.

It has taken this author over three years to research all of the existing materials of Bruce Lee (although in truth, I've been studying Lee and his writings for well over two decades), and another year to edit them into the manuscript that became this book. I have kept my own thumbprint off the body of the text, so that, apart from this prefatory material, it is only Bruce Lee's words that you will be reading, recorded here exactly as he spoke or wrote them. Where Lee simply jotted down a thought or a sentence, it has been left to stand exactly as he wrote it in the hopes that the spirit of his intention will be fully preserved.

Lee was in the habit of sitting down and writing whatever came into his head. He didn't do this as a flight of fancy, but rather in an attempt to get in touch with his real feelings on various issues, without the guise of public celebrity or self-image, but simply the honest expression of his innermost thoughts and feelings in a completely spontaneous and unedited fashion. He once wrote:

> I have to say I am writing whatever happens to be popping into my mind. It might be incoherent to some but, what the heck, I don't care. I'm just simply writing whatever wants to be written at the moment of its conception. If we communicate, which I sincerely hope; it's cool. If not, well, it can't be helped anyway.

And again at another sitting:

> I don't know what I will be writing but just simply writing whatever wants to be written. If the writing communicates and stirs something within someone, it's beautiful. If not, well, it can't be helped.

It is my sincere hope that this volume of Bruce Lee's personal writings will indeed "communicate" and "stir something within someone" reading this book, to the point that it will serve to help that someone in their own process of becoming both a better martial artist and, more importantly, a better person. That, dear reader, would be a very "beautiful" thing, indeed.

—John Little

INTRODUCTION

Martial art, like any art, is an expression of the human being. Some expressions have flavor, some are logical (perhaps under certain required situations), but most martial arts are the mere performing of a sort of mechanical repetition of a fixed pattern.

This is most unhealthy because to live is to express and to express you have to create. Creation is never merely repetition. Remember well my friend that all styles are man-made and man is always more important than any style. Style concludes. Man grows.

So martial art is ultimately an athletic expression of the dynamic human body. More important yet is the person who is there expressing his own soul. Yes, martial art is an unfolding of what one is—his anger, his fears—and yet under all these natural human tendencies (which we all experience, after all) a "quality" martial artist can—in the midst of all these commotions—still be himself.

And it is not a question of winning or losing but it is a question of being what is at that moment and being wholeheartedly involved with that particular moment and doing one's best. The consequence is left to whatever will happen.

Therefore to be a martial artist also means to be an artist of life. Since life is an ever-going process, one should flow in this process and to discover, to actualize, and to expand oneself.

—Bruce Lee

Part 1

COMMENTARIES ON THE MARTIAL WAY

REFLECTIONS ON COMBAT

Martial art—a definition

Martial art includes all the combative arts like karate, judo, Chinese gung fu or Chinese boxing, aikido, Korean karate—I could go on and on and on. But it's a combative form of fighting. I mean, some of them became sport, but some of them are still not. I mean, some of them use, for instance, kicking to the groin, jabbing fingers into eyes, and things like that.

An animal jumps at every sound . . . a leaf responds to every push of air . . . but an enlightened man in combat moves only when he chooses—only when necessary—actually, the movement before it is necessary. He is not tensed but ready, he is never set but flexible.

Bruce Lee's

JEET KUNE DO
截 拳 道

Professional
Consultation & Instruction-------*$275 per Hour*
Ten Sessions Course ---------------------------------*$1000*
Instruction Overseas $1000 a week plus expenses

I am known as a teacher and a notoriously expensive one at that. For when my time is demanded of me, my learners pay for their worth. Time means a lot to me because you see I am also a learner and am often lost in the joy of forever developing.

Unfortunately, now in boxing people are only allowed to punch. In judo, people are only allowed to throw. I do not despise these kinds of martial arts. What I mean is, we now find rigid forms which create differences among clans. And the world of martial art is shattered as a result.

The other weakness is, when clans are formed, the people of a clan will hold their kind of martial art as the only truth, and do not dare to reform or improve it. Thus they are confined in their own tiny world. Their students become machines which imitate martial art forms.

As a matter of fact, they each have their strong points and weak points. They all need self-evaluation and improvement. They are too narrow-minded. They can only see their strong points, but not their weak points and other's strong points. A man confined in thought and scope will not be able to speak freely. Therefore, if he wants to seek for truth, he should not be confined by the dead forms.

The successful martial artist
The successful martial artist will be one who is able to:
1. Possess fluid speed—tenseness tightens and slows reaction time.
2. Possess confidence-plus—at all times.
3. Sock it—everything there, as soon as the opening is there.
4. Puzzle the opponent—never do the same thing twice. Whenever the opponent gets set to hit, move. Each combatant has his own gears (speed, etc.).

Qualities
1. Natural instinctive primitiveness
2. The technique should be a natural blending with stillness and sudden (as well as violent) destructiveness.

A quality martial artist is always ready for any move and trains oneself invincible.

A little learning is a dangerous thing.

Don't ever telegraph your move—that's just common sense in martial art.

Timing! A good martial artist keeps his eyes open.

When the opponent advances, one intercepts!

Anger blinds!

Controlled balance of speed of changing of both firing posture and delivery with *speed* and *power*!

Talking tactics

Pretend inferiority and encourage his arrogance (technique of deception—action—once or twice—down!). Arrogance corrupts.

If you are among those who are unable to understand the dangers inherent in combat then, like them, you also are either unsure or simply unable to understand the advantageous ways of fighting.

All martial art is simply an honest expression of one's body—with a lot of deception in between.

Retaliation to a bluff

I never met a conceited man whom I did not find inwardly embarrassed.

The ultimate in disposing one's skill is to be without ascertainable shape. Not only that emptiness can never be confined, but also the fact that gentleness cannot be snapped—action—and the most penetrating weapons cannot pry in nor can the wise lay plans against you.

A man with a weapon is the one at a disadvantage

The man who pulls a knife on you is at a disadvantage. He will clearly lose the fight. The reason is very simple. Psychologically, he only has one weapon. His thinking is therefore limited to the use of that single weapon. You, on the other hand, are thinking about all your weapons: your hands, elbows, knees, feet, head. You're thinking 360 degrees around him. Maybe you're considering some form of escape, like running. He's only got a lousy knife. Now he might throw it at you. Let him. You still have a chance to avoid it, block it, or he may miss you. You've got all the advantages when you think about it.

Against a man with a club

He's holding something with two hands. I mean, what's he going to do: swing, thrust, jab? He's got a problem. What's he going to do with his feet? He'll be off-balance if he holds the staff and tries to kick you. That's *his* disadvantage.

On martial art and success

In the beginning, I had no intention whatsoever that what I was practicing, and what I'm still practicing now, would lead to this. But martial art has a very, very deep meaning as far as my life is concerned because, as an actor, as a martial artist, as a human being, all these I have learned from martial art.

Use karate, judo, aikido, or any style to build your counter-offensive. It will be interesting!

On sparring

Every Monday, Wednesday, and Friday, I work on my legs. Every Thursday and Saturday I work on my punch. On Wednesdays and Sundays, I have sparring sessions.

The best way to learn how to swim is to actually get into the water and swim; the best way to learn jeet kune do is to spar. Only in free sparring can a practitioner begin to learn broken rhythm and the exact timing and correct judgment of distance.

In sparring the mind must be quiet and calm; the attention concentrated, and the energy lowered. Besides, straightening the head and body, hollowing the chest, raising the back, lowering the shoulders and elbows, loosening the waist, setting right the sacrum, and keeping the waist, legs, hands, and other parts of the body in perfect harmony are all important. The postures must be natural, capable of stretching and drawing as intended without any awkward strength, and responding immediately after sensing.

Pointers on sparring
- Requires individuality rather than imitative repetition
- Efficiency is anything that scores (in primary freedom one utilizes all ways and is bound by none, and likewise any technique or means which serves its end).
- Simplicity of expression rather than complexity of form
- Turn your sparring into play—but play seriously.
- Don't take your sparring too seriously.
- Totality rather than partiality
- Dissolves like a thawing ice (it has form) into water (formless and capable to fit in with anything—nothingness cannot be confined . . .)
- When you have no form, you can be all form. When you have no style, you can fit in with any style
- In sparring there is no answer; truth has no future, it must be understood from moment to moment. You see, to that which is static, fixed, dead, there can be a way, a definite path but not to that which is moving and living. There is no conviction or method, but perception, a pliable and choiceless awareness.
- To have a choiceless awareness, one should have the totality, or emptiness—all lines, all angles.

- If one is isolated, he is frozen and paralyzed. To be alive is to be related. Action is our relationship with our opponent.
- Action is not a matter of right and wrong. It is only when action is partial, not total, that there is right and wrong.

Economy of motion

In kicking and striking, especially when launched from the ready position, eliminate all unnecessary motions and muscle contractions which slow and fatigue you without accomplishing any useful purpose. Much energy is wasted by the unrelaxed opposing muscles in resisting the movement—learn and feel proper contraction and recovery (otherwise your physiological engine is racing, but the brakes are on).

Acquire the kinesthetic perception in tension-creating situations—distinguish between the relaxed and the tense states. Practice controlling the body responses voluntarily and at will. Use only those muscles required to perform the act, using them as economically as possible, and not using the other muscles to perform movements which do not contribute to the act or which interfere with it. Expend constructively both the mental and physical energy (economical, neuromuscular, perceptive movement). In coordinated, graceful, and efficient movement, the opposing muscles must be relaxed and lengthen readily and easily.

It takes perception, practice, and willingness to train the mind into new habits of thinking and the body into new habits of action. A champ is one who makes every motion count, and he accomplishes maximum results with a minimum expenditure of energy.

You and your opponent are one. There is a coexisting relationship between you. You coexist with your opponent and become his complement, absorbing his attack and using his force to overcome him.

Forms and katas are not the answer

I think simply to practice gung fu forms and karate katas is not a good way. Moreover, it wastes time and does not match the actual (fighting) situation. Some people are tall, some are short, some are stout, some are slim. There are various kinds of people. If all of them learn the same boxing (i.e. martial art) form, then who does it fit?

The highest state is no form

I think the highest state of martial art, in application, must have no absolute form. And, to tackle pattern A with pattern B may not be absolutely correct. I feel that martial art should not be limited in a circle. That will produce in the students a wrong idea, thinking that a certain pattern will achieve the same result in fighting as in practice.

On what is the "best" martial art

There is no such thing as an effective segment of a totality. By that I mean that I personally do not believe in the word *style*. Why? Because, unless there are human beings with three arms and four legs, unless we have another group of beings on earth that are structurally different from us, there can be no different style of fighting. Why is that? Because we have two hands and two legs. Now the unfortunate thing is that there's boxing, which uses hands, and judo, which uses throwing. I'm not putting them down, mind you—but because of styles, people are separated. They are not united together because styles become law. The original founder of the style started out with hypothesis. But now it has become the gospel truth, and people who go into that become the product of it. It doesn't matter how you are, who you are, how you are structured, how you are built, or how you are made . . . it doesn't seem to matter. You just go in there and become that product. And that, to me, is not right.

Nationalities don't mean anything

Many people will come to an instructor but, most of them, they say, "Hey man, like what is the truth? You know, would you hand it over to me?" So, therefore, one guy would say now, "I'll give you the *Japanese* way of doing it." And another guy would say "I'll give you the *Chinese* way of doing it." But to me that's all baloney because unless there are men with three hands or there are men with four legs, then there [cannot be] a *different way* of doing it. But since we only have two hands and two legs, nationalities don't mean anything.

A constant process of relating

When I see a Japanese martial artist, for example, I can see the ad-

vantage and I can see the disadvantage. In that sense, I am relating to him. Man is living in a relationship, and in relationships we grow.

Because martial art is my career, I want to use it as a means to express my ideals. A real fighter should fight for righteousness. Moreover, when he decides to fight, he must be sincere and fight wholeheartedly to the end. Only in such a way can he develop good character and total truth and sincerity.

Understand.

Dueling ultimately is simply a test in individual "essence."

Not being stuck mentally and not abiding oneself is the root of life.

Strategy of distracting attention

Focus on movement, greater speed—in other words, subjectively in time for the signal, don't focus full attention on signal, though necessary. This way one can time the rhythm of the signal, or the starter's pattern, so that he can start with the signal, not react to the signal.

Auditory signals and reaction time

Experiments indicate that if the cue to act can be made auditory instead of visual, the athlete's response is more rapid. Make use of it together with visual if possible.

Strategy of distracting attention

Repeat—for most rapid perception, attention must be at the maximum focus on the thing to be perceived.

Vision awareness factors that all martial artists should consider

1. Awareness in attack 2. Awareness in counter 3. Awareness in combination

You see, the kicks and punches are weapons not necessarily aimed toward invading opponents. These tools can be aimed at our fears, frustrations, and all that. Martial art can help in your process toward growth.

Truth is the daughter of inspiration; intellectual analysis and partialized debate keep the people away from truth. It is like a finger pointing a way to the moon. Don't concentrate on the finger or you will miss all that heavenly glory.

You can be a slave in the form of a holy mind to live. We do not live for, we simply live.

The head is a united part of the human body.

If one prepares to the front, his rear will be weak. If he prepares to the left, his right will be vulnerable. And when he prepares everywhere he will be weak everywhere.

Quick temper will make a fool of you soon enough.

A coward will easily be captured. Also a reckless one can be killed.

The true power of our skill is as self-knowledge—the liberation of the self—not as a weapon.

Commentaries on the Martial Way

External pride is not the thing, it's internal self-sufficiency.

Your instinctive skill should be well-tempered with self-inquiries and judgments.

I thought we had discovered that tournaments are places where human beings are playing a protecting game of pride.

Let's cut out the verbal threatening. To be a true martial artist is not to try to avoid what is your lot.

Psyching-out dialogue (based on Sun Tzu's Art of War)

1. Pretend inferiority after an evasive move to encourage an opponent's arrogance for your advantage.
2. Your brain is the general of your head and if the general is angered his authority can easily be upset.

In combat we understand, we converse by using normal power to engage, and use the extraordinary to win.

On challenges

When I first learned martial art, I too have challenged many established instructors and, of course, some others have challenged me also. But I have learned that if challenging means one thing to you, it is "What is your reaction to it? Where does it get you?" Now if you are secure within yourself, you treat it very lightly because you ask yourself: "Am I really afraid of that man? Do I have any doubts that that man is going to get me?" And if I do not have such doubts and such fears, then I would certainly treat it very lightly, just as today the rain is coming down very strong but tomorrow, baby, the sun is going to come out again. I mean it's like that type of a thing.

Well, let's face it, in Hong Kong today, can you have a fight?—I mean a no-holds-barred fight? Is it a legal thing? It isn't, is it? And for me, a lot of things, like "challenging" and all that, I am the last to know! I am always the last to know, man. I always find out from newspapers, from reporters, before I personally know what the hell is happening.

On my fighting ability

All the time, people come up and say "Bruce—are you *really* that good?" I say, "Well, if I tell you I'm good, probably you will say that I'm boasting. But if I tell you I'm not good, you'll *know* I'm lying."

I have no fear of an opponent in front of me. I'm very self-sufficient, and they do not bother me. And, should I fight, should I do anything, I have made up my mind that, baby, you had better kill me before I get you.

To tell the truth, I could beat anybody in the world.

Someone once asked me, what I am going to do when I am fifty or sixty. I replied "Man, there ain't going to be no fifty or sixty-year-old that can push me around."

On why Hollywood's elite want to learn martial art

The way that I teach it, all types of knowledge ultimately mean self-knowledge. So therefore, these people are coming in and asking me to teach them, not so much how to "defend themselves" or how to do somebody in. Rather, they want to learn to express themselves through some movement, be it anger, be it determination, or whatever. So, in other words, they're paying me to show them, in combative form, the *art of expressing the human body*.

Don't look for secret moves. Don't look for secret movements. If you're always hunting for secret techniques you're going to miss it. It's you. It's your body that's the key.

Complete determination—the mark of the real fighter

You must be fierce, but have patience at the same time. Most important of all, you must have complete determination. The worst opponent you can come across is one whose aim has become an obsession. For instance, if a man has decided that he is going to bite off your nose no matter what happens to him in the process, the chances are he will succeed in doing it. He may be severely beaten up too, but that will not stop him from carrying out his objective. That is the real fighter.

A lesson in attitude

Suppose you come home and find some guys have battered a friend. First, you're going to think about *what* you should do. Then you're

going to try and figure out *how*. But suppose, instead of a friend, you come home and find your mother battered. Wham! You're ready—that's pure attitude.

On wu-hsin (no-mind) in martial art

What man has to get over is consciousness. The consciousness of himself.

Jeet Kune Do

The story of the centipede

The fluidity a martial artist seeks can best be described by the story of the centipede. The many-footed creature was asked how it managed to walk on all its feet. When it stopped to think about how it managed its daily function, it tripped and fell. And so, life should be a natural process, in which the development of the mind is not allowed to throw the natural flow of life out of balance.

On being whole

When a man is thinking he stands off from what he is trying to understand. Feeling exists here and now when not interrupted and dissected by ideas or concepts. The moment we stop analyzing and let go, we can start really seeing, feeling—as one whole. There is no actor or one being acted upon but the action itself. I stayed with my feeling then—and I felt it to the full without naming it that. At last the I and the feeling merged to become one. The I no longer feels the self to be separated from the you and the whole idea of taking advantage or getting something out of something becomes absurd. To me, I have no other self (not to mention thought) than the oneness of things of which I was aware at that moment.

I could not feel a conceptually defined pattern, and the essential quality of feeling life lies simply in the feeling. Do not, as when in the midst of enjoying yourself, step out for a moment and examine yourself to see if you are getting the utmost out of the occasion. Or, not content with feeling happy, you want to feel yourself feeling happy.

Longstreet: Wait a minute. Let me think.

Lee: If you have to think, you still do not understand.

It is when you act with unconscious awareness, you just act. Like when you throw a ball to me and, without thought, my hands go up and catch it. Or when a child or animal runs in front of your car, you automatically apply the brakes. When you throw a punch at me, I intercept and hit you back, but without thought. "It" just happens.

On guns versus martial artists

Nowadays, I mean you don't go around on the street, kicking people or punching people. Because if you do, they will pull a gun out of their jacket and bang! That's it. I mean, I don't care how good [in martial art] you are!

On my martial origins

When I started studying the martial arts I was thirteen years old. I studied under Yip Man. It was a Chinese art. The form of the martial art that I studied was Wing Chun. Some have called gung fu "a Chinese form of karate," but you cannot really call it that because karate came after Chinese gung fu. I mean karate, and all these things, came after that, you see.

MARTIAL VARIETY AND ASSESSMENTS

On gung fu
The word *gung fu* includes techniques of hands, feet, knees, elbows, shoulders, head, and thighs, the thirty-six throws, the seventy-two joint locks, and the eighteen different weapons. Swordplay is the most difficult of all arts in gung fu. It requires at least ten years of hard training to be a master of it. The sword must be united with the mind, and be used as the limb of the body.

Classical gung fu analyzed
1. Classically inclined—hand position, ritualistic and unrealistic techniques
2. Rhythmic training—forms, two-man cooperation
3. Partial in structure—the nucleus and the circumference

On the difference between Chinese boxing and Western boxing
Well, first, we use the feet. And then we use the elbow. You name it, man, we use it! We use it all, you see, because that is the expression of the human body. I mean *everything*—not just the hands! When you are talking about combat, well, I mean, if it is a sport [i.e., like Western boxing], then now you are talking about something else; you have regulations, you have rules. But if you are talking about fighting, as it is—with no rules—well then, baby, you'd better train every part of your body!

On boxing versus real fighting
If you put on a glove, you are dealing in rules. You must know the rules to survive. But in the street you have more tools in your favor—the kick, the throw, the punch.

On board breaking

Boards don't hit back. This matter of breaking bricks and boards with the edge of your hand: Now I ask you, did you ever see a brick or a board pick a fight with anybody? This is gimmick stuff. A human being doesn't just stand there and wait to be hit.

Polemics from the traditionalists

Most of them [the instructors of the traditional martial arts approach] are so doggone stubborn. I mean, [their attitude is] "Well, two hundred hundred years ago it was taught like this—therefore . . . " you know? To [still] maintain that type of attitude, you've had it! I mean, you will never grow because learning is a discovering thing; it's a constant discovery thing. Whereas if we follow the old method, it is a continuous repetition of what was being handed down several hundred years ago.

The traditional teacher says, "if your opponent does this, *then* you do this, *and then* you do this *and then* you do this." And while you are remembering all the "*and thens*" the other guy is killing you.

On the limitations of wrestling and judo

1. A sport (no foul tactics)
2. Lacks long-range tactics (kicking, hair-pulling, butting, finger jab, kneeing, elbowing, stomping on shin or instep, grabbing groin, pinching skin, pulling ears, biting, etc.)

On the limitations of Thai boxing

1. A sport (no foul tactics)
2. No grappling
3. Lacks economy structure and scientific leads
4. Unaccustomed to advance targets attacks to eyes and groin—the delicate movements

On the limitations of street fighting

1. Lack of finesse in structure
2. Efficient sharpening of "tools" generally lacking
3. Correct mental attitude

Commentaries on the Martial Way

How to deal with various arts

A question [to ask]: What are their most favorite techniques? (ease and safety and efficiency)

Western boxing

Thai boxing

karate

tae kwon do

wrestling

judo

   • Attacking same • Countering same • When in doubt

Pros and cons

Western boxing

PRO 1. Efficient footwork

     2. Variety of punches:

       • Jab • Hook • Cross • Uppercut

     3. Shoulder/chin in protection (plus all-purpose parry and block stance)

     4. Conditioning

     5. In-fighting

     6. Head and body movements

CON An evaluation: It has its set of restrictions and is designed to defeat an adversary in a certain manner.

Wrestling

PRO 1. Leg tackle 2. Uncrispy, economy rush 3. Protective shell while moving in 4. Strangulation 5. Holds, locks 6. Ground fighting

CON Need to add: • Hair pulling • Groin grabbing • Eye poking (front) • Shin pinching (Study especially the old-time illegal holds.)

Karate

PRO Tool development:

     • Balance • Form

CON Need to stress greater mobility and aliveness

PRO Front kick

    • Snap • Thrust

CON Need to modify upward snap—compare with savate

Tae kwon do

PRO 1. Kicking flexibility 2. Turning heel kick 3. Head ram

CON 1. Lacks contact 2. Lacks broken rhythm and aliveness

    3. Lacks variety

Judo

PRO 1. Balance 2. Osoto 3. Foot-sweeps

    4. Mat work

    • Locks • Chokes

CON Need to add:

    • Hair pulling • Groin grabbing • Eye poking

    • Shin pinching

      Note: Study a few practical throws.

both are at grips in the right natural posture. Take his lower part of left elbow with your right hand; while approaching push in your body.

while approaching your right foot nearest to the rear of your left heel, pull him round before its left side the moment you make his left foot advance onward, when strengthen the lower part of abdomin with the upper part of body straight and the balance lowered.

Float and break him in the rear while stepping to his right foot side with the left foot. When the waist settles firm, pull and break him with the left hand and at the same time push him up with the right hand; then throw him down by a hair breadth.

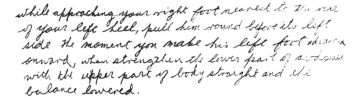

Thai boxing

PRO 1. Elbows 2. Knees 3. Actual combat

CON 1. The punching is not of a high caliber: the "left jab" is poor, the "uppercut" almost nonexistent, the "hook" is inadequate.

2. Gloves prevent the use of the finger jab and the palm smash.

3. Lead foot attacks lacking: no shin/knee lead attack and groin attack.

4. No grappling tactics.

5. No "under the belt" tactics.

6. Scientific economical structure is lacking. Plus lack of sophistication in cadence, timing, broken rhythm.

7. No hair pulling or scratching.

Specialized all-in fighting

PRO 1. Poking Eyes

  • Long range jab • Close range poke

2. Pulling Hair

  • As immobilization • As release • As assist

3. Biting

  • As release • To disable • To attack in close

4. Practice forearm pinching to hurt

5. Grabbing groin

6. Specialize in under-the-belt attack with kicks, strikes, punches, and grappling

Gung Fu Styles—Wing Chun

PRO 1. Teaches the economy of straight line

2. Nucleus fighting

3. Chi sao—two halves of one whole

CON 1. Over simplification 2. Lacks variety

Gung fu styles—tai chi

PRO 1. Esoteric 2. The flow

Gung fu styles—northern styles

PRO 1. Palm strike 2. Variety to liberate

CON 1. Needs to add power 2. Needs to be more compact

Western fencing

PRO 1. Skillful use of front lead (study auxiliary supplemented guarding hand in each position) 2. Timing and cadence

3. Foil 4. Saber 5. Epee

Kendo

PRO 1. The Zen approach

2. The determined clash

3. The footwork

Aikido

PRO 1. The flow 2. The two halves of one whole 3. The footwork

CON 1. Needs to work on idea of adding uncrispyness to snap (in their concept of flow)

Research your own experience

A thought: because of formalized styles of yesteryear:

- Simple things don't work. However, from some formalized schools, like Shotokan, tae kwon do, Thai boxing, Western boxing, how can I draw their "essence" and make them work for me (attitude, economy, good form, speed, power, etc.)?

List some of these "essences" of other schools:

Shotokan

ESSENCE a. Direct route b. Master in basics c. Spirit

DISADVANTAGE (Your comments) _____

_____

Tae kwon do

ESSENCE a. Flexibility b. (Your comments) _____

_____

DISADVANTAGE (Your comments) _____

_____

Thai boxing

ESSENCE (Your comments) _____

_____

DISADVANTAGE (Your comments) _____

_____

Boxing

ESSENCE (Your comments) _____

_____

DISADVANTAGE (Your comments) _____

_____

Make Notes On

1. Gung fu 2. Fencing 3. Aikido 4. Kendo 5. Karate 6. Thai boxing 7. Savate

Part 2

JEET KUNE DO—THE FUNDAMENTALS

JEET KUNE DO—
ORIGIN AND DEVELOPMENT

On the origin of jeet kune do

In case you have missed the recent news, Bruce Lee's jeet kune do—of which he is the founder—has been elected and accepted into the "Black Belt Hall of Fame" in America. This marks the first time a recently developed form of martial art is nationally accepted. No, jeet kune do is not thousands, or even hundreds of years old. It was started around 1965 by a dedicated and intensified man called Bruce Lee. And his martial art is something that no serious martial artist can ignore.

I've been teaching my brothers and some friends gung fu at my house. They are very enthused over the whole deal. I, too, am working on my transformation of simplicity to yet another, more free-flowing movement of no limit as limitation.

I'm having a gung fu system drawn up—this system is a combination of chiefly Wing Chun, fencing, and boxing. As for gung fu training, I'll have them written down when it is finished. Boy it will be *it*!

What is jeet kune do (JKD)? Chinese martial art, definitely! It is a kind of Chinese martial art that does away with the distinction of branches, an art that rejects formality, and an art that is liberated from the tradition.

Before I explain what JKD is, we have to know what "traditional martial art form" is first. All ancient, traditional martial art has a legendary tradition. People may say that one kind of martial arts was passed on to a monk from a deity through a dream. Or, when its founder saw two animals fighting, he imitated their actions, and consequently, created a kind of martial art. So the people after him imitated that kind of action and form, and did not care whether it fits their needs and environment or not.

Use your brain to overcome your enemy

The two most important aspects of martial arts are "the essence" and "the practical usage." Essence refers to the foundation. It is only on a sound basis that practical usage of gung fu can be realized. Swiftness, strength, and persistence are the keywords to martial arts.

Jeet kune do rejects all restrictions imposed by forms and formality and emphasizes the clever use of the mind and body to defend and attack.

It is ridiculous to attempt to pin down so-and-so's type of gung fu as "Bruce Lee's jeet kune do." I call it jeet kune do just because I want to emphasize the notion of deciding at the right moment in order to stop the enemy at the gate.

If people are determined to call my actions "do" [the Way], this action can be called jeet kune do: In *Fist of Fury* [*The Chinese Connection* in North America] I had a fight with Robert Baker. In the film, he once locked my neck with his legs so that I became unable to move. The only movable part of my body was my mouth, so I gave him a bite! I am not joking. Really there is no rigid form in jeet kune do. All that there is is this understanding: If the enemy is cool, stay cooler than him; if the enemy moves, move faster than him; be concerned with the ends, not the means; master your own manipulation of force, don't be restricted by your form.

Very often when people talk about JKD, they are very much concerned about its title. Actually, the title is not important. It's only a symbol for the kind of martial art we study. It's just like the X, Y, and Z in algebra. The emphasis should not be put on its title, but on its effect, because that is a good mirror in which to reflect the power of JKD.

It is not simply mixing arts

- X is jeet kune do.
- Y is the style you will represent.
- To represent and teach Y one should drill its members according to the preaching of Y.

- This is the same with anyone who is qualified and has been approved to represent X.
- To justify by interfusing X and Y is basically the denying of Y—but still calling it Y.
- A man, as you put it, is one who is noble to stick to the road he has chosen.
- A garden of roses will yield roses, and a garden of violets will yield violets.

The Jun Fan method (structure)

Totality (circle without circumference)

1. Sticking to the nucleus
2. Liberation from the nucleus
3. Returning to original freedom

Jeet kune do and Thai boxing

Sure, it's a little like Thai boxing, except that if you had a gung fu fight, there'd never be any "round three." Somebody would be lying on the floor.

Martial art should not be passed out indiscriminately. So far I have only three assistants teaching for me when I cannot personally be there. Taky Kimura, a friend and quality assistant (and most capable pupil/teacher) for over ten years, teaches occasionally in Seattle. James Lee, an ex-gung fu instructor, closed his school and has a club in Oakland, and Dan Inosanto teaches as a hobby here in his home in southern California. Both Taky and James are more steeped in the (Wing Chun) Chinese system because they met me at the earlier stage in my development and, consequently, whenever I see the two of them, I try to liberate them more from one way to walk the pathless path. Dan, a dedicated professional, met me during the midst of my evolution though he has less training than either Taky or James. During the last ten years, Chinese martial art

Training In Jeet Kune Do 截拳道

1). Exercise for Power :-
    1) FUNCTIONAL POWER :- a) LEG b) hand c) elbow d) knee
    2) BASIC STRENGTH - a) arm b) leg c) big muscle groups.

2) Exercise for Speed :- 1) repetition of technique, simple technique
    2) Combination

3) Exercise for timing & coordination :- 1) sparring

4). Exercise for flexibility :- 1) basic flexibility
    2) leg flexibility

5). Exercise for Endurance :- 1) vascular endurance
    2) pending & sticking (muscular) Endurance

6). Exercise for agility :- 1) basic agility Exercise with weight
    2). jumping with or without bar

7). Exercise for basic fitness - 1) stomach
    2) leg
    3) back.

8). Nutrition & Rest.

has always been a major part of my activity, though I am now in a new field, the field of acting. My achievement in the

Fundamental Exercises :-

1). Exercises for strength :- a) basic strength (power)
   b) functional strength (power)

2). Exercises for speed :- a) repetition of basic movements & technique

3). Exercises for timing & coordination - a) sparring
   b)

4). Exercises for flexibility :- a) leg b) stretching

5). Exercises for endurance :- a) sparring endurance
   b) running (muscular/fitness) muscular

6). Exercise for agility :- a) agility exercises with light weight
   b) jumping with kicking

7). Nutrition & rest :-

8) Exercise for basic fitness :-
   1) stomach :- ① sit up ② leg raise ③ side bend ④ twist ⑤ isometric a) tension b) arch
   2) leg. :- ① squat ② isometric squat ③ jumping squat (with weight)
   3). back :- ① deadlift ② forward & ways bend

martial art is most satisfying and the word *Chinese* has come a long way in the circle of martial art due to the fact that all three of the US karate free style champs are studying under me [Chuck Norris, Joe Lewis, and Mike Stone].

I've lost faith in the Chinese classical arts—though I still call mine Chinese—because basically all styles are products of dry-land swimming, even the Wing Chun school. So my line of training is more toward efficient street fighting with everything goes; wearing head gear, gloves, chest guard, shin/knee guards, etc. For the past five years now I've been training the hardest and for a purpose, not just dissipated hit-miss training.

I've named my style jeet kune do—reason for my not sticking to Wing Chun is because I sincerely feel that my style has more to offer regarding efficiency.

To reach me, you must move to me. Your preparation of attack offers me a directional commitment to intercept you.

I have never discontinued studying and practicing martial arts. While I am tracing the source and history of Chinese martial arts, this doubt always comes up: Now that every branch of Chinese gung fu has its own form, its own established style, are these the original intentions of the founder? I do not think so. Formality could be a hindrance to progress; this is applicable to everything, including philosophy.

The founder of any branch of Chinese gung fu must be more ingenious than the common man. If his achievement is not carried on by disciples of the same ingenuity, then things will only become formalized and get stuck in a cul-de-sac; whereby breakthrough and progress will be almost impossible.

Neither formality nor branches

It is this understanding that makes me forsake all that I have learned before about forms and formality. Actually, I never wanted to give a name to the kind of Chinese gung fu that I have invented, but for convenience sake, I still call it "jeet kune do." However, I want to emphasize that there is no clear line of distinction between jeet kune do and any other kind of gung fu, for I strongly object to formality, and to the idea of distinction of branches.

I stress again, I have not created or invented any kind of martial art. Jeet kune do is derived from what I have learned, plus my evaluation of it. Thus, my JKD is not confined by any kind of martial arts. On the contrary, I welcome those who like JKD to study it and improve it.

This time I intercepted your emotional tightness. You see, if only one can just punch—from the head to the fist, how much time is lost!

Jeet kune do uses all ways and is bound by none, and likewise uses any technique or means which serves its end. Efficiency is anything that scores.

Jeet kune do is fitting in with one's opponent, but there is no path, no self, and no goal.

———

Jeet kune do's first concern is about its experience and not its modes of expression.

———

As to martial arts, I still practice daily. I train my students and friends twice a week. It doesn't matter if they are Western boxers, tae kwon do students, or wrestlers, I will train them as long as they are friendly and don't get uptight. Since I started to practice realistically in 1966 (protectors, gloves, etc.), I feel that I had many prejudices before, and they are wrong. So I changed the name of the gist of my study to jeet kune do.

———

Jeet kune do is only a name. The most important thing is to avoid having bias in the training. Although the principle of boxing is important, practicality is even more important.

———

True observation begins when one is devoid of set patterns.

———

Freedom of expression occurs when one is beyond system.

———

A style is a classified response to one's chosen inclination.

———

Truth cannot be structured or confined.

———

Remember that a martial art man is not merely a physical exponent of some prowess he may have been gifted with in the first place. As he matures, he will realize that his side kick is really not so much a tool to conquer his opponent, but a tool to explode through his ego and all those follies. All that training is to round him up to be a complete man.

———

In order to cope with what *is*, one must have the awareness and flexibility of the styleless style. When I say "styleless style," I mean a style that has the totality without partiality; in short, it is a circle without circumference where every conceivable line is included.

Because, after all, an opponent is capable of throwing all lines (in all kinds of broken rhythm) and if one is partial only to dealing with the straight, then he will run into friction with just the right line that will screw up his straight line. Let's remember the word *relationship*: To do a technique is to study oneself in action *with* the opponent, which is relationship.

How on earth can we truthfully understand and feel relationship if we merely follow the one straight line—here we have merely isolation in an enclosed idea of a straight line; such an idea, no matter how noble, concentrates only on a partial aspect of combat and is fitting with the opponent through a screen of resistance. True that a straight line is definitely valuable; take the pendulum—in order to swing to one side (the side one favors), you need to initiate the movement from the other side. Why are we isolated out from one side? Indeed, why don't we look at one continuous swing as one whole!

In order to cope with what *is*, one must be equipped with flexibility of line and fit in from moment to moment, depending on what is being given. Having the two halves of one whole, which is the straight and the curve, we can truly have the choiceless awareness, and choiceless awareness can lead to reconciliation of opposites in a total understanding of combat in its suchness. Thus, in the highest stage, one is in the center of a circle and there he stands while *yes* and *no* pursue each other around the circumference. One can achieve that because he has abandoned all thought of imposing a limit or taking sides; he rests in direct intuition, which is returning to original freedom.

Fighting and instruction

Instruction should comprise the fighting as well as the technical training. Fighting training should be given for each stroke before going on in the study of a new one.

- *How* it is done
- *Why* it is done
- *When* it is done

Jeet kune do—not a mass art

Of my art—gung fu and jeet kune do—only one of 10,000 can handle it. It is martial art. Complete offensive attacks. It is silly to think almost anyone can learn it. It isn't really contemporary forms of the art I teach. Mainly that which I work with—martial attack. It is really a smooth rhythmic expression of smashing the guy before he hits you, with any method available.

On closing my schools

I was teaching martial art in the United States. I had three schools; one in Oakland, one in Seattle, and one in Los Angeles. And then later on I just closed them, you know, and just taught private lessons. I do not believe in "schools."

I've disbanded all the schools of jeet kune do because it is very easy for a member to come in and take the agenda as "the truth" and the schedule as "the Way."

The problem of styles

I do not teach because I do not believe in styles anymore. I mean I do not believe that there is such a thing as, like, "the Chinese way" of fighting or the "Japanese way" of fighting . . . or whatever "way" of fighting, because unless a human being has three arms and four legs, there can be no different form of fighting. But, basically, we only have two hands and two feet. So styles tend to separate man—because they have their own doctrines and the doctrine became the Gospel Truth that you cannot change! But, if you do not have styles, if you just say "here I am as a human being. How can I express myself totally and completely?"—now that way, you won't create a style because style is a crystallization. That way (the opposite of style) is a process of continuing growth.

I mean "styles" kind of restrict you to one way of doing it and therefore limit your human capacity, you know?

A path and a gateway have no meaning or no use once the objective is in sight.

Let me give you a good example of why I don't like cults or sects in the martial arts. Let's take stances. Okay, now look at the way a crane just stands there on one leg. So suppose you have something like that invented by a cripple? In five thousand years everybody is a cripple.

Ah Sahm: Why do you do that?
Cord: Do what?
Ah Sahm: Chew twenty-one times on the left side of your jaw, twenty-one times on the right, before you swallow.
Cord: I was taught that in the monastery.
Ah Sahm: Does it serve a purpose?
Cord: It exercises the jaw. It prepares the stomach to receive the food. It extracts the essence of each mouthful.
Ah Sahm: Yet a hungry man, disciplining himself in this manner, might starve to death while still counting.

On why man is always more important than any established style

Man is always in a learning process. Whereas "style" is a concluding, established, solidified something, you know? You cannot do that because you learn every day as you grow on, grow older.

The way of "no way"

When there is a Way, therein lies the limitation. And when there is a circumference, it traps and if it traps, it rottens; and if it rottens it is lifeless.

Man is constantly growing. And when he is bound by a set pattern of ideas or Way of doing things, that's when he stops growing.

The highest art is no art. The best form is no form.

In martial art cultivation there must be a sense of freedom. A conditioned mind is never a free mind.

Conditioning is to limit a person within the framework of a particular system.

To be bound by traditional martial art style or styles is the way of the mindless, enslaved martial artist, but to be inspired by the traditional martial art and to achieve further heights is the way of genius.

I'm telling you it's difficult to have a rehearsed routine to fit in with broken rhythm!

Rehearsed routines lack the flexibility to adapt.

Jeet kune do is not a method of concentration or meditation. It is being. It is an experience, a Way that is not a Way.

Pure being

Jeet kune do is the awareness of pure being (beyond subject and object), an immediate grasp of being in its "thusness" and "suchness" (not particularized reality).

Mind is an ultimate reality which is aware of itself and is not the seat of our empirical consciousness—by "being" mind instead of "having" mind ("no mind and no-mind"; "no form and no-form").

Converge with all that is.

Do not seek *it*, for it will come when least expected.

Random thoughts on JKD

My JKD is something else . . . more and more I pity the martial artists that are blinded by their partiality and ignorance.

On what it all amounts to

Unless there is another group of beings on earth that are structurally different from us, there can be no different style of fighting.

Why is that? Because we have two hands and two legs. The important thing is, *how can we use them to their maximum* [potential? This leads us to study our selves] in terms of [the potential] paths [our weapons can travel. And once we've analyzed that we discover that] they can be used in straight lines, curved line, up, round lines. The [round line, for example] might be slow but, depending on the circumstances, sometimes that might not be slow. And in terms of legs, you can kick up, straight—same thing, right? [You're studying yourself] physically, then, [which leads] you to ask yourself: how can I [learn to make my weapons become maximally efficient in a] very well coordinated manner? Well, that means you have to [train like] an athlete—using jogging and all those basic ingredients. And after all that, you [must] ask yourself, *how can I honestly express myself at this moment?* And being yourself, when you punch you really want to punch—not trying to punch [out of fear of being struck] or to avoid getting hit, but to really be in with it and express yourself. Now this to me is the most important thing. That is, *how in the process of learning how to use my body can I come to understand myself?*

The trouble is that circumstances must dictate what you do. But too many people are looking at "what is" from a position of thinking "what should be."

The "space" created between "what is" and "what should be." Total awareness of the now and not the disciplined stillness.

More and more I believe in [the fact that] you have two hands and two legs, and the thing is how to make good use of yourself—and that's about it.

PRINCIPLES AND STRATEGIES

The art of offensive defense
Though your style should
be a combination of offense
and defense, I often stress
that offense should be the
more emphasized. This does
not mean that we should
neglect defense; actually, as

the reader will later realize, into every jeet kune do offense, defense
is also welded in to form what I term "defensive offense."

In attacking, you must never be halfhearted. Your main concern is
with the correct and most determined execution of your offensive.
You should be like a steel spring ready at the slightest opening to set
the explosive charge of your dynamic attack.

Every attack you make should be penetrating, disturbing your
opponent's rhythm and bringing pressure upon his morale. Remember

though that your hands are not a hatchet (a common image nowadays) to chop your opponent down. Rather, they are keys to unlock your opponent's defense, and a different lock requires a different key.

It is easy to learn the mechanics of an attack, but to apply that attack in time with the opponent and at the correct distance takes a lot of practice.

Thus in order for an attack to be successful requires this fitting in with the opponent. To attack correctly, you must have a keen sense of timing with the opponent, a good judgment of distance between you and him, and the right application of speed and rhythm with the reactions of your adversary.

There is no effective trick to stop a properly timed simple attack, and always remember the best technique in offense or defense is the simple one properly performed.

"Defense is offense, offense is defense" is a phrase uttered by many systems. But looking at it closely, all of these systems devote themselves on a passive block and then an active offense. Though aggressive parrying is used occasionally in jeet kune do, the best parry is still the kick and the blow.

Aggressive defense
The leading right shin/knee stop kick
When your opponent attacks you, he has to come to you, and his action of coming toward you offers you to apply the theory of attack given in the previous section, that of using the longest against the closest. When your opponent advances toward you, he presents to you his "advanced target" of his shin and knee. Before his attack is halfway through, you can stop kick him and check his attack.

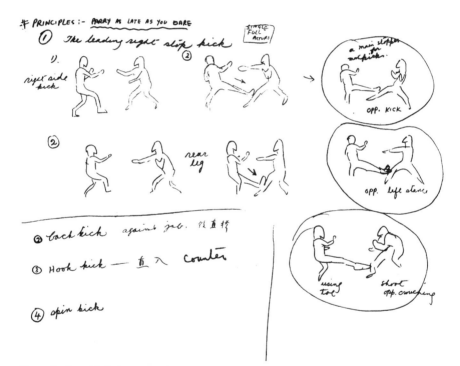

THE ELEMENT OF ~~DEFENCE/OFFENCE~~ *offensive defense.*

"JEET KUNE DO" *signifies aggressive defense*

\# *By defence, every means of frustrating and punishing one's opponent's lead.*

\# *Does not necessarily mean the attacking man will land the kick or blow*

\# *The successful avoidance of a blow presents on most occasions the opportunity for a counter attack*

\# *Best defense is not to let the attack get started, to keep opponent continually on the defensive*

\# *Aggressive defense — each defensive move must be accompanied by a counter attack or be followed immediately by a counter attack*

\# *Gung Fu is not primarily defensive but indicates that knowledge of this art results in a person being able to defend himself.*

\# *It doesn't mean trading punches, nothing so crude*

\# PRINCIPLES :- PARRY AS LATE AS YOU DARE

① *The leading right stop kick*
1). right side kick

②

SINGLE FULL PICTURE

a man slipping for indicate
OPP. KICK

②

rear leg

opp. left stance

② *back kick against jab.* 挡直拳

③ *Hook kick* — 直入 *counter*

④ *spin kick*

using toe   *shoot opp. crouching*

Figure 1. A and B facing each other.

Figure 2. Awareness is most important in the success of any stop hit or kick, though the stop kick is easier, allowing the defender more time due to the longer kicking distance between him and his opponent. The second A is aware of B's initial onslaught, A immediately shoots out his shin/knee stop kick while arching back for power and safety distance.

The side kick

The longest of all kicks, this side rear kick can be a strong defensive weapon, especially against all-hand attacks, round-house kicking, or rear leg attack of the opponent.

The hook kick

A good counter kick, especially against hand attacks.

The finger jab

Using footwork

Additional aggressive defense factors that all martial artists should consider

The inside high parry

The outside high parry

The inside low parry

The outside low parry

The element of offensive defense

Jeet kune do (JKD) signifies offensive defense.

Every attacker must have within himself a touch of the gambler. Never attack halfheartedly—penetrate in, concern yourself only with the correct and most determined execution of your offense.

Offensive defense pointers

1. Use the longest (weapon) against the closest (target).
2. Use leg first in attack, then having bridged the gap, use the hands.
3. Make indirect attack out of them, feint head first if hitting low (this is not always the rule)—do not set pattern which will allow your opponent to time you.

[By defense, every means of frustrating and punishing one's opponent's lead.]

Does not necessarily mean the attacking man will land the kick or blow.

The successful avoidance of a blow presents on most occasions the opportunity for a counterattack.

Best defense is not to let the attack get started, to keep the opponent continually on the defensive.

Aggressive defense—each defensive move must be accompanied by a counterattack or be followed immediately by a counterattack.

Gung fu is not primarily defensive but indicates that knowledge of this art results in a person being able to defend himself.

It doesn't mean trading punches, nothing so crude.

Principles
Parry as late as you dare.

Weapons and targets

There is only one basic principle of self-defense: You must apply the most effective weapon as soon as possible to the most vulnerable point of your enemy. You'll find in this note diagrams showing the most effective weapons given to you by nature and the most vulnerable points of the body.

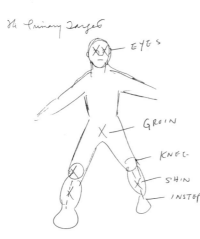

A jeet kune do weapons arsenal

JKD kicks from a right stance:

Side kick
1. Downward side kick (shin/knee and thigh)
   - Right simple side kick to knee/shin
   - Right simple side kick to thigh or rib

Parallel side kick (ribs, stomach, kidneys)
- Right simple side kick to head
- Angle in high side kick (to left stance)
- Angle in low side kick (to left stance)

Upward side kick (solar plexus, head)
- Reverse left side kick
- Leaping side kick

- Jumping side kick
- Slide in dropping side kick
- Step-back side kick

Leading straight kick
- Right high straight
- Right medium straight
- Right low straight
- Right angle in (to left stance)

JKD groin kick
Right rising kick (knee and/or wrist)
Step-back straight kick

Hook kick
1. Right simple high hook
2. Right simple medium hook
3. Right simple low hook
4. Reverse left high hook
5. Reverse left medium hook
6. Reverse left low hook
7. Right one-two hook
8. Reverse left one-two hook
9. Jumping hook
10. Step-back hook
11. Double leading hook
12. Three foot sweeps

Spinning back kick
1. Left simple spinning back kick high
2. Left simple spinning back kick low
3. Left simple spinning back kick medium
4. Jumping reverse spinning back kick
5. Step-back spinning back kick

Heel kick (stiff-legged or bent)

1. Right simple high heel kick
2. Right simple medium heel kick
3. Right simple low heel kick
4. Right one-two heel kick
5. Reverse left one-two heel kick (to left stancer)

Reverse straight kick

1. Reverse left high straight kick
2. Reverse left medium straight kick
3. Reverse left low straight kick
4. Reverse left angle in high straight kick
5. Reverse left angle in medium straight kick
6. Reverse left angle in low straight kick
7. Reverse left cross stomp
8. Step-back reverse straight kick

Jeet kune do hand techniques

Leading finger jab

Leading right

1. High 2. Medium 3. Low
4. Double 5. Slanting right
6. Slanting left

Right hook

1. High
2. Medium
3. Low
4. Tight
5. Loose
6. Upward

Left cross
1. High 2. Medium 3. Low
4. Overhand 5. Left hook

Right backfist
1. High 2. Medium
3. Low 4. Reverse backfist

Right quarter swing
1. With palm
2. With back fist
3. Reverse left quarter swing
4. Inward finger fan

Uppercut
1. Right 2. Reverse left

The pivot point
1. Left pivot
   • Forearm
   • Back fist
   • Elbow

Additional striking weapons

Elbow

1. Right upward smash
2. Right downward smash
3. Right elbow smashing left
4. Right elbow smashing right
5. Right inward elbow smash
6. Right backward elbow smash
7. Reverse left upward smash
8. Reverse left downward smash
9. Left swing right
10. Left swing left
11. Inward left elbow swing
12. Left back elbow
13. Pivot elbow blow

Knee

1. Right upward thrust
2. Right inward thrust
3. Reverse left upward thrust
4. Reverse left inward thrust

Head butt

1. Lunging forward
2. Lunging left
3. Lunging right
4. Lunging back

Throwing, tackling, locking, and choking

1. Hook throw (soto) with or without arm drag
2. Left foot sweep (right and left stance)
3. Right foot sweep (left and right stance)
4. Kick back (left and right stance)

FAKE HIT HEAD THROW AND KNEE

FAKE

KNEE THRUST TO BAK DISC

STOMACH THRUST, HEAD AND LEG THROW, FOLLOWED BY A BACK BREAKER.

The spread Eagle groin shot.

1   2   3   4

5   6   7

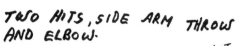

TWO HITS, SIDE ARM THROWS AND ELBOW.

L block/hit

H'T

elbow, hand
rake, right
thrust if necessary

Foot twist or toe hold (into left and right stance)

1. Single leg tackle and trip (standing or lying)—single leg lock
2. Double leg tackle—double leg and spine lock turn over

LEG BAR – TO NECK CRACKING.

NECK BREAK.

ARM BAR CHEST TAREDOWN

踏つ Stomp

leg split

Joint locks

1. Outside armpit lock (left and right stance)
2. Wrist lock A and B (A = cross wrist lock/ B = elbow wrist lock)
3. Lying cross-arm bar lock (after hook throw)
4. Reverse wrist lock (to double arm lock)

Lee's first mass fight (in a set-up)

1. Natural instinctive primitiveness
2. The technique
   - A natural blending of stillness with sudden, violent destructiveness
   - The triple kick (maybe not)
3. Lee's deadliness
4. Body slam to opponent

Note: After a quick dispersal of attackers, set up each opponent separately for each spectacular technique.

Sudden

(1)

匚步 twist drag

Arm scissors to neck break

go behind toe
hold

(speed)

 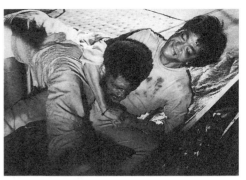

Chokes

1. Rear chokes
2. Lean-over stranglehold
3. Side stranglehold

Foul tactics

1. Hair pulling in infighting (for control)
2. Foot stomps in infighting (to hurt)
3. Skin pinching (to hurt) or ear pulling (for control)
4. Groin grabbing

Target areas

The body is the easier target to hit for the simple reason that it covers a far larger surface than the jaw (the groin might be a better target and is definitely harder to block) and is less mobile.

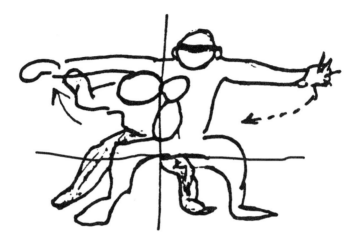

To intercept a head lock, or a head-immobilization attack by your opponent, block the locking arm with the arm that is furthest away from your opponent, while simultaneously slipping your left leg in behind his right leg. With a quick twist to the left, lift your opponent's right hand and trip him by pushing him over your left knee.

Progressive charts
1. Progressive target 2. Progressive tools 3. Lead side

Progressive target factors that all martial artists should consider
1. Distance and footwork (see sections on distance and footwork) in long-range fighting
2. The importance of fluid [interchange of] long-range fighting and close-range fighting and vice versa

---

The choice of stroke
1. Should deceive opponent's stroke
2. Offensive action should move in the same direction as those of the defense. Otherwise the blades are bound to meet while turning in the opposite circle.

To find out the reaction of habit in your opponent
1. Quick simple attack
2. Feints preceded by attacks on hand
3. False attack with a half lunge

The role of techniques
Though they play an important role in the early stages, the techniques should not be too mechanical, complex, or restrictive. Remember, you are expressing the techniques and not doing the techniques. When attacked, your response is not technique 1, 2, 3, 4, 5— rather you simply move in like sound and echo, without any deliberation. React as when I throw something to you, you catch it. Nothing else.

In most cases the same tactics for each maneuver must be drilled on the opposite side of the body for the proper balance in efficiency.

When your feeling is more involved in the technique your technique improves.

The three stages of a technique

Stage I (synchronization of self)

a. Correct form
b. Precision (augmenting speed progressively)
c. Synchronization of the whole

Stage II (synchronization with opponent)

a. Timing—the ability to seize an opportunity when given
b. Distance—correct maintenance of space

Stage III (application under fighting conditions)

a. Mobility
b. The physical ability to lengthen movements of arms and legs, in other words to increase reach
c. Resistance to fatigue, i.e., stamina
d. Spring and resilience
e. Physical and mental alertness
f. Imagination and anticipation
g. Courage to take chances
h. Speed progression • Strength progression

Repetition of the same parry can spell disaster.

Observe, deduce, and apply.

Speed and cadence

Speed must be regulated very carefully to fit in with the speed of execution of the opponent.

The regulating of one's speed to correspond with that of the adversary is known as cadence.

With each adversary the first thing to find out is his cadence, as even a simple attack can fail if that has been ascertained.

It is a great advantage to be able to impose one's own cadence on the opposition.

Men of experience often change their cadence, and effectively hinder the opponent in his effort to regulate his.

Certain styles and tactics

The Golden Principle: Each movement of yours must correspond to those of the opponent.

On the need to vary your attacks

The stronger man will be he who, if necessary, is able to vary his strokes and kicks.

The more experienced the opponent, the more varied will be the strokes and kicks.

Sometimes PIA works, sometimes HIA—in other words, depending on the opponent's tactics and reaction. It takes two to play.

When you are in range, in order to be safe:
a. You can apply the pressure by attacking (well-covered attacking!)
b. You can lodge yourself in blind sides of opponent
  • Both sides—HIA
  • Boxing safety position (to shoulder—attack groin—leg immobilization attack)
  • Gap pressing
c. Sidestep to both sides to limit opponent's direct rush—be watchful of all possibilities to counter from the positioning relationship—like rear cross, spin kick, etc. (immediate) and the opposite hand and kick (secondary).
d. Watch your opponent with "all-inclusive playful seriousness."

Question
A good artist is one with:
a. An all-inclusive attitude without gap—playfully serious
b. Totality in equipment
c. Ability to supply and regulate with the object (opponent) C with (a) and (b)

It is impossible to vary one's offensive actions if the adversary does not vary his parries.

Watch for the opponent's styles, habits, and movements and use them for your advantage.

When faced with an opponent who has a decided advantage in reach, it is often a mistake to try to keep still further away from him.

He also may dislike to have his measure shortened, and it may be worthwhile to make a shortstep forward on his offensive action. His measure being shortened, he may not be able to achieve speed and penetration of attack through his development. He also may be inclined to miss.

Tactics to use against hand/hair-immobilization attack (HIA)

At first sight, the answer appears to be to deceive his attempt and stop hit him, or to attack during his preparation, but it is unlikely that all his attacks on the hand will be deceived, and his heaviness, coupled with the numerous hand deceptions which have to be made, will finally tire one's hand. It is wiser, against such an adversary, to spar with absence of touch; that is to say, by adopting a low front leading hand, where he will find difficulty in making contact.

Additional notes on the feint (PIA)

Never pause on a feint—a feint should always be followed up.

Feints with a short lunge are also very useful to keep an aggressive at bay. Sometimes the opponent can be caught off his guard and unprepared by such feints; one can immediately follow up.

We must not allow our hand to be found while feinting. If we do, it must be intentionally and because we are hoping to score with another tactic.

Counter-time

Counter-time is the answer for an opponent who continually attacks into one's attack—a quick leaning forward of body, or a false attack.

Striking

It should be focused clearly and distinctly, and have the penetration ability to strike from any angle and from any distance—develop a sense of focus that will enable you to control and direct it.

Stance

The stance is slightly shorter in order to keep the leading foot and leg out of range of a sudden low kick—also, use small and rapid steps for gaining and breaking ground.

The on-guard position

1. Short stance for mobility—on balls of feet
2. Front hand slightly lowered with center low line protected—ready

The distance is governed by the amount of target to be protected and the parts of the body which are most easily within the adversary's reach.

The practitioner must be made to advance or retire before, while, or after the strike or kick at which he is working has been executed.

Two counter-offensive actions—stop hit and time hit —to make the adversary respect his distance.

Stop hit
Counter defense/offense against an opponent who attacks wildly, with insufficient care to covering, or who comes too close.

To take advantage of faulty execution or overconfidence.

The stop hit oftentimes necessitates a step forward in order to land ahead. It is advisable at least to lean forward as if to meet the attacker.

The time hit
1. The final line in which the attack is delivered must be anticipated.
2. The executant must be covered.
3. The timing of the stroke must be perfect.

The time thrust

A time thrust is a simple attack made against the adversary at the same time that he is making an attack; closing the line where he intends to finish his attack with the same hand or with a supplementary guard accompanying.

The time thrust is a simple straight or disengage attack made against the attacker, closing the line which he intends to finish his attack.

The stop thrust

The stop thrust is usually made by straight thrust or disengage. It can be made safer by shifting the body out of line to evade the original, or the continuation of the original, attack. Stepping to the side or ducking under the opponent's attack are two such possibilities.

The stop thrust is designed to score a hit in the midst of the attacker's action.

a. Opponent steps forward to prepare kicking or punching

b. Preoccupying with feinting

c. Complicate combinations

d. In between two moves of a complicated combination

Stop thrust—used against

1. A slow complicated attack

2. A direct attack incorrectly made, with a bent arm or hesitation

3. A preparation for an attack, such as taking of the hand, slapping the hand, etc.

4. An attack advancing

Applying the technique

It is advised that the stop hit should be, in fact, a time hit. The time hit must fulfill several conditions (see page 93).

Consider training aids in perfecting the time thrust and stop hit.

Attack

If a fighter concentrates sufficiently, senses the moment to attack, and acts upon it swiftly and decisively, the prospects of success are greatly enhanced.

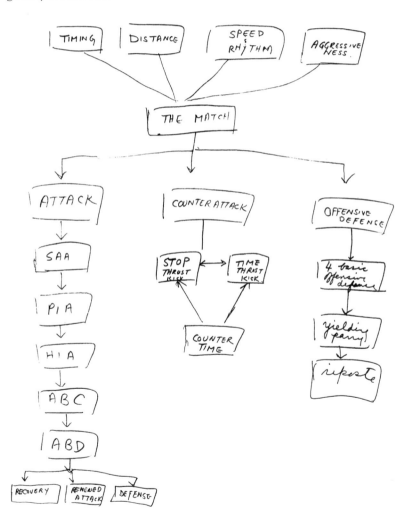

The three factors in a successful attack
1. A fine sense of timing
2. A perfect judgement of distance
3. A correct application of cadence

A compound attack badly executed
a. With a bent arm (before it is stretched)
b. With wide, badly directed hand actions (as it opens)
c. By feinting in the on-guard position and lunging with a second disengagement (on the first feint before lunging with real attack)
d. Incorrect wide movements before immobilization (direct or indirect—depends)
e. The preparation of stepping forward
f. Opponent feints very wide exposing his guard

Because of the large area, fighting is a careful game; it will be readily understood that each hit must be painstakingly and patiently prepared.

Because the success of your attack depends on the opponent's reaction, there are various means to find them out:
1. The feint 2. The false attack 3. The beat 4. The economical full-fledged attack

It is generally fatal to start a bout with a set plan.

Solutions to attack problems
Before adopting a particular plan of attack, one must find out, for instance, whether the adversary parries, stop hits, or gives ground.

Those that parry
a. PIA
b. False attacks then
  • Timed stroke
  • HIA
  • Close-range tactics

Those that stop hit

a. Counter-time b. Shift to grappling

Those that give ground

a. Sudden change of rhythm, uncrispy entrance
b. Preparation (live close), hand/hair-immobilizing attack, occasionally followed by progressive indirect attack, simple-angle attack
c. Speedy simple attack when appropriate distance is secured, followed by renewal or combination attack

---

Opponent assessment

1. For instance, does he parry feints, or does he wait for the final attack?
2. Does he riposte automatically after each parry?
3. Does he try to engage, or is he quite happy in a position of absence of touch?
4. Are his stop kicks (hit) spontaneous or premeditated?
   - His cadence has to be assessed
   - His rapidity of footwork
   - His lightness or heaviness of hand
   - His habitual preferences

Dealing with the novice

The novice is often much more difficult to deal with because he may make uncoordinated movements and fail to respond normally (or at all) to orthodox feints or other forms of attack. Also, he starts his movements from the most unorthodox angles. This danger will be aggravated if his main asset is a good sense of distance.

Such beginners should be treated with respect and kept at a distance until one has been able to make some assessment of their cadence and sense of distance. Use second-intention techniques and induce them to attack either out of distance, or in a desired way, by pressing them with determined feints and judicious variation of the fighting measure.

Courage and decision are essential factors to success in fighting.

Don't simply rely on what comes easiest to you

There is a great temptation to exploit favorite strokes to the neglect of most others. While this may bring initial success, it is unlikely to enable one to gain regular results in the highest-class competitions. All too soon one's opponents will find the answer to a limited game; a routine system of defense, for instance, plays into the hands of an observant opponent.

There is always a temptation to rely too much on a small repertoire of favorite strokes which particularly suit one's temperament or physical advantages. This must be resisted if one is to progress be-yond a few initial successes in battle and, indeed, to enjoy fighting with all its subtlety, speed, and variety to the full. You must be able to exploit a wide variety of strokes and tactics, even though some movements will always suit your game best.

Variations of cadence and distance are excellent tactics of fighting—for example, deliberate slowing down of some movments so as to deliver an indirect or compound attack or riposte in broken time can be an effective tactical move, especially against an opponent who is superior in speed to oneself.

Lightness and speed in footwork and a proper sense of balance through a sound on-guard position are obvious essentials. False attacks are much used to distract the opponent while gaining ground in order to obtain proper measure, even momentarily, to successfully launch an attack under the best conditions. Variation of the length of steps backward and forward is used for the same purpose, steps backward often being designed to draw the opponent within distance.

Fighting is often based on subtlety of conception and speed of execution.

The essential attributes
In martial art the essential attributes are:
1. The choice of the right stroke
2. The ability to execute it not only correctly, but at the right moment and at the right speed or cadence

Exploratory moves
The exploratory moves are:
1. Feints
2. Simple economical attack
3. False attack with half lunge
4. Preparation on leg or hand

(*Note:* All these are safe if one is sharp at correct distance, if used with economy, and well-covered.)

The nature of feinting

Feinting is the art of using the body in feinting attack at one point, and then attacking another. It involves footwork, knees, hands, eyes, arms, and trunk.

When obtaining the inside position, drive both hands to opponent's groin.

The false moves are called feints.

In total fighting, all evasive kicks and/or hits are used:
a. To time opponent's last extending commitment
b. To time gaps between two exertions
(*Note:* (a) and (b) are means to take the play away from the aggressor, or to initiate grappling)

Attack

The final choice of stroke should be based on the observation of the opponent's:
1. Reaction 2. Habits 3. Preferences

Observe, deduce, and apply the three factors in attack

1. A fine sense of timing
2. A perfect judgment of distance
3. A correct application of cadence

Attacks on preparation

When the opponent makes a preparation for an attack he is, for a fraction of time, concentrated on attack rather than defense. This is a propitious moment for you to launch an attack.

An attack on preparation is often effective against an opponent who maintains a particularly accurate distance measure and is difficult to reach—a good tactic for this type of opponent is to induce him to prepare an attack by a short step back.

An attack on preparation is not an attack into attack; rather, it is launched during the opponent's preparation and before the attack begins.

To be successful, you must have a very exact choice of distance and careful timing. Of course, sharp awareness is the foundation.

Distance influences the choice of movements as well as the tactics to be used. Rarely close enough to his adversary to reach him with a lunge, the fighter has to await the opportunity to attack until the former comes within distance with preparation.

Attacking on opponent's preparation to attack
1. His stepping forward
2. His feintings
3. His process of trapping hand
   - Curving in (while moving out of line or shifting body) to intercept
   - Thrusting through loopholes
4. Finding exact physical (balance) and psychological (psyche out or carelessness) moment of weakness.

During a preparation the fighter increases his vulnerability:
1. Because he is closer to his opponent
2. Because his mind is usually concentrating on his offensive action as a whole
3. Because one cannot, simultaneously, step forward and backward

Don't just charge in blindly; you've got to listen—listen!

Attack on preparation is one of the best forms of attack.

Change of engagement is very useful when the opponent presses against the hand in engaging or preparing to attack.

Consider training aids to attacks on preparation.

Disturb opponent's rhythm by causing him to lose a period of gung fu time.

The function of an attack
1. To move ahead of the opponent's defense
2. To put the opponent on the defensive
3. To control *timing* and *distance*
4. To control the play
5. To build confidence

An attack must be *determined* and *continuous* until it ends either in a hit or in being parried.

Attack options

Two-feint attacks, counter-ripostes, and compound ripostes, ending in quarte, will have a reasonable chance of success against the left-stancer.

Counter-time can be used to draw the left-stancer's stop hit.
1. Use parries of fourth (quarte) and counter-fourth
2. Engage him in fourth (quarte)

JKD's five ways of attack

1. Simple angle attack (SAA) *Simple attack (SA)*

Once mastering this difficult accomplishment, he can, without any further instruction whatever, dispose of any "sparring" gentleman or unskilled opponent with the utmost ease.

A direct thrust can only be made when the opponent is uncovering any line.

Maintain in-line punching for straight punching, and utilize feints in curve and hook.

Do not attack from out of range; be sure to obtain your correct distance and launch it at the precise moment when the opponent leaves the line open.

By passing over, or under, the opponent's arm, the attacker can direct his offensive toward a part of the body away from which the defender is moving—indirect attack.

It is composed of a single hand movement.

opponent in left stance

Attack by disengagement

Attacks and ripostes, however well designed and executed, will generally fail unless they are delivered at the right moment and at the right speed (cadence). A simple example of the right choice of time is provided by an attack by disengagement.

From the normal on-guard position, a disengagement can be parried by a lateral movement of the hand which travels a matter of a few inches, while the attacker's hand has to travel several feet to reach the target. Under these conditions the fastest attack should be parried by even a slow defensive movement, and this disparity in time will be aggravated if the attack is directed toward a side of the target toward which the defender's hand is already moving to close the line.

It is obvious that the attack should be timed to move toward a part of the target from which the opponent's hand is moving away; that is, into an opening rather than a closing line, if it is to have the best chance of overcoming the disadvantage of time and distance to which it is always subject. Similarly, an excellent moment to launch an attack is when the opponent is himself preparing an attack. His intention and hand movement will then be momentarily concentrated more on attack than defense.

Counter-disengagement

To be able to seize an opportunity and, therefore, to time a movement well, the fighter must never allow himself to tense.

Simple attacks are those executed without any preceding feints or threatening motions against opponent's hand!
1. Straight thrust, hook thrust (covered)
2. Disengage 3. Cut over

Attack while your opponent is in the process of covering up one line, by entering into his opening line.

Let simplicity be the keynote of your offensive (e.g.: direct attack, HIA, movement preceded by one feint, etc.).

Simple attack can be made from a "small phasic bent-knee stance" ("phasic" meaning "a stage or interval in a development or cycle") or, on rare occasions, a motionless, well-covered, on-guard position, or by timing the moment of departure after threatening movements of the body or feints by the opponent (small [not large] phasic is hard for opponent to time).

Small phasic bent-knee stance (SPBKS) in simple attack

Small: Small quick steps for speed and controlled balance in bridging gap. *Phasic:* Constant small changing starts the motor rhythm in ready gear, a tuned state for any change of direction. *Bent-knee stance:* Insures readiness in motion.

Two effective means of simple attack

Fighting is a game of timing, tactics, and bluff. Two of the most effective means to this end are:

The simple attack from immobility

This will often surprise the opponent, especially after a series of false attacks and feints have been executed, so that the defender is subconsciously expecting a preparation or more complex movement and fails to react in time to the swift and unannounced simple movement.

The variation of rhythm or cadence

Made prior to, or during, an attack. This may achieve the same element of surprise. For example, a series of judiciously slowed-down feints to the leg and slow gaining and breaking ground may be used (to "put the opponent to sleep"). A final simple movement which suddenly erupts at highest speed will often take him unawares. Again, some rapid feints followed by a deliberately slowed-down or broken-time final movement will often disconcert a vigilant opponent. Sometimes a number of feints in the high lines can pave the way for a sudden disengagement to the knee.

Some fighters form the habit of withdrawing the hand or foot when a hit is directed toward it. Such fighters are vulnerable to an immediate renewal of the attack by a quick lunge.

Preparation on the knee and trapping hand while obstructing opponent's leg are often used to reduce the movement time factor—conversely, attacks on preparation are particularly effective.

A broken-time attack—making a pause before delivering the final movement, can be very effective in deceiving the opponent as to the attacker's intention.

One way to find the opponent's reaction is to launch a simple attack just out of distance but still he will have to parry—wait for his riposte, which will be deflected—and carefully select the target area for the counterattack.

Simple attacks are undoubtedly difficult to bring off and have a better chance of success when they are preceded by an attack on the leading leg or hand, which will produce some form of reaction and permit a period of time to be gained. But whether or not these simple attacks are preceded by preparation, they are dependent on:

a. Attack with confidence

b. Attack with accuracy

c. Attack with great speed

In retrospect, all aggressive arm actions, no matter how simple or complex they become, stem from three fundamentals:

1. The beat or a preparation on the lead hand of opponent

2. The disengagement

3. The simple thrust

Any elementary offense or defense through proper strategy and ring generalship may under certain conditions be used in the most advanced type of fighting.

Simple-attack factors that all martial artists should consider

1. Simple attack in attack

2. Simple attack in countering

3. Training aid in simple attack
   - Hundreds of repetitions on the mechanics of each technique to acquire instinctive initiation in good form with great speed is the basis for simple attack.

Examples of simple attack

1. Leading shin/knee side kick
   - Deep—with finger jab, lead, and back fist
   - Fast—with finger jab, lead, and back fist

2. Leading finger jab

3. Leading right jab

4. Lead hook
   - With finger jab • With right lead • With back fist • With rear left cross

To ensure the success of simple attack

a. Coordinate all into powerfully one.

b. Must develop a continual condition of relaxation.

Note: Any tension when awaiting the opportunity to launch the attack (through correctly found distance) will only give a short and jerky movement; or moving too soon; or giving indication of one's intentions.

Types of opponents

a. One who uses distance to passively run away—use cool combinations and double step and, if capable, use smooth simple economical attack.

b. One who uses distance as a means to counter—feint and evasive score

c. One who guards and parries with distance

d. One who mainly guards and parries and is ready to crash

e. One who presses forward

Note: Develop smooth, expressive speed.

Simple attack (SA; aka simple angle attack or SAA)

All simple attacks should be made in one continuous movement, keeping your hand as close to the opponent's as possible.

Simple attacks should not be launched until the right distance is gained. Then go full blast.

The essential attributes (proper timing and exact distance are essential)

Speed

Speed is dependent on quickness in blending the hand with the advance into one continuous action—hand leading foot slightly.

Simple attack points to keep in mind (maintain that continuous looseness throughout)

Before initiation • Loose but poised

Initiation • Economical • One continuous movement

Initiation + exploding force = scored!

During initiation • Economy use of movement and force

• Most direct line attack backed up by tight covering

After initiation • quick natural flow to recovery (SPBKS)

Additional SAA factors that all martial artists should consider

1. The SAA in attack 2. The SAA in defense 3. The SAA in combination 4. Countering SAA 5. Training aid

2. Hand-immobilization attack

(Add leg-immobilization attack, hair-immobilization attack, and head-immobilization attack

- Close own boundaries while closing distance
- Watch out for opponent's stop hit or kick
- Be ready to angle strike when opponent opens or backs up
- Feinting before immobilizing is recommended for double safety and success

The immobilization attacks

1. Hand-immobilization attack (HIA)
2. Leg-immobilization attack (LIA)
3. Head- and/or hair-immobilization attack (HHIA)

LIA *factors that all martial artists should consider*

1. Leg-immobilization attack as attack
2. Leg-immobilization attack in defense
3. The leg-immobilization attack in combination
4. Countering leg-immobilization attack
   • Frontal • Front oblique left • Front oblique right
(*Note:* Utilize hair control combined with biting—followed by . . .)
5. Training aid

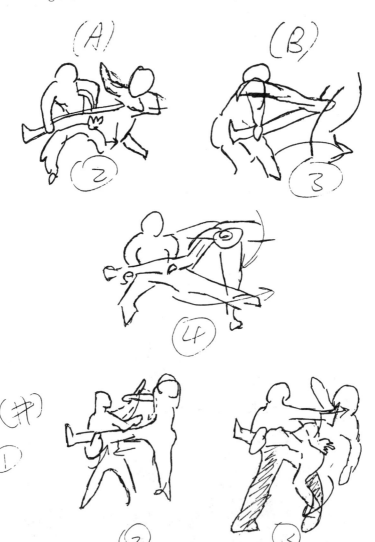

HIA factors that all martial artists should consider

1. Hair immobilization as attack
2. Hair immobilization as defense
3. Hair immobilization as combination
4. Countering hair immobilization
5. Training aid

HIA factors that all martial artists should consider

1. HIA—as attack
2. HIA—in defense
3. HIA—in combination
4. Countering HIA

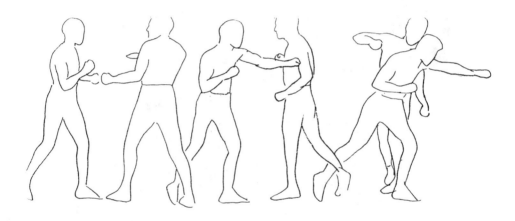

Stopping

Stopping is the pinning of an opponent's hand or arm so that he is unable to deliver a blow. It may be used:

a. As a preventive measure when attacking with one hand while pinning the other

b. As a preventive measure when slipping or countering

c. When an opponent actually intends to deliver a blow

(Used in this manner, it requires a knowledge of when an opponent is going to lead, and depends on speed and skill for execution.)

3. Progressive indirect attack (PIA)

- Whenever possible move out of line or suddenly change your level—for added safety and surprise.
- Boundaries close accordingly.

High to low

a. Right strike to low right jolt

b. Right strike to right groin toe kick

c. Right strike to left strike or kick

d. Left strike to right strike or kick

Low to high
a. Right strike to high right jolt or hook
b. Right groin kick to high right strike
c. Right groin kick to high hook kick
d. Left strike to high jolt or hook

Left/right or right/left
a. Right strike to right hook
b. Left strike to right thrust
c. Tangle leading hand with right and left cross
d. Right lead draw snap back and cross

Progressive indirect attack (PIA)

I've added in a progressive indirect attack to the original chi sao, which is close-quarter combat. Progressive indirect attack is the link to achieve chi sao. Progressive indirect attack is used against an opponent whose defense is tight and fast enough to deal with simple attacks like straight blast, finger jab, pak sao, and hit. Progressive indirect attack (PIA from now on) is based on feinting, and feinting is to draw the opponent to the execution of a parry or block.

Remember that although feinting consists mainly of two movements (sometimes three, but no more than that!), they must be one smooth, flowing action. The following notes will help you to understand the execution of feinting, which will make you advance into your opponent's defense faster and safer:

a. The first movement (feint)—must be long and deep (by that I mean penetrating) to draw the parry. The second real movement (attack) must be fast and decisive allowing the defender no possibility of recovery—long-short; even in the delivery of attack with two feints, the depth of the first feint must force the opponent to move to the defense—long-short-short.

b. Gain distance—to shorten the distance the hand has to travel by a good half with your feint, and leave to your second movement only the second half of the distance—known as progressive attack.

c. Gain time—(by deceiving the parry so that even if you are slower you can still strike him). To time this movement of arm crossing from left to right (right to left, up to down, down to up) for the execution of the attack means that for a moment the defense is moving in an opposite direction to that of the attack—it is while the opponent's arm is traveling across that he must start his offensive action. Thus the second movement (in other words, the attack after the first movement which is the feint) should move ahead of the opponent's parry that is being deceived by your first movement, the feint.

I hope after much thinking on the above note you will begin to feel the progressive indirect attack. Remember that speed must be regulated to coincide with the opponent's movement.

Progressive (to gain distance) indirect (to gain time) attack (to move ahead of opponent's defense).

To close in on opponent so that he has to commit thus bringing hands in line.

The use of feinting in progressive indirect attack

Object: to provoke the execution of a block.

Progressive: to shorten the distance the measure has to be closed by a good half with your first feint, and leave to your second movement only the second half of the distance.

Indirect: do not wait for the block before completing your attack; keep ahead of it but prolong your feint enough so that the opponent has time to react.

Except in rare cases, all movement should be made as small as possible, that is with the least deviation of the hand necessary to induce the opponent to react.

Caution demands that attacks should, whenever possible, be completely covered.

Disengagement works best against a defender who:
a. Habitually crosses his arm from one side to the other
b. Is exerting pressure on your hand as he does so

HIA moves toward hand, while PIA moves away from hand (combine them to the situation)—effective use of PIA, or tackling, or direct attack.

Disengage and hit should be made in one movement, passing the hand very closely under or over the adversary's hand. If the disengagement is to be made from the low lines, the point must pass over the adversary's hand, and if from the high lines, under his hand.

The disengage can be parried by an opposition, a counter-parry, or change of distance.

Double, which is a feint of disengage and deceives the counter-parry. Double, one-two, etc. (one sort of preparation of attack).

To make PIA with the leg more effective try
1. The first attack is deep, sudden (with opponent), economical (with self), well covered, and above all, well balanced.
Note: Distinguish between the initiation for power (like reverse hook) and straight initiation.
2. "And a half" (1/2). The second halves must select
   • Those kicks that are fast and powerful
   • Those that do not deviate too much from the on-guard position as infighting can be initiated

On reaching your target
To reach the target the attacker must deceive the adversary's
a. Going forward balance
b. Rooted balance
c. Unpreparedness (physical and mental)
d. Guards and parries

Feints (PIA)

1. Object: to provoke a parry.
2. Be ready for counterattack; protection hand up.
3. Do not wait for the parry before completing your attack: keep ahead of it.
4. Prolong your feint enough so that the opponent has time to react.

The first action of a PIA is intended to open a line which is closed, so as to hit in that line on a subsequent action.

Principal use of PIA

1. To overcome a strong defense against simple attack
2. To offer variation in one's pattern of attack

On the value of surprise in both SA and PIA

Surprise is essential both in SA and PIA. Any motions, hesitations, or telegraphing on your part that might betray your intention to attack must be avoided. Otherwise, you leave yourself wide open to stop thrust, time hit or kick, or parries retreating.

Keep control of opponent's hands and legs at all times.

Never attack before bringing the distance that you have to cover to some measure of equality with that of your opponent, the defender—principle of PIA.

PIA factors that all martial artists should consider

1. PIA in attack (see five ways of attack)
2. PIA in defense
3. PIA in combination
4. Countering PIA
5. Training aid in PIA

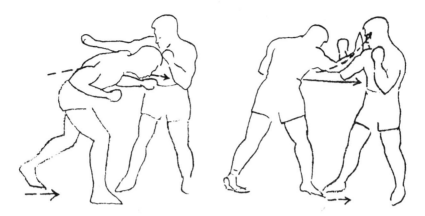

4. Attack by combination (ABC)

In Western boxing there are five methods of attack commonly employed. Each of these attacks is frequently varied by feinting the usual first punch and delivering the second punch of the combination which comprises the attack. So the five standard attacks become ten.

In each attack there must be coordination of length of step, body sway, and punch delivery. As always, you must fight from a balanced center. Each punch you throw must leave you in position to shoot another. The position of your opponent, his physical condition, and his weaknesses are considerations in determining which attack to use.

As a matter of generalship you should try to fight a type of contest which least suits the fighting abilities of your opponent. Simply stated: If he is a clever boxer, make him slug it out toe to toe. Boxing is fighting by skill and maneuver, having as your object to hit your opponent as often as possible and to get hit yourself as few times as possible.

To be a first-class fighter, you must be able to box or slug efficiently. You must be a two-way fighter.

Tight boundaries—speed and surprise—determination

a. The o-n-e-two

b. The o-n-e-two—hook

c. Right body/right jaw/right jaw

d. The straight high/low

e. Right jaw/ hook jaw/left jaw

The importance of range in fighting

If you do your best fighting at long range you should keep your opponent away with right jabs and left crosses and occasionally vary your attack with hooks from body to head. Once in a while work in close and drive a straight left to your opponent's body and follow this with a hard right hook to his jaw. Surprisingly, some boxers miss the boat trying to hit close targets with their sixteen-inch guns. In overshooting they throw themselves off center, lose their hitting position, and become easy marks for opponents who correctly adapt their punches to the proper style.

Some combination attacks (*Western boxing's punch combinations*)

The one-two

Stepping well forward and swaying slightly to your left, shoot a straight right jab to your opponent's jaw and follow with a hard, straight left cross to his jaw, allowing your body to then sway to the right as your left is delivered. This is the famous one-two punch combination and the blows are fast, long-range punches. Follow up as success indicates.

The lead low/lead high

Crowding your opponent, step forward and shoot a short straight right or a right hook to his body, shifting the weight of your body forward and slipping your head to the left to avoid his probable right lead jab. Follow this with a hard right hook to your opponent's jaw, shifting your weight to the ball of your left foot and twisting your body to the left in a pivoting motion. Follow up if it works.

Sometimes vary this attack by feinting the first right and hooking instantly to the jaw.

Rear low/lead high

Crowding your opponent, step diagonally right and forward and drive a short left to your opponent's body, swaying your body to the right and keeping your right fist and forearm well up as when you use the left-hand body blow. Follow this with a hard right hook to your opponent's jaw, swaying your body to the left. Follow up as your success warrants (this is used against a foe who has a strong facial defense but who has an opening in the lower regions and can also be used as a counter to the lead jab).

Lead low/rear high

Crowding your opponent into a corner, step forward and swaying your body to the left to avoid his right lead jab, shoot a right hook to his body. Follow this punch with a hard left rear hook to your opponent's jaw, swaying your body to your right and twisting at the waist to get your weight into your punch. Follow up if indicated.

Rear high/lead low

Crowding your opponent into a corner, step forward and, swaying your body to the right, drive a hard left rear hook to his jaw. Follow this punch with a hard right hook to his body, swaying your body to the left and twisting at the waist to get your weight into the punch. During both punches work your head in close to your opponent's right shoulder to protect yourself from his counterpunches. Always follow up if your attack succeeds.

One-two-three

This combination is known as the "jab-cross-hook." To the one-two combination, add another punch, a right hook. Send right jab out. Before it lands, start the left cross going, pivoting on the ball of the left foot. This will bring your left shoulder nearer to your opponent than your right shoulder, which should be drawn back with your right hand on your chin, elbow protecting your cocked side arm. Then shift your body toward the left, sending the right fist out in hook fashion, pivoting on your right foot. As the right goes out, the left cross goes back to defensive position. These combinations must be done with a great deal of speed. Practice them as much as possible.

Jab/hook

Send your right out in jab fashion, shuffling in with your right foot, followed by left foot. After the jab lands, step in fast again. As you do, cock your elbow and shoot out fast in hook fashion. While doing this, make sure you do not drop your left hand. You will notice when you jab an opponent that his head will snap back a little. This will put his jaw in perfect position for a well-timed hook. To add further force to this combination, send a left cross over after the jab and hook. This must be done fast.

Jab/rear hammer

This is a good combination against an opponent who ducks a lot. As you send your right lead hand out in jab fashion, your right foot slides forward simultaneously a few inches in the same direction as the jab. Before your right has reached its mark, prepare your left hammer blow to crash explosively on the back of his neck. If he straightens up, follow with a right hook.

Jab/low cross/hook

This combination is useful when fighting one who is constantly turning quickly to the right, leaving his left kidney an open target.

Attack-by-combination factors all martial artists should consider

1. Attack by combination in defense and counter
2. Countering attack by combination
3. Training aid

5. Attack by drawing (ABD)

Attack-by-drawing factors all martial artists should consider

1. Attack by drawing—in attack
2. Attack by drawing—in defense
3. Attack by drawing—in combination
4. Countering attack by drawing
5. Training aid

Causing your opponent to lose a movement or time

1. Progressive indirect attack (PIA)
2. Immobilizing attack (feet or hand—HIA)
   - Drawing reaction (for PIA or SA)
   - Disturbed rhythm of attacks of opponent (leg obstruction)
   - Jam or check and control
   - Deflect and score
3. False attacks followed by time attack on exposed area or advanced targets.

Attacks from ready stance: Hand attacks

1. One-two
   - Head • Body
2. Low/high lead
   - Straight • Hook (high/low lead)

3. Two-three (rear low/high lead hook)

4. Low lead/high rear cross

5. Rear cross lead/low lead shovel hook

6. Feint cross/lead hook

7. Feint lead/spin back blow

8. Low/high back fist

Counter-hand considerations

a. Under what circumstances

b. Special reminder of tips

c. Its possible kick combination

d. Its natural follow-up

e. The "landing" facilitation

---

1. Snap back with return jab

2. Left slip and straight

3. Left slip and palm strike

4. Reverse stance palm strike

5. Side step right and strike

6. Parry outward with return jab

7. Downward deflect with return jab

8. Push aside lead with shovel hook

9. Lead versus rear swing

10. Slip right with low cross counter

11. Cross-counter—with and without slip

12. Rear cross-counter versus lead swing

13. Duck with low rear cross to opponent's rear cross

14. Parry with lead crosses with rear (high/low)

Note: Study rigid and loose hand explosion (snap and thrust/snap)

---

1. Right elbow loosely resting on the hip for delivery

(*Study:* chin kept well inside lead shoulder)

Balance

Right straight lead

1. Advance 2. Backward 3. Left 4. Right 5. Snap back 6. Feint low then . . . 7. Feint high, then . . . 8. Double lead

Right hook (followed with left cross)

1. Forward hook (step forward)

2. Long hook (left foot step sideways)

3. Shovel hook

4. Horizontal hook

(*Note:* Bent leg crouch to spring in with hook: first with • Low lead feint • Low rear feint • After jab.)

Backfist

1. High 2. Low 3. Vertical

2. Left-hand cross

Preparation of attack

Obtain an opening for a riposte and may precede a simple or a compound attack or riposte (forcing commitment).

Broken rhythm attack

Broken rhythm attack is: 1. Economical flash 2. Time thrust
or 1. Economical flash 2. Counter-time

An example would be indirect immobilization—to draw opponent's reacting commitment—simple attack.

The gaining of distance has to be "covered up" by some hand action which will, momentarily, distract the opponent's attention.

The use of preparation

1. The fighting measure is long, especially when kicking is included, particularly to shin/knee.

2. There is the ever-present possibility of the stop kick or hit being used as a means of defense.

Remember that the success of an attack on the shin/knee depends largely on the element of surprise.

The trapping of the hand or obstructing the leg as a preliminary step is very effective because it tends to reduce the possibility of a stop thrust—especially when it is done with economy and surprise. A preparation of attack is the action taken by a fighter to make an opening for his attack:

a. To trap or deflect the opponent's lead

b. To obtain a desired reaction

c. To make a change of distance

(*Note*: A preparation may equally be used to obtain an opening for a riposte and may precede a simple or a compound attack or riposte.)

The taking of the blade

If the opponent always keeps his guards in line, we can remove them by two different ways:

1. The first by force, through the beat, the press, etc.—against weak opponents

2. The second, a more subtle way, by feints—against rigid and stiff opponents

The beat

There is the direct beat and the change beat, the latter being preceded by a change of engagement.

Leg attack (from ready stance)

1. Simple knee/shin side kick

2. Feint high/hook kick low

3. Feint hook kick low/strike high

4. Pursue double side kick (left and right opposing stance)

5. Feint side, spinning back kick

6. Step through forward rear front kick

7. Feint side, hook kick

8. Left straight feint, right hook kick

9. Left foot sweep feint with right hook

Consider leg attack options.

Leg attack: simple
1. Shin/knee side kick 2. Simple side kick 3. Simple hook kick
4. Simple spin kick 5. Rear straight thrust kick 6. Simple heel
wheel kick

Leg attack: double
1. Pursuing double side kick 2. Pursuing hand-block hook kick
3. One-two-one

Infighting
1. HIA 2. Shifting blasting

Direct attacks (right stance)
Kick

a. Right sweep kick to head b. Right side kick to ribs
   side kick to knee
   side kick to shin
   side kick or stomp kick to instep
   left foot sweep to back of knee or heel
c. Right hook kick to head d. Right hook kick to ribs
   side kick or hook kick or spin kick to face
   hook kick to groin

   1. Right stance—progressive kicking paths
   2. Left stance—progressive kicking paths
   3. Right stance—progressive striking path

4. Left stance—progressive striking path

5. Right stance—in close tactics

6. Left stance—in close tactics

7. Right stance—combination (feet)

8. Left stance—combination (feet)

9. Right stance—combination (hand and feet)

10. Left stance—combination (hand and feet)

11. Infighting loose play

12. Out-fighting loose play

Double leads

1. Lead and rear at head

2. Lead and rear at body

3. Lead at head and body

A compound attack is used when the opponent cannot be hit by a simple attack.

It is wise not to launch an offensive without having come to some conclusion regarding the probable reaction on the part of the opponent.

Defense (blocking)

Your blocking should be accomplished at the correct time. Not too soon. Never too late—block as late as you dare—in other words, your blocking should not occur too soon, but before the attack has been fully entered into and the attacker has extended himself into it. Once the attacker is fully committed, control of his hand is possible.

Parrying

As a general rule, parries should be assisted by a change of distance—stepping back with the parry sufficiently so that the attack will fall short. This distance should not be so great that a riposte (return attack) cannot easily reach.

Counter-striking

The more forceful the attack, the more you are required to bring your hand out of line in order to control the attack. It must be remembered, however, that the farther your hand goes out of line, the longer, and hence slower and more difficult, will be your counter.

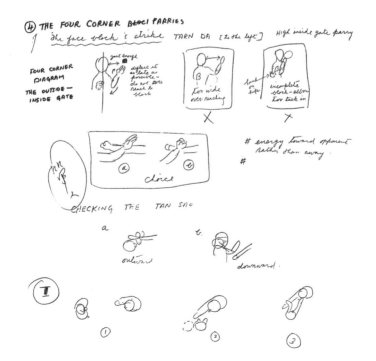

The four corner counters

To maintain control of the opponent's hands in order to prevent a continuation or retaking of the attack, make your counter with opposition, and vary your parries.

Do not hesitate with your counter. It must be a continuous action, with the exception of a delay counter.

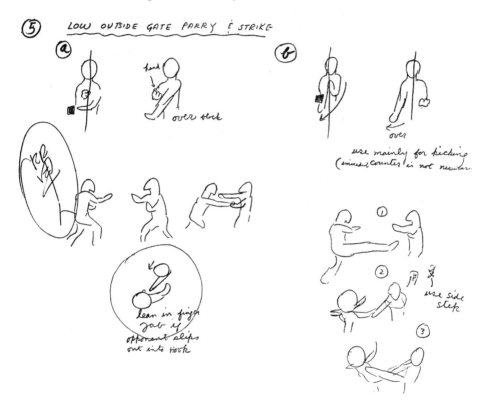

⑤ LOW OUTSIDE GATE PARRY & STRIKE

Counter-time

Counter-time is one method of dealing with the opponent who likes to try for the time thrust or stop thrust. It consists in deliberately feinting to draw such a reaction from him, parrying it, and countering.

The action to draw the time or stop thrust—it may be a half lunge, a deliberately uncovered feint, a step forward, an attack on the hand,

⑥ WARN PARK DA (Cross *parry* strike or high outside gate par...

① when opp. in right stance

middle

hit low

② when opp. in left stance

if opponent withdraw or drop R hand

⑦ HA· PARK DA — LOW INSIDE GATE STRIKE

upper cut to stomach

SEE THE ELBOW
IN DEFENSE IN
CHI SAO

or a combined action—must be forceful enough to really do so, and
the person using counter-time must allow his opponent to commit
himself to the counterattack before making his defensive move.

When an attack is made "in time," in the correct distance, and with maximum speed, the probability of bringing this attack to a successful finish is 99 percent.

Distraction and rhythm (watch for alertness to decline)

Standing up or sinking in the on-guard position, making an advance or retreat, recovering from an attack, making a feint without the intention of hitting, returning from a feint; engaging the opponent's hand, disengaging the opponent's hand, beating or any other action against hand without intention of striking, changing from one guard position to another.

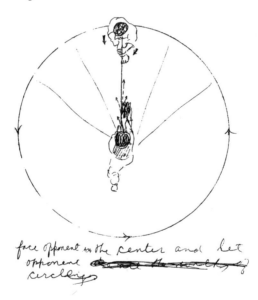

face opponent in the center and let
opponent ~~circling~~
circling

The circle of combat

Stand still and extend one leg out in front of you as far as it will go. Mark this spot with a piece of chalk. Now slowly pivot your extended leg around while simultaneously drawing a chalk circle around the circumference, the length of your extended leg. Make a mental image of this circle, realizing that as long as your opponent remains outside of the radius of your circle, he can do you no damage. Therefore, it is silly to jump and waste energy if he gestures or makes threatening movements outside of your circle. Additionally, you can move your circle backward should he advance so that he is, again, no threat to you. Let your opponent do all the walking around the circle and simply adjust yourself to his movement with economical moves. Keep in mind that if through movement and adjustment you can keep your opponent on the outer periphery of your circle, he will never get close enough to do you any harm, which should allow you to relax somewhat in this situation. However, when your opponent is inside your circle and you cannot or will not retreat or adjust any further, then you must fight. But until then, you should maintain your control and your distance.

Commentaries on hand-to-hand combat

If one determines to risk his life to bite his enemy's nose off, there is a great chance he may succeed. He may be heavily hurt, but this cannot prevent him from achieving his ambition. A real fighter should have this quality.

In fighting one's enemy, one should fight with all strength and all attention. His actions in desperation will press his enemy under heavy psychological burden. Even if he loses finally, he will be regarded as an honored loser.

In comparisons of strength, the stronger one will certainly beat the weaker one. However, if the weaker one fights with all his effort and finally loses, his courage can win admiration from the stronger. Thus, one of the most important factors in fighting is morale.

Fighters must have alert eyes like an eagle, a cunning brain like a fox, swift action like a cat, fierceness and toughness like a leopard, swiftness like a cobra, patience like a camel. He who obtains all these advantages will be a perfect fighter.

In practicing jeet kune do, we must practice swiftly and actively. But in real fighting, we have to keep our brain calm. Don't let your mind be conquered by stupid thoughts. Just regard the fighting as if it were nothing.

Practice makes perfect. After a long time of practicing, our foot-work will become natural, skillfull, swift, and steady.

Our eyes should not stare at only one point. See your enemy in whole and anticipate his action, so that you can evade his attacks and carry out counterattacks.

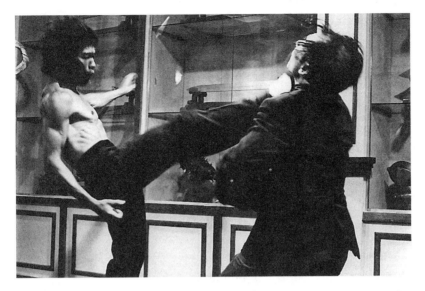

Many people make a big mistake in fighting against an enemy by thinking too much about winning or losing. Practically speaking, they should allow none of these sentiments to invade their mind. They need only to act as circumstances demand. When they act naturally, their hands and feet will suitably function.

A fighter with bad movement is a horseman without a horse. We depend on our hands to attack. But before we attack, we have to keep our body in balance, so that our attack can be effective and powerful.

Movement is the skill of fighting and the timing of movement is even the skill of skill. But only timing is not enough, movement should cooperate with hands and feet to carry out defense of attack. Furthermore, it should keep one's body in balance.

In fighting, if one could command a natural stance, swift movements, and powerful attacks, he already effects the best defense.

"Rehearsing" stunts every day: It doesn't work because the techniques are organized despair. Idealistically arranged and ritualistically practiced.

Dissecting a corpse—holding one's breath.

Half rhythm—*the half* beat—the broken rhythm, is never present in stylized form.

1. Too idealistic—doesn't happen like so
2. Unrealistic—dissecting dead corpse
3. Too classical—ritualistic

Simplicity—directness

Distances
1. Kicking 2. Finger jab 3. Punching 4. Combinations

Long-range tools and techniques
Kicks
1. Side shin/knee kick
2. Hook kicks—groin, knee, head
3. Side thrust kick

Combination kicking
1. Double step shin/knee side kick
2. Hook kick/side kick
3. Side kick/hook kick

Hand techniques
1. Finger jab 2. Right jab 3. Left cross 4. Right palm hook

Striking combinations
One-two

Long-range tools
1. Kicking
   • Leading shin/knee side kick

- Leading shin/knee hook kick
- Leading hook kick (tight)

Combination kicking
- Double side kicks: • Shin/knee • Thigh or rear leg

2. Hitting
- Leading right finger jab • Right jab • Right palm • Right hook

Combination hitting
The one-two

Grappling and throwing factors that all martial artists should consider
1. Grappling and throwing as attack
2. Grappling and throwing as counters
3. Grappling and throwing and hitting/kicking (or vice versa) as attack
4. Grappling and throwing and hitting/kicking (or vice versa) as counter
5. Counter to grappling/throwing—right stancer
6. Counter to grappling/throwing—left stancer
7. Training aid

Joint-lock factors that all martial artists should consider
1. Joint lock—standing attack
2. Joint lock—standing counter
3. Joint locks with grappling/throwing and/or hitting/kicking or vice versa—as attack
4. Joint locks with grappling/throwing and/or hitting/kicking or vice versa—as counter
5. Counter to joint locks—right stancer
6. Counter to joint locks—left stancer
7. Training aid

Ground-lock factors that all martial artists should consider

1. Ground subduing with hitting/kicking and/or grappling/throwing and/or joint locks or vice versa—as attack
2. Ground subduing with hitting/kicking and/or grappling/throwing and/or joint locks or vice versa—as counters
3. Countering ground locks and subduing
4. Training aid

Wrestling notes (matwork grappling)

When your opponent is facing the ground

1. Upper body
   - Strangulation • Grab hair • Or both
2. Lower body
   - Toe hold • Stomp lower back • Kick or grab groin

When your opponent is facing up

1. Upper body
   - Stomp
2. Lower body
   - Single leg lock • Double leg lock • Kick to groin or punch

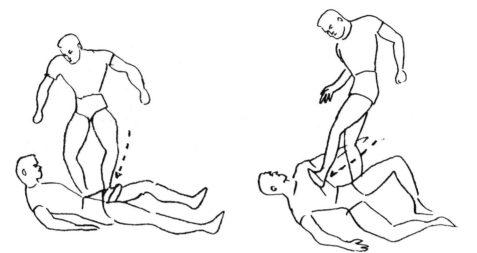

From takedown

The one-foot lead stance

All-infighting

a. All-infighting does not replace any known system of close fighting, nor does it evolve about any single style of defense and counterattack. It makes use of all known forms of personal combat, and any other means that will accomplish a quick kill.

b. Good conditioning and athletic ability

c. Scientific training of a boxer—fine coordination, sense of timing and distance

d. Sophistication of a fencer

e. Attitude and mental development of Zen, Taoism, etc.

f. It simply is a cold, efficient means of overcoming your enemy in a manner most suitable to the performance of your situation or the saving of your life. It has but one simple objective—to win!

Look into hair pulling

- Standing and on deck
- Control for strangulation

Concerning attacks

No plan of attack can be put into execution without first of all having taken the probable system of defense into consideration.

The success of attack depends on

a. A fine sense of timing

b. A perfect judgment of distance

c. A correct application of speed (rhythm)

The attack has to remain as simple as possible.

Attacks of more than one feint become dangerous, particularly if they are directed toward the body.

Head-butting factors that all martial artists should consider

1. Head butt as attack
2. Head butt as counter
3. Head butt combined with close-range tactics as attack
4. Head butt combined with close-range tactics as counter
5. Counter to right-hander's head butt
6. Counter to left-hander's head butt
7. Training hint for head but

The importance of fluidity

The importance of fluidity in the interchanging of:

1. Hitting/kicking
2. Grappling/throwing
3. Joint locks
   - Standing
   - On the ground
   - Immobilizing techniques for standing and on the ground

Close-range factors that all martial artists should consider

1. Counter to a close-range fighter—in right stance
2. Counter to a close-range fighter—in left stance
3. Training aid for close-range fighting

Infighting (kicking, striking, stomping) factors that all martial artists should consider

1. The high/low (or vice versa) lead in close-range fighting
2. The high/low (or vice versa) lead in close-range fighting—as attack
3. The high/low (or vice versa) lead in close-range fighting—as counter
4. The high/low (or vice versa) lead combined with close-range leg tactics (or vice versa) as attack (with lead hand or elbows and knee)
5. The high/low (or vice versa) lead combined with close-range leg tactics (or vice versa)—as counter
6. Counter to high/low (or vice versa) lead while infighting—from right stance.
7. Counter to high/low (or vice versa) lead while infighting—from left stance
8. Training aid for the high/low (or vice versa) leads
9. The lead low/rear high (or vice versa) in close-range fighting
10. The lead low/rear high (or vice versa) in close-range fighting—as attack
11. The lead low/rear high (or vice versa) in close-range fighting—as counter
12. The lead low/rear high (or vice versa) combined with close-range leg tactics or vice versa—in attack
13. The lead low/rear high (or vice versa) combines with close-range tactics or vice versa—as counter
14. Counter to lead low/rear high (or vice versa) in close-range fighting—opponent in right stance
15. Counter to lead low/rear high (or vice versa) in close-range fighting—opponent in left stance
16. Training aid for lead low/rear high (or vice versa) while infighting

Putting it all together

1. The right beginning
   - Krisnamurti • Emptiness—Zen
2. Aliveness
   - Being so of itself
3. Economy
   Simplicity and nontelegraphic (see progressive chart on page 205)
   - Stance
   - Attacking
   a. Feet b. Hand c. Counter d. Defense
4. Footwork
5. The basic weapons
   - Feet • Hands • Grappling
6. Some combinations
   - Long range–progressive chart • Close range/grappling
7. Broken rhythm and rhythm
   - Cadence
   - Timing
   - Speed
   - Distance
8. The five ways of attack
   - SAA
   - PIA
   - HIA
   - ABC
   - ABD
9. Counters
   - List counter to every attack and counter-time to counter.
10. Defense: the last resort
    - Stop hit (counter but emphasize again here!)
    - Slip
    - Duck

- Footwork
- Parry
- Smother

11. The leading straight
    - As offense
    - As counter
    - As retreating stop hit
    - As return after parry

12. The shin/knee side kick and other attacks on lead leg
    - Offense (stop kick!)
    - Counter
    - Obstruction
    - While infighting
    - Cross stomp (long and short, right and left)

13. The groin kick (a good mix-in)

14. The leg tackle (a preparation for maiming)

15. The high/low attack

Long-range and close-range adjustment

    a. Lead and shin/knee
    b. Lead and hook kick
    c. Reverse of (a)
    d. Reverse of (b)
    e. Lead and hand to groin (long and infighting)
    f. Hand to groin and to face (long and infighting)

16. Accompany each toot with training suggestion

17. Have three volumes—corresponding as though to the three stages—ending with the highest meaning of them

Note: In each technique comment on:

1. The general idea behind each technique

2. Itemized details as to:
    - Economy starting
    - Progressive details
    - Counter to watch for (e.g., right lead counter: remember the simple done right has no counter—economy starting, etc.)

Setting up (with kicking)

1. Hook sweep with palm shove and side low thrust (to left stancer)
(*Note:* Be sure to set up by using leg to fill in with hand attack. If jammed, reverse is also true when hand fails to bridge.)

Immediate counterattack

(Build up action with emphasis)

1. Flying side kick attack (from immobility) and study of posture for attack
2. Spinning back kick—from opponent's pursue—from own side thrust kick—to arrest attention.
3. Drop side kick—soft (to feel out opponent)—to irritate opponent
4. Rear leg thrust
5. Front hand blinding (abruptly!)
6. Front speed hook to "suddenly" drop opponent with his own preparation

The one-two

One-two factors that all martial artists should consider

1. The one-two (high lead/low rear or low lead/high rear or two high) as attack
   - The one-two to head (to right stancer)
   - The one-two to head (to left stancer)
2. The one-two lead as attack
   - The low/high one-two (to right stancer)
   - The low/high one-two (to left stancer)
   - The high/low one-two (to right stancer)
   - The high/low one-two (to left stancer)
3. The one-two (high/low or vice versa or two high) as counter
   - The one-two to head (to right stancer)
   - The one-two to head (to left stancer)
   - The low/high one-two (to right stancer)
   - The low/high one-two (to left stancer)

4. The one-two as counter
   - The high/low one-two (to right stancer)
   - The high/low one-two (to left stancer)
5. The one-two combined with kick or vice versa
   - As attack
   - As counter
6. Counter to one-two (right stancer)
   - The one-two to head
   - High/low one-two
   - Low/high one-two
7. Counter to one-two (left stancer)
   - The one-two to head
   - High/low one-two
   - Low/high one-two
8. Training aid for one-two

How can I be a master fighter?

1. The natural and direct expression of kicks and punches
2. The increasing development of the organic feel of efficiently "laying on right" of the physical tool
3. Obtaining "direct body feel" of devastating
   - Throwing
   - Left side kicking and punching
   - Ground fighting
   - Hara in changes
4. The mastering of economic mechanics under all situations
   - Speed/power
   - Form/naturalness
   - Balance/agility
5. The development of functioning from "root" with dynamic mellow continuity.

Be instinctively familiar with all possibilities.

Be instinctive with distance and timing with opponent's distance and timing.

What is my counter for:
1. A left stancer's right forward straight kick before and during initiation.
   - Those that overstep ground
   - Those that are right
2. It's coming
3. It's snapped

What is my counter for a left stancer's right rear hook kick?
1. Before or during initiation
(*Note:* for good and over-reaching initiation.)
2. It's coming
3. It's snapped

What is my counter for a left stancer's left side kick?
1. Before or during initiation
2. It's coming
3. It's snapped

What is my counter for a left stancer's right reverse punch as attack?
1. Before or during initiation
2. It's coming
3. It's snapped

What counter can I use for a left stancer's right reverse punch as counter to
- My hook kick (work on how not to let this happen)
- My side kick (how not to let opponent use this counter)
- My reverse hook (how not to let his counter work)

Look into initiating foot sweep

a. Long range (with or without hand work) as counter and attack

b. As combination in medium range with or without hand work

(*Note:* As attack and counter.)

c. In close range—with or without hand work; as attack and as counter.

d. How to counter left-stancer's foot sweep (left lead and rear)

(*Note:* Also at different range.)

e. How to counter right-stancer's foot sweeps (right lead and left rear)

(*Note:* Also at different range.)

Basic considerations in combination (points to ponder)

a. *When* should you incorporate rear leg and straight thrust? (Hint: one possibility is when opponent twists his body in rear hand thrust commitment.)

b. *How* does one get body-feel to toss the loose high speed explosive "padding" tool? (By "padding" we mean "right force absorption positioning tool.")

(*Note:* Be aware of the "foundation point of on-guard position" and get "body feel" to acquire lightning recovery and "sudden economical initiation" to protect oneself from countering or losing the play.)

Facts (things to do!)

Select and design most direct path to:

1. Combination kicking
   - Most economical (for self) and most direct ("to" opponent)
   - With on-guard position as the basis for guidance, controller, filling the gaps, etc.
   - The wanting to thrust and bust through from the correctly measured firing range (*Note/comment:* "Firing range" with hook kicking and also comment on ease as a refining element for clear awareness and not being erratic and the on-guard position as extra safety. To chase and measure speed and effort toward shifting and obvious target.)
2. Combination of kicks and hands
   Note: Reexamine the idea of:
   - Most economical for self
   - Most direct to opponent in the fight of "between" combination of kicking tools and striking tools

---

1. Examine leg to hand
   - Long-range leg with long-range hand
   - Kicking and HIA
2. Shifting from hand to leg
   - To shin/knee and instep
   - To groin
   - To head
   - To body
3. The nursing of the on-guard position and examining all the physical movements in order to facilitate the:

- Speedy return to the on-guard position
- Ability to attack and defend from where you end up and in the transition to this point

Some "direct to the path" kicking

To disorganize

1. Hook kick to knee and low stomping side kick with right toss finger jab to eyes (at different levels) and left cross (or HIA)
2. To direct speed groin hook kick

(*Note*: Don't take eyes off opponent. Don't commit to the point of difficulty in recovery. Remember your on-guard positioning.)

3. Shin/knee counter stop kick
   - At opponent's initiation
   - During development
   - At completion (1½ beat)
4. Low hand crouch to high hook kick (to right stancer)
5. Low hand crouch to high reverse hook kick

To direct harassment

(*Note*: Compare with HIA in the sense of moving compactly toward lines or opponent)

a. A direct speed groin hook kick and:
   - Don't take eyes off opponent
   - Don't commit to point of slow wide recovery. Remember the on-guard positioning!
b. A direct speed shin/knee side and...

Also question

a. If opponent is on way back
b. If opponent is caught flat-footed

(Thus the follow up would be affected by (a) and (b) above.)

To force

a. Double-step shin/knee side kick

b. Reverse hook and side kick

c. Reverse hook and hook kick

Natural follow-ups between

Right hand
• Jab • Hook • Back fist • Shovel hook path

Left hand
• Straight • Cross • Overhand • Hammer

Right leg
• Side • Hook • Straight • Upward • Reverse (groin variation, vertical variations) • Examine Thai crescent kick

Left Leg
• Straight thrusts (various heights)
• Hook kicks (various heights)
• Spin kicks (various heights)

High/low
• Safety triple
• In relationship to all phases of footwork

Questions in examining all tools

1. If left cross falls short within hand distance:
   • What is the natural follow up?
   • What do you accompany with it and with what defensive means?
   • What types of opponents react to it?

2. If left cross really misses opponent who retreats to kicking distance:
   • What is the natural follow up?
   • What do you accompany it with and by what defensive means?
   • What is the type of opponent who reacts to it?

3. Also, arrange natural follow up as to:
- Most direct
- Secondary choice
- During venture

a. Deep-penetrative-fast combination
b. Short-fast combination
c. Crispy combination
d. Uncrispy combination
(All strive to exert maximum force for what they are worth. That is why some need more forceful reinforcement; thus, the idea of combination.)

Be exposed to the various paths of combinations and to change of path during one path.

During gaps of combinations insert
a. Noncommitment to distract or improve
b. Delicacy to score without destroying the overall balance and flow of the combination (finger jabs, finger fan, finger flicks, back fingers, palm thrust)

Long-range combat factors that all martial artists should consider
1. Attacking the long-range fighter (right stancer)
2. Attacking the long-range fighter (left stancer)
3. Counters to a long-range fighter (in right stance)
4. Counters to a long-range fighter (in left stance)
5. Training aids for long-range fighting

Some combination with feinting in the initial progression and then loosely changing to second intention:
- Pay particular attention to the efficient gap bridging of the two moves

a. To get speed

b. To get power

Note: Use both of the following in attacking:

a. A fleeing opponent

b. An aggressive counterattacker

Right stancer

a. Low/high hook (lead with low hook first)

b. Low hook to high reverse hook

The root

Physical

Compare with subtle finger play of Western fencing to subtle use of hip, path, force, etc., and obtain the findings to check for all particular tools (i.e., side, hook, reverse hook, spin, rear thrust, etc.)

Mental

To cultivate continuous relaxation of mental subtlety for movement in a moment's notice. (*Note:* In order to seize an opportunity and, therefore, to time a movement well, the fighter must never allow himself to tense. This fact cannot be stressed too often. Relaxation will bring about smoothness, precision, and speed. Let us never forget this!)

Notes for Monday, November 16, 1970

Look into attacking the joints and limbs (investigate each department as well as to what part of the joint and limb).

Breaking by

a. Directed kicking (thrust kicks, push thrust, snap kick)

b. Directed striking

c. Limb locks by pressure

Practice relaying snapping forearm smash—add to tools possibilities.

Investigate by "body feel" to relay different parts of foot tools (heel, ball, instep) to target. Relay and time "what you are throwing" to "where."

Would one "no committing" followed by "well-placed commitment" (regarding full range of tool) be the safest measure?

Note: Requirement for the above is still the economical initiation.

Motto: Do not attack until he has obtained or created a rewarding movement from his enemy.

1. In attack
2. In counter

Question: Experiment on the following mechanics and feeling of footwork

1. Footwork to be evasive and soft if opponent is rushing
2. Footwork to avoid contact point (as if opponent is armed with knife)

Note: The ultimate aim is still to obtain the "brim of fire-line" on opponent's final real thrusts.

Investigate into butting (body feel)

1. With head 2. With hips and buttocks 3. With shoulder

Investigate

1. Elbowing
2. Kneeing (body feel)

Kicking range to counter rushes by kick or punch (pressures)—a difference from leisure "pecking."

Study opponent's delivering method—signs of telegraphing.

Develop the ability to

a. Read opponent's moment of helplessness.

b. Attack instantaneously with correct self-synchronization, right distance, and fight timing as one.

c. Learn to time opponent's second, third moves; read his style and solve the problem should simple attacks fail.

d. School yourself to execute tools and movements with speed, force, and precision—which presuppose a strong and flexible body.

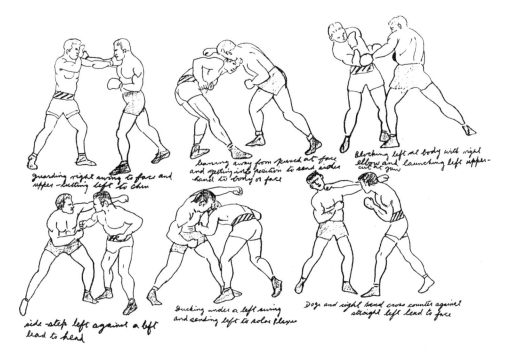

guarding right swing to face and upper-cutting left to chin

leaning away from punced at face and getting into pecision to send sides hand to body or face

Blocking left at body with right elbow and launching left upper-cut at jaw

side-step left against a left lead to head

Ducking under a left swing and sending left to solor plexus

Doge and right hand cross counter against straight left lead to face

Investigate into fighting from ground (sudden change of level)

1. As attack into opponent
2. As counter
3. Using legs mainly
4. Using legs and hands

Develop such mastery that one can fight safely from ground.

Ideas

1. By thrusting to advanced target
2. Other possible means
3. Develop strong fast kicking tools
4. Develop instinctive, fast maneuverability

Note: Thus the:

a. Orthodox scientific core b. Effective off-beat for rich variety

Study "distracting hand" to conceal the art of kicking

a. Obstructing method

b. Sound method (two hands slap, one extended/the other slap thigh)

Note: Investigate "covering method" during weak areas in combination.

Study attack, counter, and parrying in terms of:

1. Skillful frontal attack (countering same)
2. Skillful sideways attack (countering same)
3. Skillful dodging and shifting attack (countering same). Use them all in attack, parry, counter as one whole.

1. Investigate into clawing with attempt to tear apart the
   - Throat
   - Groin
   - Hair
2. Investigate into hand hook to pull opponent down backward.

Develop and exhibit a speed of hand and leg movements second to none! (Combine top physical fitness to keep one's conscience or whatever unblemished.)

Study body feel to get speed, fluidity, and power.

Note: Learn to put "energy flow" to rise from unaccustomed squatting postures.

Use attitude to create:

a. Evasiveness with every light movement (but not passive!)

b. Devastating attacks c. Speed d. Natural dynamics

e. Deceptive and slippery f. Sticky and direct g. Complete ease

(*Note:* (a) through (d) are as one ease)

Remember on the day of the 14th of December, 1970

The speedy delivery of kicks to "jump" opponent's consciousness.

a. To find attitude of loosening antagonistic muscle prior to delivery; find a continuous one rather than a "preparatory one" and also a "waiting one" (depending on opponent's commitment).

b. To "arrest" opponent's "moving away from neutrality."

c. To "watch" the delivery, landing, and recovery with continuous awareness, reinforcing and "almost watchful" hand guard (balancing center).

Concerning a big, tall, powerful opponent who is marching menacingly forward at all times to trap

a. To pace him as well as "inflicting respect" if he continues to bridge firing-line gap.

b. If he initiates a fast combination.

c. If he forces on uncrisply.

d. What one should be doing.

e. One must mix attack, counter, defensive footwork. Defense as one whole.

f. What about moving in to attack very weak point?

Group One: The basic blows

1. Straight right (high and low)—long and short range

2. Straight left (high and low)—long and short range

3. Gliding slant punch

4. Back fist

5. The hook

(All of the above with footwork)

Group Two: The basic kicks

1. Straight kick (medium and low)

2. Side kick (medium and low)

3. Toe kick (straight and hook)

4. Round house (high) kick (for practice only)

(All of the above with footwork)

Group Three: Basic defense

1. The finger stop strike

2. The high guard and strike

3. The low guard and strike

4. The inside parry and strike

5. The low parry and strike

6. The moving out of line and strike

7. The swallowing in and strike

8. The side-step strike

Group Four: Basic footwork

1. Advancing 2. Retreating 3. Circling right 4. Circling left

Group Five: Classical techniques

1. Slapping hand strike

2. Hook jerk (single and double)

3. The back-fist strike (left and right)

4. The slapping hand strike and hook jerk back fist

5. The double back fist

6. Hook jerk strike and right straight (opponent slaps)

7. Knuckle-first back fist and side kick

8. Entering inside gate right and left punch

9. Entering inside gate right fist inside slap

Group Six: Self-defense techniques

1. Grab collar

2. Left punch (boxer stance)

3. Right punch (opponent left stance)

4. Pushing

Group Seven: Basic combinations

1. High/low strike (hand)

2. High/low strike (hand/foot)

3. Low/high strike (hand)

4. Low/high strike (foot/hand)

Group Eight: Forms

The three facts of jeet kune do

1. Nonclassical

a. No classical postures

- No unrealistic footwork

- No mechanical bodily movements

- Aliveness

- No dissections of movement like a corpse

- Example of sitting down

b. No rhythmical mess

- No two-men cooperation

- Comparison of rhythmic form and broken rhythm of shadow boxing in Western boxing.

- Example of Bob Hayes

2. Directness

a. No passive defense

- Blocking is considered the least efficient

b. Everything stripped to their essentials
  - No fancy decoration or ornamentation—if someone grabs you, punch him!
  - See reality in its suchness
  - Example of throwing objects

  3. Simplicity
a. Daily minimize instead of daily increase
  - Being wise doesn't mean to "add" more, being wise means to be able to get off sophistication and be simply simple.
b. The three stages in jeet kune do:
  I. *Sticking to the nucleus*
  II. *Liberation from the nucleus*
  III. *Returning to the original freedom:* Before I studied the art, a punch was just like a punch, a kick just like a kick. After I studied the art, a punch is no longer a punch, a kick no longer a kick. Now that I understand the art, a punch is just like a punch, a kick just like a kick.

The triple blows

The triple blows are combinations of three different punches which have slipping as their basic technique. Always the first two blows are to the body, followed by a blow to the chin. There are two triples, one which starts with a slip to the inside guard position, and one which starts with a slip to the outside guard position. The first two blows are designed to bring down the guard to create an opening for the final blow.

The one-two-three series

The one-two-three series is a series of three blows which have as their basis rhythm, timing, and power. They are blows which seem to follow each other naturally. One series, that is, the jab, cross, and hook is intended to narrow the opponent's guard and create an opening for a hook from the outside. The jab, hook, and cross series is designed to create an opening for a final straight blow to the chin. Both series can be used effectively.

The high/low

The high/low are a series of blows which have rhythm as their basis in punching first to the body and then to the head, or vice versa. The wide hook is used to open a path for the final straight blow. The main thing to remember is that the last blow will be to the spot of the first blow. If the first blow is to the jaw, the last blow will also be to the jaw.

Set-up options

Note: Relate the possibility of kicks with the following blows or in place of:

The inside triple

1. Use only against a right lead. Action must be fast and continuous.
2. Slip inside with a straight left to the body. Use a stop for the opponent's left.
3. Step sideways with the left foot, moving the foot up even with the right.
4. At the same time, shift the weight over the left leg and hook the right hand to solar plexus.
5. Straighten the body and cross the left to the opponent's chin, weight shifting to the right foot.
6. Keep the body low until the final movement. Weight is shifted first to the right leg, then to the left leg, and back again to the right leg.

The outside triple

1. Use on a right lead.
2. Bend the body to the left under the right lead and hook the right to the opponent's midsection.

3. Move the right foot sideways and forward as the body moves to the inside guard position.
4. Hook the left to opponent's ribs, at the same time stopping the opponent's left with the right hand.
5. Then straighten the body and whip the right hand to opponent's chin.
6. Keep the body low until the final blow. The weight is shifted from the left foot, to the right, then back to the left.

The one-two

1. Jab with the right hand and step with the right foot.
2. Follow by moving the left foot to the fundamental position and driving the left arm out into complete extension.
3. The rhythm is o-n-e—two!
4. Be sure to jab high with the right hand to block vision. Then drive the left hand to chin.

The jab hook

1. Jab with the right hand
2. Without moving the hand, shift the weight back to the left foot and hook the right hand in an arc toward the left shoulder.
3. Hold the left hand off the right shoulder.

The jab, step, and hook

1. Jab, without stepping with the right foot.
2. Hold the arm extended and walk to the arm. Elbow is thus bent to position of a hook and held off the right shoulder.
3. Whip a short hook to opponent's chin.
4. Perform the movement fast! Successful execution depends upon deception and speed.

The jab, cross, and hook

1. Drive a one-two to the opponent's chin.
2. Then step to the side with the left foot and whip a right hook to the opponent's chin.

The jab hook, and cross

1. Use the jab hook to the chin, weight shifting back to the left leg with the hook.
2. Shift the weight to a straight right leg and drive a straight left to the opponent's chin.
3. Fold the right arm ready to stop the opponent's left hand blow.

The straight high/low

1. Fling the right arm upward and forward.
2. Quickly drop the body forward and drive a straight left to the ribs.
3. Hold the right arm ready to stop the opponent's left-hand blow.

The high/low and cross

1. Remember that if the first blow is high, the last blow is high.
2. Lead a wide hook to the chin. Hesitate, and hook to the body. Then drop a straight left to the chin.
3. The rhythm is one . . . , two, three!
4. The first two blows are designed to clear the path for the last blow.

The low/high and uppercut

1. Lead a wide right hook to the body. Hesitate, then hook a right to the chin. Follow immediately with a left uppercut to the solar plexus.
2. Rhythm is the same, one . . . , two, three!

Deception and evasion

Deception is the drawing (by feint) of the opponent's parry—thus causing him to commit himself. Evasion is used against an opponent who attacks with a prepared hand technique. The deception and the evasion have one thing in common—there must be no contact with the opponent's hands while they are being executed.

The feint is composed of a false thrust and a real evasive thrust.

The preparation by a series of false attacks and feints, executed at a normal rhythm, has the effect of lulling the opponent into a false sense of preparedness. It accustoms his reaction to a cadence other than what will be used for the attack itself. Then the movement comprising the attack is suddenly accelerated and more likely to find him lagging behind.

An effective variation

A very effective change of cadence is to slow down, instead of speed up, the final action of a compound attack or riposte—attacking, or riposting, in "broken rhythm"—this change of cadence, by slowing down, can be pictured as a strike whose delivery is begun, halted in its path forward, and continued when the adversary leaves the threatening line for another in the hopes of finding the hand.

Practice

Feinting is best practiced before a full-length mirror. Practice each possibility and notice the deception of each.

Feinting factors that all martial artists should consider

1. Feints in attack 2. Feints in defense 3. Feints in counter
4. Feints in combination 5. Training aids in feinting

Ducking to avoid a strike

Jeet Kune Do

Ducking is for swings and hooks (hands or feet), and the rear heel is twisted when ducking under a hook, a detail which aids the alacrity of the whole movement.

While the punches are coming, keep your eyes open every minute. The punches will not wait for you. They will strike unexpectedly, and unless you are trained well enough to be able to spot punches, they will be hard to stop.

Weaving

Note: The weave is rarely used by itself. Almost invariably the weave is used with the bob.

Weaving is an advanced defensive tactic which means moving the body in, out, and around a straight lead to the head, making the opponent miss and using the opening thus created as the start of a two-fisted counterattack.

Body-sway (bob and weave) factors that all martial artists should consider

1. As attack to a right stancer
2. As attack to a left stancer
3. Ducking as counter: the outside duck to right stancer
4. Ducking as counter: the inside duck to right stancer
5. Ducking as counter: the outside duck to left stancer
6. Ducking as counter: the inside duck to left stancer
7. Countering a right-stancer's outside duck
8. Countering a right-stancer's inside duck
9. Countering a left-stancer's outside duck
10. Countering a left-stancer's inside duck
11. Bob and weave in combination with four-corner tactics
12. Training aid

Slipping a strike

In attacking with the lead, the first few inches of advancing, the head remains in line; after that, the head should adapt.

Notes on slipping

Slipping is avoiding a blow without actually moving the body out of range. It is used primarily against:

a. Straight leads b. Counters of opponent

It calls for exact timing and judgment and to be effective, must be executed so that the blow is escaped only by the smallest fraction. Performed suddenly the slip contains an element of surprise and leaves the opponent wide open at the mercy of a terrific counterattack.

Because slipping leaves both hands free to counter, it is the method preferred by the expert.

It is possible to slip either a left or right lead, although more often used and safer against a right lead. The outside slip, that is, to the left of an opponent's right lead, or to the right of an opponent's left lead, is the safest position, leaving the opponent unable to defend against a counterattack.

Slipping is an invaluable technique, the real basis of counter-fighting upon which depends the science of attack. So do take advantage of the opening and do not slip passively all the time.

Slipping factors that all martial artists should consider
1. Slipping in attack to a right stancer
2. Slipping in attack to a left stancer
3. Slipping as counter to a right stancer
4. Slipping as counter to a left stancer
5. Slipping in combination
6. Countering a right-stancer's outside slip
7. Countering a right-stancer's inside slip
8. Countering a left-stancer's inside slip
9. Countering a left-stancer's outside slip
10. Training aid on slipping

④ THE FOUR CORNER BLOCI PARRIES

the face block & strike   TARN DA [to the left]   High inside gate parry

FOUR CORNER DIAGRAM
THE OUTSIDE — INSIDE GATE

just enough
deflect it as late as possible — do not over reach to block

Too wide over-reaching

hand on hip
incomplete block – elbow Too tuck in

The art of parrying
Against most attacks the defender has the choice of three forms of parry to deflect any single offensive action from his opponent. For example, engage in quarte, opponent engage into sixte.

a. Circular parry of counter quarte

b. Direct parry of sixte

c. Semicircular parry of septime

["Septime" is fencing nomenclature for "seven" or "defense of the low inside line."]

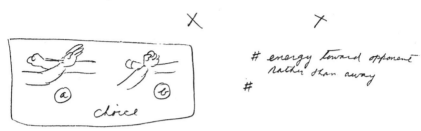

CHECKING THE TAN SAO

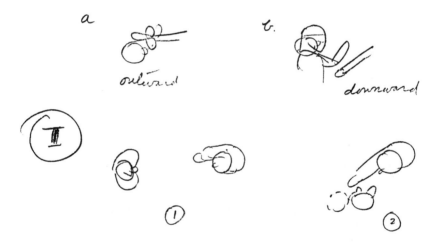

Against experienced men, one must vary his parries and keep his opponent guessing as to what form of defense he is about to take. This will cause a certain amount of hesitation on the part of the attacker, whose offensive action will suffer in his confidence and penetration.

Remember that to land a hit, whether it be with the edge or with the point, the defense has to be avoided. Excessive speed can catch up with the opponent's parries. The attacker is then known as "having parried himself."

Simple parry

The uncontrolled use is conducive to large arm movements and slashing actions.

Against an inexperienced fighter who lacks the variety of defense, one cannot use greater variety of attack that will not correspond to such fighter's defense.

Make sure these instinctive parries are well controlled. Make sure they are not wild and are performed neatly.

Right-stancer parrying factors that all martial artists should consider

1. Simple parry (the right-stancer's front hand)
   - Outside high (with lead right hand)
2. Simple parry countering right-stancer's
   - Outside high (with lead right hand)
   - Outside low (with lead right hand)
   - Countering a right-stancer's outside low (with lead right hand)
   - Simple parry: the right-stancer's cross block to inside high (with right lead hand)
   - Countering to right-stancer's cross block to inside high (with right lead hand)
   - Simple parry: right-stancer's cross parry to inside low (with right lead hand)
   - Countering to right-stancer's cross parry to inside low (with right lead hand)
   - Right stancer using left rear hand to block
   - Simple parry: right-stancer's left lateral parry to inside high (using rear left hand)
3. Countering right-stancer's
   - Left lateral parry to inside high (using rear left hand)
   - Simple parry—right-stancer: left lateral parry to outside high (with rear left hand)

- Countering to right-stancer's left lateral parry to outside high (with rear left hand)
- Simple parry: right-stancer's left downward parry to outside low (with rear left hand)
- Countering to right-stancer's left downward parry to outside low (with rear left hand)
- Simple parry: right-stancer's left downward parry to inside low (with left rear hand)
- Countering to a right-stancer's left downward parry to inside low (with left rear hand)

Left-stancer parrying factors that all martial artists should consider

1. Simple parry: the left-stancer's front hand
   - Outside high (with lead left hand)
2. Countering left-stancer's:
   - Outside high (with left lead hand)
   - Right-stancer's outside low (with lead left hand)
   - Countering left-stancer's outside with left lead hand
   - The left-stancer's simple parry: the cross parry to inside high (with left lead hand)
   - Countering to left-stancer's cross parry to inside high (with left lead hand)
   - Simple parry: left-stancer's semicircular parry to inside low (with left lead hand)
   - Countering left-stancer's semicircular parry to low (with left lead hand)
3. Left-stancer's using right rear hand for simple parry
   - Left-stancer's rear right lateral parry to inside high
4. Countering left-stancer's
   - Right lateral parry to inside high (using rear right hand)
   - Left-stancer's simple parry: right lateral parry to outside high (with rear right guard)
5. Countering to left-stancer's right lateral parry to outside high (with rear right guard)

6. Left-stancer's simple parry: right semicircular downward parry to outside low (with rear right hand)

7. Countering to left-stancer's right semicircular downward parry to outside low—with right rear guard

8. Left-stancer simple parry: right semicircular downward parry to inside low (with right rear guard)

9. Countering to left-stancer's right semicircular downward parry to inside low—with right rear guard.

10. Simple parry in attack

11. Training aid

Defenses in "filling the gaps" (parry)

a. While attacking

b. Counterbalance parry to defensive parry

c. Successive parries in combination

What to do should an opponent grab your hand or sleeve

a. Apply leverage stop

b. Spin, pull, lead away while in balance to hit, kick, counter grapple

---

Get body feel on the forearm as destructive weapon (use as loose snap or club) alongside with elbowing.

Right-stancer circular parry factors that all martial artists should consider

1. The right-stancer's right circular parries—clockwise and counterclockwise

2. The right-stancer's right front circular parries
   • Leading right clockwise circular parry

3. Countering right-stancer's leading right clockwise circular parry

4. The right-stancer's right front circular parry: leading right counterclockwise parry

5. Countering the right-stancer's leading right counterclockwise parry

6. The right-stancer's left rear circular parries—clockwise and counterclockwise
7. The right-stancer's rear left circular parry
   • Left circular clockwise parry
8. Countering the right-stancer's left circular clockwise parry
9. The right-stancer's left circular counterclockwise parry
10. Countering the right-stancer's left circular counterclockwise parry.

Left-stancer circular parry factors that all martial artists should consider

1. The left-stancer's front left circular parry—clockwise and counterclockwise
2. The left-stancer's left front circular parry—leading left clockwise circular parry
3. Countering left-stancer's leading left clockwise circular parry
4. The left-stancer's left front circular parry—leading left counterclockwise parry
5. Countering the left-stancer's leading left counterclockwise parry
6. The left-stancer's right rear circular parries—clockwise and counterclockwise
7. The left-stancer's rear right circular parry—right circular clockwise parry
8. Countering the left-stancer's right rear circular clockwise parry
9. The left-stancer's right rear circular counterclockwise parry
10. Countering the left-stancer's right rear circular counterclockwise parry
11. Circular and semicircular parry in attack

The semicircular parry
Semicircular parries are generally used against attacks into the low line.

Defensive awareness
1. Stop hit, kick, and finger jab 2. Deflect and strike

1. The stop hit or kick
2. The all-purpose striking and/or kicking
3. The four-corner counter
4. The leg obstruction

Self-defense techniques

1. The collar grasp (left or right hand)
2. The push (left or right hand)
3. The shove (two hands—or after being shoved—kick)
4. The straight right
   - The right swing • The right uppercut • The right twisting curve
5. The left jab
   - The left hook • The left uppercut • The left swing • The left twisting curve

Body-feel in defense

a. To draw opponent off balance into one's sensitive aura while keeping yours
b. To be able to express efficiency while moving backward and experiment with all possibilities (side, curve, etc.—to be in balance for finishing blows and kicks
c. Take advantage of common tendency to reach with spent tools

The art of riposting

1. Direct riposte (on final part of the attack)
   - Direct riposte into direction combination
   - Direct uncrispy riposte to adhere and remain
2. Delayed riposte to study reaction for score
   - Delayed riposte into combination attack
   - Delayed riposte into PIA attack
3. The disengage riposte

Applications of simple riposte

1. The direct riposte—is executed against a fighter who, when on the lunge, commits the error of bending his arm prepatory to recovery, thus leaving himself exposed in the line of the parry.

2. The riposte in low line—is the choice made against an opponent who ends his attacks correctly covered, and who recovers with his arm extended, thus only leaving his lower target open.

3. The disengagement and cut over ripostes—are used against an opponent who, when on the lunge, or while recovering, bends his arm and covers in the line of the parry, in anticipation of a direct riposte.

4. The riposte by counter-disengagement—is made against an opponent who, when on the lunge or recovering, does not remain in the line of the parry, but changes his engagement; in other words, takes a counter.

Simple-riposte factors that all martial artists should consider

 1. From inside high to right-stancer's kick
 2. From inside high to right-stancer's punch
 3. From inside high to left-stancer's kick
 4. From inside high to left-stancer's punch
 5. From outside high to right-stancer's kick
 6. From outside high to right-stancer's punch
 7. From outside high to left-stancer's kick
 8. From outside high to left-stancer's punch
 9. From inside low to right-stancer's kick
10. From inside low to right-stancer's punch
11. From inside low to left-stancer's kick
12. From inside low to left-stancer's punch
13. From outside low to right-stancer's kick
14. From outside low to right-stancer's punch
15. From outside low to left-stancer's kick

16. From outside low to left-stancer's punch
17. Riposte after HIA using "all measures" to advanced targets and vital targets to maim or control
18. Training aid on ripostes

Direct riposte and riposte by disengagement

The choice of a direct riposte is made against the attacker who commits the error of bending his arm on the lunge. However, for an attacker who, expecting a direct riposte, covers in the line in which he has been parried, sometimes he covers intentionally, often it is merely an instinctive movement. Whatever the reason may be, if this covering is successful, the riposter must anticipate and deceive it by a simple disengagement.

Riposte-by-disengagement factors that all martial artists should consider

1. From inside high to right-stancer's kick
2. From inside high to right-stancer's punch
3. From inside high to left-stancer's kick
4. From inside high to left-stancer's punch
5. From inside low to right-stancer's kick
6. From inside low to right-stancer's punch
7. From inside low to left-stancer's kick
8. From inside low to left-stancer's punch
9. From outside high to right-stancer's kick
10. From outside high to right-stancer's punch
11. From outside high to left-stancer's kick
12. From outside high to left-stancer's punch
13. From outside low to right-stancer's kick
14. From outside low to right-stancer's punch
15. From outside low to left-stancer's kick
16. From outside low to left-stancer's punch

Riposte by counter-disengagement

Riposte by counter-disengagement is the riposte which deceives the change of engagement taken by the attacker when recovering from his attack. It is not uncommon to meet fighters who, when returning to guard, take a change of line (or counter).

(*Note:* This form of riposte is particularly useful when dealing with left-hander stance.)

Sometimes the riposte must be sent out immediately as soon as contact has been made (as though one smooth thrust). At other times it is necessary to hold the attacking thrust for a moment before speeding the riposte on its way (delayed).

Parrying/riposting on the final portion of the attack

Generally the immediate riposte is the most effective as it forces the opponent on the defensive. To ensure its effectiveness, the parry and riposte must be made just as the attack is ending, and before the opponent has an opportunity of changing from offense to defense.

Counter-time

Counter-time is of the essence in the tactical art of Epee. Counter-time is the surest way to draw the opponent's blade into a position in which it can be dominated, in such a way as to score a hit without oneself being hit.

The counter-time is a time thrust made into the feint in time.

Counter-time (second-intention attack) consists of
A. Drawing a stop hit or time hit
B. Parrying it and scoring with a riposte

Watch out for his launching of his stop hit as a feint, and he will parry the riposte and score with a counter-riposte (he might induce one to use counter-time by an apparent predilection for stop hit.)

Practice
a. Student stamps his foot to indicate a false attack
b. The teacher stamps his foot to indicate the feint
c. Then student lunges with the time hit while teacher tries to finish the feint attack with a short lunge. Both complete the action with the lunge.

In counter-time, the artist draws the counterattack by one of the various means at his disposal, i.e., step forward, beat, take the hand. Then he will attack with a lunge, after having parried, beaten, or taken the hand (immobilization).

Counter-time is the strategy by which an opponent is induced or provoked to attack in tempo, with the object of counter-timing or alternatively taking possession of the opposing hand or detaching it and executing a subsequent attack or riposte.

Counter-time is an action of "second intention"—it lies not so much in drawing the stop cut as in correctly timing the parry which deflects it. The speed of the opponent's reactions will have to be found and his cadence judged.

Measuring distance
Distance must be judged correctly to minimize the danger of being hit, while still being within reach of the opponent in order to land the final movement of the counter-time sequence, which is the riposte.

Counter-time is "the action of drawing a stop hit, parrying, and riposting it"—counter-time can combine with HIA, PIA, etc.

It might be wise to riposte with opposition and switch to HIA or varying body positions to avoid opponent's continuation of the stop hit.

Counter-time as a basic tactic

It is not wise at all to attack without first of all having gained control of the opponent's movement time or hand position. Thus, a smart fighter uses every means at his disposal, patiently and systematically to draw the stop hit. It brought the adversary's hand or leg within his reach and gave them the opportunity of gaining control of it.

The second-intention attack

The second-intention attack (counter-time), as its name implies, is a premeditated movement, generally used against a fighter who has formed the habit of continually attempting stop hits or who attacks into the attack. That is to say, one who launches an attack as soon as his opponent makes any offensive movement.

The success of a counter-time movement largely depends on concealing one's real intentions and inducing the opponent to make his stop or time hit with conviction so that he has little opportunity to recover when it is parried before the riposte lands.

Drawing a stop hit

The stop hit may be drawn in a variety of ways:

a. By use of invitation

b. By intentionally uncovered feints

c. By making false attacks with a half lunge or merely by stepping forward

Counter-time is of the essence in the tactical art of fighting. It is the surest way to draw the opponent's hand into a position in which it can be dominated, in such a way as to score a hit without oneself being hit.

Counter-time factors that all martial artists should consider

1. Counter-time in combination
2. Counterattack to kicking
3. Counterattack in close-range tactics:
   - Elbowing and kneeing and striking
   - Joint locks (standing)

- Joint locks (on the ground)
- Throwing

4. Training aid

On neutralizing counterattack

Constant changes of varieties of attacks and defenses

Consider training aids for neutralizing counterattack.

Countering the stop hitter

An opponent who stop hits should not be difficult to deal with, especially if he is doing so out of habits. The stop hit must be drawn by a feint, a false attack, or a movement forward of the body and then counter-time his commitment.

Renewed attack

The opponent having retreated and parried:

a. An attack on the hand while recovering forward, followed by a simple or compound attack

b. The recovery forward followed by a preparation of attack, and an attack

---

When the opponent stops to counter within distance, his shin/knee is vulnerable.

The first movement in a combination should start from the small phasic bent-knee stance (SPBKS) and initiate from "economical" (nontelegraphic move from where it is) flow (smooth surprising extension with the absence of jerks caused by force that is so necessary in real attack), well covered.

Consider covering (defensive) measures after renewal of attack.

THE COMPONENTS OF A PROPER STANCE

1. Toward simplification
2. Medium crouch—knees bent slightly less than previously
3. To facilitate lightness of foot and great mobility
4. Bear weight on balls of feet (an alertness of foot will transmute into an alertness of mind), lightly poised
5. Balance in mobility

The arms and kicking leg are important only because they are the vehicles of body force (watch out for too much commitment—see finger jab, the "feeler" jab and the "feeler" kick). They, the tools, only give expression to body force when the body is in proper align-ment. *The position of the hands and arms and of the legs and feet that facilitate easy body expression is important.* The foot position is the most important phase of balance.

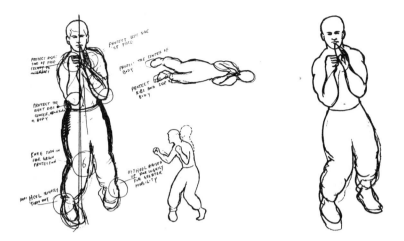

Exer-hint: develop a sense of feel for the position of the arms and legs as to:

1. Attacking in combination
    - Positions for all types of hits
    - Positions for all types of kicks
2. Retreating countering
    - Positions for all types of hits
    - Positions for all types of kicks

Forget about fancy horse stances, of "moving the horse," fancy forms, pressure, locking, etc. All these will promote your mechanical aspects rather than help you. You will be bound by these unnatural rhythmic messes, and when you are in combat it is broken rhythm and timing you have to adjust to. The opponent is not going to do things rhythmically with you as you would do in practicing a kata alone or with a partner.

Move constantly in small, shifting steps.

The position adopted should be the one which is found to give the maximum ease and relaxation, combined with smoothness of movement at all time.

Rest the left rear hand lightly upon the body. The hands may perform a "weaving" movement after the style of circles. Relax them.

Stand loosely and lightly, avoid tension and muscular contraction. Thus you will both guard and hit with more speed, precision, and power.

All punches and kicks are thrown from the on-guard position and return again to the on-guard position with all possible rapidity:
a. Necessary for speed b. Necessary for proper deception

The chin does not go all the way down to meet the shoulder, nor does the shoulder come all the way up. They meet halfway. The shoulder is raised an inch or two and the chin is dropped an inch or two.

The entire arm and shoulder must be loose and relaxed so that the boxer will be able to snap or whip out the lead in rapierlike thrusts.

The rear (loose) fist is poised about the level of the chin for defense and appropriate path to attack. The rear elbow is kept close to the body, protecting the left side and kidneys. The forearm protects the solar plexus and the fist protects the chin and left inside high line.

The close guard, including a tucked-in chin, goes a long way to neutralize a swinging blow—"going into" with a counter punch or leg tackle is best for this type of wild rushing opponent.

Caution should be observed not to telegraph your actions by any visible muscular preparation!

Delivery of hooks necessitates moving hand out of line.

Right leading hand is best positioned slightly lower and conceals the intended striking lines (straight or curve).

The solution

Thus, adopt the recommended stance previously stated and keep the potentialities of your right lead reach a secret.

Proper posture is a matter of effective internal organization of the body which can be achieved only by long and well-disciplined practice.

The head

It should be carried forward, with the chin pinned down to the breastbone. This position must never vary no matter how the body shifts. If the body turns, the head turns.

Kicking distance

Simple attack can be made efficiently from the small phasic bent-knee stance (SPBKS), and to keep that position throughout.

Additional notes on the on-guard position (JKD)

All kicking and striking are thrown from the on-guard position and end back to the on-guard at the finish.

Not too wide, not too close together.

The front hand should be up (especially for the beginners) but not so high that it obstructs his vision. It should not be too close to the body (too long a reach to the opponent) or extended too far out (not enough distance for generation of power and tires easily).

The entire arm and shoulder should be loose and relaxed and slightly moving (check diagram).

The left shoulder is pulled back, thus presenting a smaller target space—at the same time giving a longer reach to both the right lead and the right shin/knee kick.

Slight crouch—balance evenly on your right foot and the ball of your left foot, with your knees slightly bent—more on the order of a cat with his back hunched up and ready to spring (except that you are relaxed), or like a cobra coiled in a relaxed position. Like a cobra you must be able to strike so that your touch is felt before it's seen. Present little target for opponent to shoot at.

Body slightly leaning forward from the waist to facilitate drawing back from blows (to mislead distance).

In this stance, you will attack mostly with the right hand and right foot just as a boxer in his left stance uses mainly his left jab, hook, etc.

The left (protection hand) is the main defending force. In guarding, do not be afraid to let the punch come at you so you are sure of its direction. If you over reach, he will feint you or come over, under, or around your extended guard—never let guard go slack.

The left heel is up and cocked, ready to pull the trigger. It is the piston.
1. To be more agile
2. For faster footwork and drive
3. For more power in punching

When you are attacked, you can "give" by pulling back the body slightly as you sink down on the left heel without moving your feet. Thus your opponent will completely miss and is committed.

Keep elbows down and in—that makes your body hard to get at.

The best moment to attack from immobility is when your opponent advances toward you.

Your movement should be smooth—like waltzing—you are set but flexible, you are ready but not tensed, you are totally aware but not dreaming or thinking.

Do not hold your arms rigid. Keep them moving slightly in a semi-threatening manner so that your rival is kept guessing as to your intention.

All punches start and end again from the on-guard position (with all possible speed).

For more speed without wasted motion.

For proper deception without telegraphing.

Right hand returns back high without dropping and is kept high to offset a left-hand counter.

Never draw your hand back before delivery, especially the left (without hesitation!).

One hand out, one hand back (for protection and strategic purposes).

Body slightly leaning forward from the waist to facilitate drawing back from blows (to mislead distance).

Right leading hand should not stick too far forward from the torso.

The ready stance in jeet kune do is unorthodox to the traditional classical stances of martial art. It is a simple, compact, and highly mobile stance always poised for immediate action.

Many traditional classical stances assumed by the marital artists are quite a sight. They range from exotic balletlike stances to postures of squatting down in wide stances and grimacing as though laying an egg.

According to classical gung fu, the ready stance of jeet kune do is unorthodox. It is basically a simple, compact, and highly mobile stance. In this stance you are not tensed or set, but ready and flexible.

Note: Check into variations of on-guard position should footwork lose effectiveness.

Stance factors that all martial artists should consider
1. Attack—hand distance
2. Attack—close-range touching position
3. On-guard position as defense (kicking distance)
4. Defense—medium distance
5. The on-guard position, defense, close-range touching
6. On-guard position in combination
7. Training aid on on-guard position

FOOTWORK—THE ESSENCE OF FIGHTING

Moving in the on-guard (footwork)
You glide or slide, you do not run or trot.

Footwork (gaining and breaking ground)
Footwork: to remain in distance
1. Should be regulated to that of the opponent but must never be permitted to develop into a large and ungainly stride.
2. It should be under control, smooth, and rapid, never to drag the feet along the ground (especially the rear foot), nor develop the fault of jerky little jumps.
3. Constantly on the move to make your opponent misjudge distance, while being quite well aware of your own—constantly gaining and breaking in your effort to obtain the distance which suits you best.

Footwork (attacking)
The pupil must never be permitted to lean forward in attempt to reach the target. Once he has mastered the stroke from the on-guard position, he should then lengthen his distance gradually.

Make attacks on opponent's advance.

Develop great mobility—acquire sense of distance—learn breaking ground.

Footwork (gauging distance)

Distance is a continually shifting relationship depending on the speed, agility, and control of both persons.

The skilled man always keeps himself just out of distance of the opponent's attack and is constantly on the move to make the opponent misjudge his distance, while being quite sure of his own. In doing so he will obtain the distance that suits him best and when the opportunity arises he will close the distance or steal a march on the opponent's move to close in.

Use your own footwork and the opponent's for your advantage, *not* his pattern, if any, of advancing and retreating.

Vary the length and/or speed of your own steps.

③ USING FOOTWORK

1) The *shooting punch* ~~finger~~ ~~hand sweep~~ (with right side step)

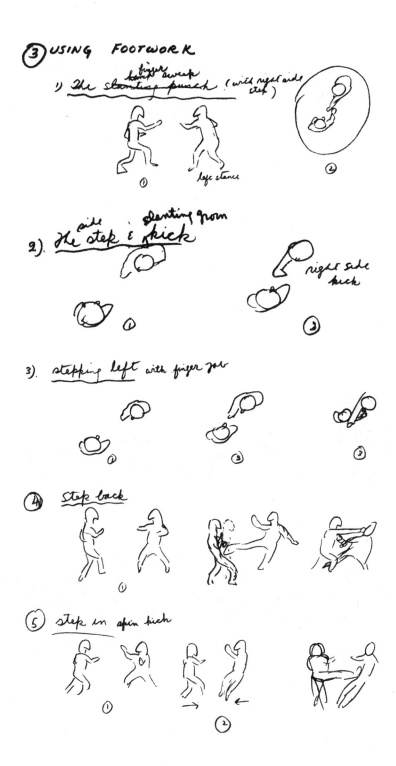

①   *left stance*   ②

2). The *side* step & *slanting groin* kick

①   *right side kick* ②

3). *stepping* **left** *with finger jab*

①   ②   ③

④ step back

①

⑤ step in *spin kick*

①   ②

Attack on the opponent's advance or change of distance.

You may retreat to draw an advance.

The length of the step forward, or backward, should be approximately regulated to that of the opponent. The steps should be smooth, rapid, springy, well balanced (evenly and easily), and controlled.

In order to lighten the feet for increased speed and mobility, the rear left heel is slightly raised with the weight on the ball of the foot. Thus, unlike the traditional flat-footed practice, the left heel is raised and cocked, ever-ready to pull the trigger and go into action.

Like a coiled spring one can release great power by pushing off the ground.

Remember we want balance in mobility. For until balance is gained, a man is ineffective in both attack and defense.

In fact, distance can be a type of aggressive deterrent during sparring.

Life is a constant movement so let us move and open that flow of existence.

The four moves
Basically, there are four moves in economical footwork from the ready stance: advancing, retreating, curving right, and curving left. The rest are just variations.

Keep relating; to move is to relate!

Footwork can beat any attack, and a properly maintained distance will baffle any skilled opponent.

Mobility and speed of footwork precede speed of kicks and punches.

Moving from a stance

In advancing, let the foot move first (it is called "footwork," after all), and do not let a shoulder jerk or a cocked hip lead the way. It might even be called the surprising step out.

The left heel is the spark plug, or better still, the piston, of the whole fighting machine.

One can only develop an instinctive sense of distance if he is able to move about smoothly and speedily.

An alertness of foot will transmute into an alertness of mind. His reaction will be all the more spontaneous.

Medium crouch, mobility—balance is mobility.

Lighten the stance so that the force of inertia to overcome will be less.

Footwork must never be permitted to develop into a large and ungainly stride because footwork should always be under control, smooth but rapid, allowing the fighter to maintain his balance evenly and easily.

The length of the step forward, or backward, should be approximately regulated to that of the opponent.

One should practice his footwork with a view to keeping a very correct and precise distance in relationship to his opponent.

Skipping and footwork

Skipping rope is a wonderful exercise to learn how to handle one's body agilely. It is a good footwork supplementary exercise.

The object of footwork

The object of footwork is to enable a fighter:

a. To move about with his opponent rapidly, and

b. At the same time always keep the right distance from him, and

c. Retain a suitable stance for resisting blows from all angles, and

d. Always maintain such a position as to enable him, while just keeping out of range, to be yet near enough to instantaneously take an opening should his opponent leave one, and this is quite impossible unless a boxer has learned to be able to move with equal facility in all directions.

All footwork must be neat and quick.

The drop shift

The drop shift—is a further refinement of the side step. It is used to gain the inside or outside guard position and is also useful in in-fighting. Mainly a vehicle for countering it requires timing, speed, and judgement to properly execute. It may be combined with the right jab, the straight left, the left hook, and the right hook.

Many fighters have found it best to use a sideways shuffle to study a foe. It keeps you out of range of the lead jab and in a position to slip past a punch. Benny Leonard used the side step extensively in circling a foe, and hit him repeatedly and deceptively with rangy left rear hands, thus keeping him guessing.

To move just enough to accomplish a purpose will . . .

1. Make an opponent strive that much harder, and

2. Thus be close enough for delivery of efficient counter blow.

Above all things, keep moving, for a moving target, especially capable of moving in all directions, is an elusive one. However, do not forget about the above-mentioned greatest phase of footwork.

Jeet Kune Do

Keep weaving and bobbing at a comfortable pace, "stepping on the gas" when necessary. Keep to the left.

Keep moving—for you can carry on a movement much more snappily than if you start from a position of rest. Also, your man will never guess what your intentions are.

Practice footwork, footwork, and then more footwork.

While shifting ground the feet must be returned to the floor as rapidly as possible. A delay can be used by the opponent to score while your foot is off the ground and you are off balance.

Your steps should be kept small and fast.

To attack him just as he is stepping forward may bring him within range.

By never getting your feet crossed you are always braced and not likely to be pushed off balance or knocked down because of bad footwork.

Footwork factors all martial artists should consider
1. Footwork in attack
2. Footwork in combination

Practice moving naturally to both sides, left and right.

The foot nearer the point to which you wish to move is shifted first.

In footwork, not stiff leg work, you should operate in the same manner as a graceful ballroom dancer who uses the feet, ankles, and calves. He slithers around the floor.

Economical footwork is the sound kind, and the boxer's aim should always be to move as little as possible.

Never move back in a straight line too far; always try to move around an opponent.

The art of sidestepping
The art of sidestepping, as of ducking and slipping, is to move late and quick (e.g., wait until your opponent's lead is almost on you, and then take a quick step forward and to the left by simply changing your legs).

When an opponent rushes you, it is not so much the rush you sidestep as some particular blow he leads with during the rush.

The stance is slightly shorter in order to keep the leading leg and foot out of range of a sudden attack.

Unless there is a tactical reason for acting otherwise, gaining and breaking of ground is executed by means of small and rapid steps.

All hand movements are combined with waist and footwork.

Classical footwork versus economical footwork in jeet kune do

Classical footwork is unrealistic.

You cannot use your hands or legs effectively until your feet have put you in a position in which you can do so—if you are slow on your feet, you will be slow with your punches and kicks.

A firm but highly mobile base, capable of being shifted in any direction at a split-second's notice.

Stay on the balls of your feet and retain the spring.

Overconfidence can often cause overbalancing.

Minimum of movement—simplicity, purposeful, not strain—moving just enough to accomplish the purpose.

Vary the length and speed of your step to confuse the opponent.

The quality of a man's technique depends on what he does with his feet.

Never move back in a straight line too far—try to move around an opponent.

The feet should be kept an easy and comfortable distance apart.

Economical footwork is the soundest kind, and the jeet kune do man's aim should always be to move as little as possible.

One should concentrate on speeding himself up. Mobility and speed is what he should seek for and, in order to increase mobility and lighten his feet, he should get away from the classical flat-footed practice and get the slight crouch with weight on the balls of

his feet (not on his toes!) and feel the floor like a spring. This is to find firmness and balance in mobility.

The length of the step forward, or backward, should be approximately regulated to that of the opponent.

Be constantly on the move to make the opponent misjudge the distance, while being quite sure of your own.

Constant gaining and breaking ground in the effort to obtain the distance which suits you best—never attack unless the distance is closed enough.

It is seeking firmness in stillness and is not the true firmness.

Mobility is vitally important in jeet kune do—present a moving target which your opponent has difficulty in hitting or kicking.

His fine sense of distance and timing prevents the opponent from attacking at normal distance, compelling him instead to come near—too near.

Energy, the first thing to be remembered is that the least possible fluid movement that achieves this object is what is required.

Moving properly means carrying out the necessary movement without loss of balance. Until balance is regained, the boxer is ineffective in both attack and defense. Therefore in all movement, balance must be retained.

Try to maintain such a position as to enable him, while just keeping out of range, to be yet near enough to instantaneously take an opening.

If you are in motion to start with, you can carry on a movement much more snappily than if you start from a position of rest.

By using footwork one can convert his attack into your attack.

"To get where you are safe—and he isn't."

Footwork will beat any punch or kick.

Footwork can add weight and power to a punch or kick.

Keep using short steps to alter the distance between you and your opponent; however, do not jump around like a fancy boxer, he is not in with the opponent, he is amusing himself. Above all, do not freeze in any position for any length of time.

Since in all hand-to-hand combat it is an operation of finding a target or of avoiding being a target, it must be a sort of movement.

Your distance depends on how much target needs to be protected.

Be aware of your own (1) footwork length, and (2) rapidity, and you can meet any tactics.

Strive to bridge for even a split second to attack.

Any attack started from a close enough distance will reach, no matter how fast the opponent can parry.

Concentrate on the opponent and the control of your tools. The leg will take care of the distance.

Correct distance (not out of distance) in parry brings about successful riposte.

There must be close synchronization between closing and opening distances and the various actions of the hand and leg.

The maintaining of the proper fighting distance has a decisive effect on the outcome of fighting.

The tactical use of changes of measure, that is stepping forward and backward, should also be studied.

Distance factors that all martial artists should consider
1. The art of bridging the distance (training aid)

Distance in combination

Organic regulation of small phasic bent-knee stance (SPBKS) of intuition—study appropriate body sway and/or head glances.

Part 3

THE TOOLS OF COMBAT— PART ONE: THE UPPER LIMBS

PRELIMINARY CONSIDERATIONS

Lead limb as striking tool
Because of their advanced position, your leading hand and foot constitute at least 80 percent of all striking and kicking (as they are halfway to the targets before starting). It is important that you can strike and kick with speed and power singly or in combination.

Jeet Kune Do consist of offensive

THE ELEMENT OF OFFENSE/DEFENSE offense

① SHOW PROGRESSIVE TARGET CHART AND LENGTH OF WEAPON CHART

your hands are not like a hatchet to chop your opponent down. Rather they are keys to unlock your opponent's defense

Every attacker must have within himself a touch of the gambler — penetrate. Never attack half-heartedly — but yourself concern yourself only with the correct and most determined execution of your offense

ⓐ USE THE LONGEST AGAINST THE CLOSEST

ⓑ use leg first in attack, then having bridged the gap, use the hands

ⓒ make indirect attack out of them, feint head first if hit low —
do not alt pattern / NOT ALWAYS THE opponent might take / RULE

It is all important that one should spend most of his time during workouts perfecting his ability to punch (and to kick) properly.

To be a complete jeet kune do man, you have to be able to strike and kick from all angles, and with either hand (and leg) to take advantage of the moment. Some of the better jeet kune do men are most unorthodox.

Factors influencing striking force

In striking, the momentum of the waist and legs, the motivation and the intrinsic energy must also be added; the hands are employed only as a means to put it through.

On striking

The leg is the more powerful weapon but, ultimately, the man who can punch better will be the one who will win.

The force of our fists must originate from the dynamic power of our waist and back. Of course, the amount of force is determined by the strength of the practitioner's muscles and his weight. If two men of different weight are equal in strength of muscle and both know the technique of using their energy, then certainly the heavier one is in a more advantageous position.

In generating maximum impact in one's punches

When you punch you've got to put the whole hip into it, and snap it, and get all your energy in there, and make your fist into a weapon.

Only when the punch begins to land should the fist be closed.

The jab and jeet kune do

In boxing, the central theme is the left jab. The left jab is used to set up other techniques and other punches. The left jab is used as a "feeler" and all punching techniques evolve around the left jab. The left jab is shot from the middle area or the high area. From the left jab, a boxer can right hook, left hook, right cross, left uppercut, right uppercut, or do a combination of the above-mentioned techniques.

According to the position of yourself and your man and the time you have to put the punch in, you may occasionally take a short step to the left, just a few inches, with your left foot (watch out for kicks). This will put even more weight into the punch, especially at fairly long range, and take you out of danger of a reply from the opponent's hands.

Hand/striking combinations to consider
1. ABC 2. PIA 3. HIA (and its variations) 4. As coordination drill

On the importance of combination punching

A good Western boxer hits from every angle. Each punch sets him in a position to deliver another punch. He is always on center, never off balance. The more effective combinations you have, the more different types of opponents you will be able to defeat.

The whole secret of hard hitting lies in accurate timing and mental application.

Keep him on the defensive and increase the pace ever so slightly. Give him no rest.

When to strike

1. Have your opponent force himself to commit to a decided step. You can then be moderately certain of what he is about to do.
2. Deprive him of the ability to change his position and guard swiftly enough to deal successfully with any offensive you may adopt yourself.
3. By his mere action of hitting out, you will or should secure an opening of sorts, can or should make him present you with a fair target at which to aim.
4. Most important of all, you will have borrowed some very considerable force from him to add to the power of your own counter-delivery.

Some observations that are applicable to all types of hitting

1. Hit as straight as possible—Step in when you punch and make your reach good.
2. Don't telegraph any punch—If you have to set your fist in a certain way for a particular punch, do it in a manner that won't warn your opponent.
3. Fight from a center and always be in a position to shoot any punch—Don't overshoot your target. For long-range fighting, jab

with your lead right and cross with your left. For short-range fighting, use hooks, left-hand body blows, and uppercuts. Sway a little as you hit. A hard punch must be delivered from a solid base; light punches are delivered by a boxer on his toes.

4. Learn to hold your fire until you can hit your opponent—Back him to the ropes or corner him before you attack. Don't waste your energy missing. If he does the leading, avoid his punches and hit back with solid counter-punches before he can get away. Keep loose and relaxed except when actually fighting. Develop speed, timing, and judgment of distance by many hard workouts with all types of sparring partners. With this practice your authority, hit confidently and hard. After hitting, instantly get back on guard. End a series of punches with a right.

THE LEAD (STRAIGHT) PUNCH

The straight punch is the core of jeet kune do, but should be reinforced and supported by other angle punches and kicks of like precision.

The blow should be thrown from the center instead of from the shoulder, which makes you a swinging fighter, and it should aim toward the front of the nose.

It's Western sword fencing—without the sword.

You should be able to deliver it at a moment's notice.

Because 90 percent of all hitting is done with the leading right hand, it is important to be proficient to whip the right to head or body, singly or in combination.

It is a potent offensive and defensive weapon because of its advanced position—it is halfway to the target before starting.

It is effective in keeping the opponent off balance and creating openings for other blows (thus it is both an offensive as well as defensive blow!).

A blow is never hit at a mark. It is driven *through a mark*. Follow-through is just as important in fighting as it is in any other sport and follow-through can only be obtained by punching through and beyond the point of attack.

Punch toward the front of your own nose and hit fiercely with each delivery, aiming in the center of the face.

The punch should start from "center" instead of from the waist or from the shoulder.

No preparatory or get-set posture before delivery. Every blow just shoots from wherever the hands happen to be at the moment. This will add speed (no wasted motion) and deception (no give away preceding movement) to your punch.

The fist should not be clenched until impact. Relaxation will give both speed and power. To be a complete jeet kune do man, you have to be able to strike and kick from all angles, and with either hand (and leg) to take advantage of the moment. Some of the better jeet kune do men are most unorthodox.

All punches should end with a snap several inches behind the target. Thus you punch *through* the opponent yet end the punch with a snap.

No hesitation before delivery, aim to snap through.

Not just arm power—strike with correct timing of foot, waist, and hip, shoulder, and wrist motion.

After delivery do not drop your striking hand when withdrawing back to the ready stance. Though you might see this being done by a good jeet kune do man, always cultivate the habit of returning back along the same path and keep it high for any possible counters.

Do not drop or withdraw the protecting hand when punching (thus hand resting on hip in classical gung fu has no place here). For example, the right hand hits high, the left should be slightly below the right elbow for protection (this is just an example, the main thing is where your opponent's hand happens to be). The same is true when hitting low with the right, the left should be held high to offset any countering on the part of your opponent.

Try to vary your head position while using the right lead.

Because 90 % of all hitting is done with the leading right hand, it is important to be proficient to whip the right to head or body, with singly or in Combination.

Combination :— to catch up with a fast-moving opponent --- to set him up.

1). The ONE - TWO
2). THE ONE - TWO ; HOOK
3). R/body — R/JAW — L/JAW
4). THE ONE - HOOK — CROSS
5). THE STRAIGHT HIGH/LOW.

Use double-right occasionally—unexpected—paves the way for follow-up.

The advantages of the lead punch

1. Faster—the shortest distance between two points is a straight line
2. More accurate—"chooses the straightest course," thus, less chance of missing and is surer than other punches
3. Balance is less disturbed—safer
4. Less injurious to one's hand
5. Greater frequency of hits—more damage can be done

Can foil the opponent's complicated attack when used as a stop hit.

Reduces the chances of missing because opponent has less time for blocking.

The effectiveness of the right lead depends on the speed and surprise with which it is delivered.

On initiating the lead punch

The punch should, and this applies to all punches and kicks, start from the ready stance without any unnecessary motions. The beginners should watch out especially for the drawing back of the hand before shooting it out; it starts from where it is, and returns to where it begins. In other words, practice your punching from the ready stance and finish in the ready stance.

The essential qualities of the lead punch

1. Economy of correct form
2. Accuracy
3. Speed
4. Explosive power

The right lead is the opening gambit in any hand combat.

The extended side automatically becomes the speediest and most natural way of reaching the opponent.

It can be termed very effective and valuable to keep an opponent at a respectable distance.

The lead keeps the line. The whole aim of attack in swordplay is to get past this line, for until it is passed, no point can be made.

A reinforcing weapon is the rear hand, poised for immediate action.

It should be so well-timed as to reach its mark at the utmost of its owner's power. That is, with the maximum reach at his command, including shoulder extension (to obtain maximum reach), a movement that comes up from his left leg, continues across his shoulders and along his right arm.

Whenever striking with the right lead either to the head or the body, it is important to sway (snap) slightly to the left. The head should slip in the same direction.

It is usually best, whenever possible, to "draw" your opponent into leading before hitting out on your own account.

The lead right—in action

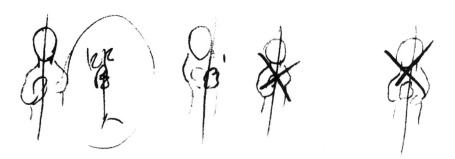

(5) The LEADING RIGHT — Long ; MEDIUM.
(refer to section on the straight punch for more detail)
usually use after bridging the gap

LONG PUNCH

Figure 1. (top) A and B sparring for opening. A should hold his right arm loosely and moving slightly, and keep his footwork flexible for any sudden move.

Figure 2. (bottom) A timed B's advance and shoots his right lead straight out. Remember to shoot it out simple and direct without any unnecessary movements. Its success depends on its unexpectedness and timing with the opponent's unawareness—like stepping forward, dropping the hands, changing position, etc.

Right-lead factors that all martial artists should consider

1. Attack to right stancer
2. Attack to left stancer
3. Defense (as counter) to right stancer
4. Defense (as counter) to left stancer
5. Combined with kicking (and vice versa) as attack to right and left stancer
6. Counter to right lead with kicking (or vice versa) from four-corner range to right and left stancers
7. Counter to right lead
8. Counter to left-stancer's jab

The lead right to the body

Most people are weak in low-line defense and the right to the body will also set up for the same punch to the head. It's success depends on its sudden change of level and catches the opponent off his guard.

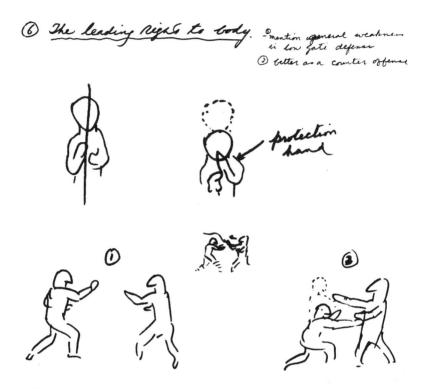

⑥ *The leading Right to body.* ① mention general weakness in low gate defense ② better as a counter offense

protection hand

① ② ③

Figure 1. A and B facing each other.
Figure 2. A advances straight in toward B and B is ready to strike A's head.
Figure 3. Suddenly A drops and changes his level during the advance and strikes B with a right to the solar plexus.

Remember to drop suddenly and level your shoulder to your punch. Your head should turn slightly to your left during delivery but don't leave sight of your opponent. This right to the body is a better counter than a lead.

Counters to be aware of
When leading with your right hand, look out for the following counters:

1. Left hand to the body
2. Left hand to the jaw (over or inside your elbow)
3. Right hand to the body
4. Right hand to the jaw

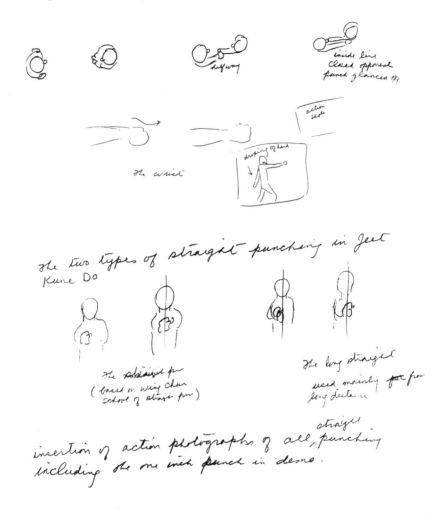

inside line
Closed opponent
punch glances off

action
shot

drifting of hand

the wrist

the two types of straight punching in Jeet Kune Do

The straight jab
(based on wing chun
school of short jab)

The long straight
used mainly for from
long distance

straight
insertion of action photographs of all punching
including the one inch punch in demo.

Right-lead-to-the-body factors that all martial artists should consider

1. The right lead to groin (or body) as attack (to right stancer)
2. The right lead to groin (or body) as attack (to left stancer)
3. The right lead to groin (or body) as counter (to right stancer)

4. The right lead to groin (or body) as counter (to left stancer)
5. The right lead to groin (or body) with kick (or vice versa) as attack
6. The right lead to groin (or body) with kick (or vice versa)—as counter.
7. Counter to right lead to groin (or body)—right stancer
8. Counter to right lead to groin (or body)—left stancer
9. Training aid

High/low straight-lead factors that all martial artists should consider
1. The high/low (vice versa) straight lead
2. The high/low lead (or vice versa) as attack (to right stancer)
3. The high/low lead (or vice versa) as attack (to left stancer)
4. The high/low lead (or vice versa) as counter to right stancer
5. The high/low lead (or vice versa) as counter to left stancer
6. The high/low lead (or vice versa) combined with kick or vice versa—as attack
7. The high/low lead (or vice versa) combined with kick or vice versa—as counter
8. As counter to the high/low lead (or vice versa)—opponent in right stance
9. As counter to high/low lead (or vice versa)—opponent in left stance
10. Training aid for high/low (or vice versa)

The left-hand lead punch
1. You must never hesitate when throwing it.
2. You must not telegraph it by drawing it back or lifting it up.
3. It must be snapped in, sharp and clean.
4. The right lead must be drawn back.
5. The chin must be down and shoulder up.

The right heel should turn over to the right. Hands well up at all times, especially don't drop the left while punching with the right. Blows should start where the hands are.

Keep the right hand moving, don't hold it motionless. Let it flicker in and out like the tongue of a snake ready to strike. Above all, always threaten and worry your adversary.

Full waist and shoulder reverse with left foot sliding forward a few inches.

Aim toward the centerline to drive through the opponent.

Cross-parry (downward toward right) or draw opponent's right and slip over left shoulder and strike.

The straight left

The most important point in the delivery of the left is that there must be no preliminary movement, no drawing back, and the hand must be shot from its resting place near the chest and not on the hip.

Figure 1. A and B facing each other.

Figure 2. A advances with a straight right lead feint to obstruct B's vision as well as to draw his reaction.

Figure 3. Without a pause, A shoots his left directly behind the right and explodes on B's jaw with the full weight of the body. Note the right hand is back for protection and follow-up.

Note: The rhythm should be r-i-g-h-t - left.

The straight left to the body

As previously pointed out, most people are weak in the midsection defense, and the straight left to the body, preceded by a right feint, is quite a surprise to your opponent. The straight left is an excellent counter against the opponent's leading right.

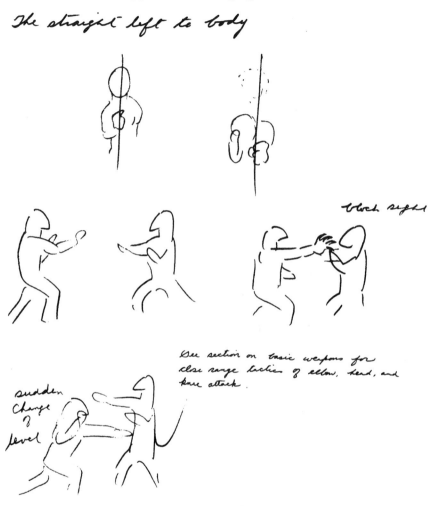

The straight left to body

block sight

See section on basic weapons for close range tactics of elbow, head, and knee attack.

sudden change of level

Figure 1. A and B facing.
Figure 2. Advancing, A feints a straight claw-like snap to obstruct B's vision.
Figure 3. Still advancing, A suddenly drops and thrusts a powerful left to B's ribs with the full twist of his body.

Study left hook to the kidney of an opponent in crouching opposition—an opponent who turns constantly to the left, leaving his right kidney an open target. The fist is looped in a half circle into the kidney.

The most important point in the delivery of the left is that there must be no preliminary movement, no drawing back, and the hand must be shot from its resting place near the chest and not on the hip.

Straight-left factors that all martial artists should consider
1. As attack to a right stancer
2. As attack to a left stancer
3. Straight left to body as counter to a right stancer
4. Straight left to body as counter to a left stancer
5. Straight left combined with kicking (and vice versa) as attack
6. Straight left body shot combined with kicking (and vice versa) as counter
7. Counter to low left body shot—right stancer
8. Counter to right body shots from left stancer
9. Training aid for rear body shot.

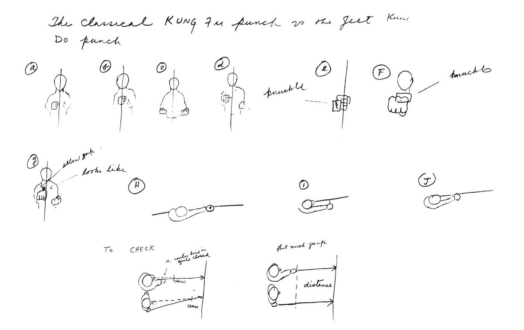

THE HOOK

A hook is a deceptive punch, especially when preceded by feints. Unlike a straight punch that comes straight, a hook comes from the side, outside the range of vision and scores by sneaking around the opponent's guard. It is a powerful blow, but oftentimes the practitioners get carried away and turn it into a swing.

Figure 1. A and B facing each other.
Figure 2. A suddenly drops his body while darting forward in what appears to be a straight to B's midsection. B reacts by low parry.
Figure 3. As soon as B's hand begins to move downward, A explodes a hook to B's jaw by going around his guard.

Tips on throwing the perfect hook

1. The hook is best employed when your opponent is coming to you (it is essentially a counter).

> *The Hook :-*
> *A hook is a deceptive punch, especially when preceded by feints. Unlike a straight punch that comes straight, a hook comes from the side, outside the range of vision and scores by sneaking around the opponent's guard. It is a powerful blow, but oftentime the people pratitioners get carry away and turn it into a swing.*

2. Much of the "kick" behind the right hook is accomplished by the footwork.

3. Like all punches the lead hook must begin from the on-guard position for added deception.

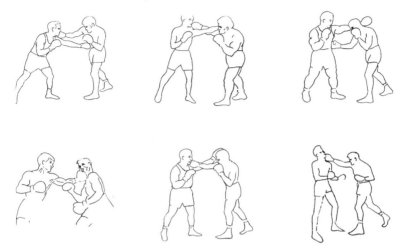

Most boxers will at first pull their right hand back too far before throwing the hook. The right shoulder is never pulled back or lowered when throwing the hook. Remember the hook is a short, snappy punch. Enough power can be put into the punch without pulling the arm far back—don't telegraph!

The hook can be used as a lead when for some reason your opponent has lost his ability to move out of the way.

Observations on the hook

1. It is basically a short-range blow— when the opponent is coming to you.
2. A good punch to combine with a side step.

Types of hooks

a. The short hook
b. The shovel hook

c. The long hook

d. The forward hook (or "corkscrew")

e. The horizontal hook

f. The palm hook

g. The upward hook

(Be ready to follow up with more punches!)

Hooking factors that every martial artist should consider

1. The hook as attack: high to right stancer

2. The hook as attack: high to left stancer

3. The hook as attack: low to right stancer

4. The hook as attack: low to left stancer

5. The hook as counter: high to right stancer

6. The hook as counter: high to left stancer

7. The hook as counter: low to right stancer

8. The hook as counter: low to left stancer

9. The hook in combination: with kicking (and vice versa) as attack to right stancer

10. The hook in combination: with kicking (and vice versa) as attack to left stancer

11. The hook in combination: with kicking (or vice versa) as counter to right stancer

12. The hook in combination: as counter to left stancer

13. The hook in combination: to counter to a regular right-lead hook (high)

14. The hook as counter: to a right-stancer's low lead hook

15. The hook as counter: to a left-stancer's left lead hook (high)

16. The hook as counter: to a left-stancer's low lead hook

17. Training hint

The hook to the body

1. The hook to the body is not as effective from a distance.

2. Remember that though the hook is an offensive weapon, one

should not lead with it. Try a straight lead or other preparation first. Always vary the punch to high/low or low/high, singly or in combination. It is an effective counter as well as a good punch while in fighting.

3. The more sharply the elbow is bent, the tighter and more explosive the hook.

Notes on the hook to the head and/or body and vice versa

- Never a wide and looping blow: a loose, easy, snappy punch.
- Always keep your left hand high as a shield to the left side of your face. Your left elbow protects your ribs.
- Remember the pivot is the key (footwork makes the punch).
- Always jab or feint first to get distance (*Note*: Feint cross to get distance and leverage).
- Body is the easier target (especially close in).
- A good punch to combine with a side step.
- Avoid telegraphing! Start and end in ready position. (It must begin from the on-guard position for proper deception.) The hand is never pulled back or lowered!

The right hook

Not only are right hooks powerful counter blows but they are one means of opening up an opponent's defense for straight blows—used mostly as a counter or "follow-on" blow, but they can under certain circumstances be used as a lead, especially after a feint—hooks come from the side, outside the range of vision as it were and will go around the guard—valuable when close in, especially after he is shook up by a straight blow.

The mechanics of the right hook

1. You must sway over to the left to put weight into the punch.
2. You must make the blow snappy; always think of speed and more speed.
3. Aim to drive through the opponent.
4. Be ready to follow up with another solid punch with either hand.
5. Above all, minimize all the above motion so that you will be moving just enough to have the maximum effect without hooking wildly.

A long body hook can be extremely effective after a shift to the left with the feet.

The experienced hooker will always jab or feint his opponent first.

The jabbing and feinting (with advance) is really a means of getting your distance.

The left hook

A good way to use the hook powerfully is to fake a left cross.

The hook is delivered when the opposition has lowered his rear hand guard. It is very effective after a right jab.

Defensive hitting is most effective against hooks and swings.

Points to remember

1. The hip comes up in a vigorous shoveling hunch.
2. Your hand is at a forty-five–degree angle. It is angled to shoot inside an opponent's defense!

Remember always that your knuckles are pointing in the exact direction of your whirling weight. The more you open an outside hook, the more it degenerates into a swing. You must keep it tight. Also, remember that when you open a hook, you open your own defense.

Shovel-hook factors that all martial artists should consider

1. The shovel hook as attack
    • High shovel to right stancer
    • Low shovel to right stancer
    • High shovel to left stancer
    • Low shovel to left stancer
2. The shovel hook as counter
    • High shovel to right stancer • Low shovel to right stancer
    • High shovel to left stancer • Low right shovel to left stancer
3. The shovel hook combined with kicking (and vice versa) as attack to right and left stancer
4. The shovel hook combined with kicking (and vice versa) as counter to right and left stancer
5. Counter to right-stancer's shovel hook
    • Right high shovel hook • Low right shovel hook
6. Counter to left-stancer's shovel hook
    • Left high shovel hook • Left low shovel hook
7. Training aid

Corkscrew-hook factors that all martial artists should consider

1. The corkscrew hook in attack
    • To right stancer • To left stancer
2. The corkscrew hook in defense
    • To right stancer • To left stancer
3. The corkscrew hook combined with kicking (and vice versa) as attack to right and left stancers

4. The corkscrew hook combined with kicking (and vice versa) as counter to right and left stancers
5. Counter to right-stancer's corkscrew hook by right and left stancers
6. Counter to left-stancer's corkscrew hook by right and left stancers
7. Training aid

Studies on the corkscrew right hook

1. It flashes in without warning.
2. If he permits his guarding left hand to creep too far forward as he blocks or parries your right jab, your corkscrew can snap down behind that guarding left and nail his jaw.
3. You can use the corkscrew to beat a sloppy left cross or a left-stancer's right.

Palm-hook factors that all martial artists should consider

1. The palm hook (bent and straight) as attack
   • High to right stancer • High to left stancer
   • Low (groin) to right stancer • Low (groin) to left stancer
2. The palm hook (bent and straight) as counter
   • High to right stancer • High to left stancer
   • Low (groin) to right stancer • Low (groin) to left stancer
3. The palm hook combined with kicks (and vice versa) as attack to right and left stancers
4. The palm hook combined with kicks (and vice versa) as counter to right and left stancers
5. Counters to right-stancer's palm hook (see counters to hooks)
   • High to right palm lead • Low to right palm lead
6. Counter's to left-stancer's palm hook (see counters to hooks)
   • Left high palm hook lead • Left low palm hook lead
7. Training aid

THE BACKFIST

A hook, in the case of jeet kune do's stances, is from right to left, while the backfist is from left to right (though there are four types of backfist—see page 73). Basically, the backfist is used from low to high or from left to right. It can be used singly—though it is more effective after your opponent blocks your straight punch. As soon as he blocks your straight punch, you roll over the guard of the opponent and strike him with the right backfist while checking his hand with your left.

Series A

⑦ The Back FIST
(blow from the side — from left to right)

often accompanied by straight

Figure 1. A and B facing each other in natural stance.

Figure 2. A suddenly drops and changes his level, coming in with a low feint straight punch to B's ribs (to offset B's counter kick, A can come in with a low left obstruction preceding the feint). B reacts to A's feinting.

Figure 3. As soon as B's hand starts to travel downward, A simultaneously traps B's hand (with his left) and whips his right into a backfist to B's temple.

Series B

Figure 1. A is in right stance, B in left stance.

Figure 2. A feints with a low straight to B's ribs by a sudden change of level while moving in. B is reacting by dropping his left lead (it doesn't matter whether B drops any hand).

Figure 3. As soon as B's hand drops, A closes the distance by jerking B's hand and whips over a backfist simultaneously.

Backfist factors that all martial artists should consider

1. Backfist in attack

- High—to right stancer • Low—to right stancer
- High—to left stancer • Low—to left stancer

2. Backfist as counter
   - High—to right stancer • Low—to right stancer
   - High—to left stancer • Low—to left stancer
3. Backfist combined with kicking (and vice versa) as attack
   - Right and left stancer
4. Backfist combined with kicking (and vice versa) as counter:
   - Right and left stancer
5. Counter to backfist
   - High—to right stancer
6. Counter right-stancer's low backfist
7. Counter to left-hander's backfist
   - High backfist
8. Counter to left-stancer's low backfist
9. Training aid

Vertical backfist factors that all martial artists should consider

1. The vertical backfist as attack
   - To right stancer • To left stancer
2. The vertical backfist as defense or counter
   - To right stancer
3. The vertical backfist
   - To left stancer
4. The vertical backfist with kicking (and vice versa) as attack

5. The vertical backfist with kicking (or vice versa) as counter
6. Counter right-stancer's vertical backfist
7. Counter to left-stancer's vertical backfist
8. Training aid

THE CROSS

A restricted use of the lead hand is the principal fault of many a martial artist.

The blow should be delivered perfectly straight on the opponent's lead at the face.

Pointers on delivering the cross

From the on-guard position with no preliminary movement, no drawing back—the hand must be shot from its resting place upon the chest or body; it generally starts from near to the left shoulder.

The start is made from regular on-guard position. The shoulder curves over the chin for protection and the chin is down. Remember: one hand out, one hand back. This is done not only for an expected counter, but also so the fighter will be in position to throw the second follow-up punch.

The left cross

For effectiveness and deception, never draw the left hand back before delivery. Don't lift the left cross before it is thrown.

Your victim musn't be given any warning as you throw it, starting from your left shoulder.

Press down on the ball of the right foot, and you must control the forward movement transferring the weight from the left to right foot before connecting. Your left foot should follow by dragging it forward.

It is best used following a right lead.

The left cross is delivered in much the same manner as the right jab in that it travels in a perfectly straight line. Your twist at the waist will be much greater.

This perfectly straight punch to your opponent's jaw is normally a long arm blow in which you use your full reach.

At the moment of impact the weight shifts forward to the right leg, which gives the power necessary for use as a finishing blow. It should be noted that the left is essentially a counter-blow (see the one-two).

Left-cross factors all martial artists should consider

1. Left cross as attack
   - To right stancer • To left stancer
2. Left cross as counter
   - To right stancer • To left-stancer
3. Left cross combined with kicking (or vice versa) in attack
4. Left cross combined with kicking (or vice versa) as counter
5. Counter to the right-stancer's left cross
6. Counter to left-stancer's right cross
7. Training aid

ADDITIONAL STRIKING OPTIONS (UPPER LIMBS)

Uppercuts and infighting

Draw a right lead then step in with a quick head twist to the right, slightly raising your right hand for obstructing the possible right hand. At the same time, all in a flash, bring up to the chin of the man leaning forward with his lead a short, sharp, left uppercut.

Study left bolo punch to left stancer's groin with right hand cuffing.

Uppercut factors that all martial artists should consider

1. The lead uppercut as attack
   - High—to right stancer
   - High—to left stancer
   - Low—to left stancer
   - Low—to right stancer
   - The lead uppercut combined with kicking or close-range tactics (or vice versa)—as attack.
   - The lead uppercut combined with kicking or close-range tactics (or vice versa)—as counter
   - Counter to right-stancer's lead uppercut—high
   - Counter to right-stancer's lead uppercut—low
   - Counter to left-stancer's lead uppercut—high
   - Counter to left-stancer's lead uppercut—low
   - Training aid

Upward lead bolo to groin factors that all martial artists should consider

1. The upward lead bolo to groin (palm, ridgehand, or fist)

• As attack • As counter

2. The upward lead bolo to groin (palm, ridgehand, or fist) combined with long- and close-range tactics

   • As attack • As counter

3. Countering the right-stancer's upward lead bolo

4. Training aid on the upward lead bolo

Reverse upward bolo factors that all martial artists should consider

1. The left reverse upward bolo (palm or fist or ridgehand) as attack

   • The right stancer • The left stancer

2. The left reverse upward bolo as counter

   • The right stancer • The left stancer

3. The left reverse upward bolo combined with long- and close-range tactics

   • As attack • As counter

4. Countering the right-stancer's left reverse upward bolo

5. Countering the left-stancer's right reverse upward bolo

6. Training aid

Reverse-uppercut factors that all martial artists should consider

1. The reverse uppercut in attack

   • High—to right stancer

   • High—to left stancer

   • Low—to right stancer

   • Low—to left stancer

2. The reverse uppercut as counter

   • High—to right stancer

   • High—to left stancer

   • Low—to right stancer

   • Low—to left stancer

3. Reverse uppercut combined with kicking or close-range tactics (or vice versa)

   • As attack • As counter

4. Counter to right-stancer's reverse uppercut
   · High · Low
5. Counter to left-stancer's reverse uppercut
   · High · Low
6. Training aid for reverse uppercut

The straight blast

One hand out, one hand back (not to the hip!) for protection and securing strategic position. Thumb up (rapid firing of both arms) and [strike with] the last three knuckles with body weight behind each blow.

The finger jab

Faced with the choice of socking your opponent in the head and poking him in the eyes, you go for the eyes every time.

The finger jab is a most effective attack.

From sparring distance it is wise to use the leg first to bridge the gap for hand techniques. Also, the shin kick can be used as a forward step to close the distance.

② *the leading* FINGER JAB (BIL JEE)

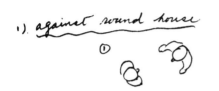

1) against round house
2) complex attack
3) telegraph attack

1). *against round house*

2) *against complex attack*

3) *against telegraph attack*

Leading right finger-jab factors that all martial artists should consider

1. Finger jab as attack to right stancer
2. Finger jab as attack to left stancer
3. Finger jab as counter to right stancer
4. Finger jab as counter to left stancer
5. Finger jab countering the right-stancer's lead finger jab
6. Finger jab countering the left-stancer's left finger jab

7. Leading finger jab with kick (or vice versa) as attack to right stancer

8. Finger jab as attack with combined tactics to left stancer

9. Leading finger jab with kick (vice versa) as counter to right stancer

10. Combined tactics as counter to left stancer

Corkscrew finger-jab factors that all martial artists should consider

1. As attack to right stancer
2. As attack to left stancer
3. As counter to right stancer
4. As counter to left stancer
5. In combination with kicking as attack to right and left stancers
6. In combination with kicking as counter to right and left stancers
7. Counter to corkscrew finger jab from right stance
8. Counter to corkscrew finger jab from left stance
9. Training aid

Leading finger-fan factors that all martial artists should consider

1. As attack to right stancer
2. As attack to left stancer
3. As counter to right stancer
4. As counter to left stancer
5. In combination with kicking (and vice versa) as attack to right and left stancers
6. In combination with kicking (and vice versa) as counter to right and left stancers
7. Counter to lead finger fan from right stancer
8. Counter to lead finger fan from left stancer
9. Training aid

Flick-finger claw factors that all martial artists should consider

1. The flick lead from medium distance as attack
2. The flick lead from medium distance as counter

3. The flick lead with kick attack

4. The flick jab with kicks "counter"

5. Counters to flick jab—right-hander

6. Counter to flick jab—left-hander

7. Training aid

Primary purpose

To kick and hit hard and fast, and to prevent the opponent from hitting back (economical initiation and speedy direct straight delivery).

Consider how the hands can combine with kicking.

Overhand-left factors that all martial artists should consider

The overhand-left punch (or palm):

1. As attack to right stancer

2. As attack to left stancer

3. As counter to right stancer

4. As counter to left stancer

5. Combined with kicking (and vice versa) as attack

6. Combined with kicking (and vice versa) as counter

7. Counter to right-hander's left rear overhand strike

8. Counter to left-stancer's right rear overhand strike

9. Training aid in the overhand-left punch (or palm)

Hammer blow factors that all martial artists should consider

1. Hammer blow as attack
   • To right stancer • To left stancer

2. The right lead hammer as counter
   • To right stancer • To left stancer

3. The right lead hammer combined with close-range tactics and/or kicking (or vice versa) as attack

4. The right lead hammer combined with close-range tactics and/or kicking (or vice versa) as counter

5. Counter to a right-hander—lead right bottom fist

6. Counter to a left-hander—lead left bottom fist

7. Training aid for lead bottom fist

Extended backfist factors all martial artists should consider

1. The stiff-armed (extended) backfist as attack
   - High to right and left stancer
   - Low to right and left stancer
2. The stiff-armed (extended) backfist as defense
   - High as counter to right and left stancer
   - Low as counter to right and left stancer
3. The extended backfist combines with kick (or vice versa) as attack
4. The extended backfist combined with kicking (or vice versa) as counter
5. Counter to extended backfist—right stancer
   - High and low
6. Counter to left-stancer's extended backfist
   - High and low
7. Training aid

Reverse bottom fist factors that all martial artists should consider

1. The left reverse bottom fist—as attack
   - To right stancer • To left stancer
2. The left reverse bottom fist—as counter
   - To right stancer • To left stancer
3. The left reverse bottom fist combined with close-range tactics and/or kicking (or vice versa) as attack
4. The left reverse bottom fist combined with close-range tactics and/or kicking (or vice versa) as counter
5. Counter to a right-hander's left reverse bottom fist
6. Counter to a left-hander's right reverse bottom fist
7. Training aid in reverse bottom fist

Left reverse spin-blow factors that all martial artists should consider

1. The left reverse spin blow (bottom fist or forearm) as attack
   - Lateral high—to right hander
   - Lateral high—to left stancer
   - Downward high—to right stancer
   - Downward high—to left stancer
   - Upward low—to right stancer
2. The left reverse spin blow (bottom fist or forearm) as counter
   - Lateral high—to right stancer
   - Lateral high—to left stancer
   - Downward spin—to right stancer
   - Downward spin—to left stancer
3. The reverse spin blow combined with kicks or other close-range tactics or vice versa
   - As attack • As counter
4. Counter to a right-hander's reverse spin blow
   - High lateral spin
   - High downward spin
   - Low upward spin
5. Counter to a left-hander's reverse spin blow
   - High lateral spin blow
   - High downward spin
   - Low upward spin
6. Training aid for reverse spin blow

Reverse elbow hook factors that all martial artists should consider

1. The reverse elbow hook in close-range fighting
2. The reverse elbow hook in attack
   - High—to right stancer
   - Low—to right stancer
   - High—to left stancer

- Low—to left stancer
3. The reverse elbow hook as counter
    - High—to right stancer
    - Low—to right stancer
    - High—to left stancer
    - Low—to left stancer
4. The reverse elbow hook combined with kicking (or vice versa) as attack
5. The reverse elbow hook combined with kicking (or vice versa) as counter
6. Counter to reverse elbow hook
    - High—to right stancer
    - Low—to right stancer
    - High—to left stancer
    - Low—to left stancer
7. Training aid to reverse elbow hook

Upward-elbow factors that all martial artists should consider

1. The upward-elbow right and left in close-range fighting
2. The upward-elbow right and left as attack (infighting)
    - The right-lead upward elbow
    - The left-reverse upward elbow
3. The upward elbow as counter
    - The right-lead upward elbow
    - The left-reverse upward elbow
4. Counter to a right hander's upward elbow
    - With right-lead upward elbow
    - With left-reverse upward elbow
5. Counter to a left hander's upward elbow
    - With left-lead upward elbow
    - With right-reverse upward elbow
6. Training aid on the upward elbow

Back-elbow factors that all martial artists should consider

1. The back elbow in close-range fighting
2. The back elbow as attack
   - High—to right stancer
   - Low—to right stancer
   - High—to left stancer
   - Low—to left stancer

3. The back elbow as counter
   - High—to right stancer
   - Low—to right stancer
   - High—to left stancer
   - Low—to left stancer
4. The back elbow combined with other close-range tactics as attack
   - High and low
5. The back elbow combined with other close-range tactics as counter
   - High and low
6. Counter to right-stancer's back elbow
   - High • Low
7. Counter to left-stancer's back elbow
   - High • Low
8. Training aid for the back elbow

Lead elbow-hook factors that all martial artists should consider

1. The elbow hook in close-range fighting (as attack)
   - High—to right stancer
   - Low—to right stancer
   - High—to left stancer
   - Low—to left stancer
2. The elbow hook in close-range fighting (as counter)
   - High—to right stancer
   - Low—to right stancer

- High—to left stancer
- Low—to left stancer

3. The elbow hook in combination with other close-range tactics (in attack)

4. The elbow hook in combination with other close-range tactics (in counter)

5. Counter to the elbow hook (the right stancer)
   - High and low

6. Counter to the elbow hook (the left stancer)
   - High and low

7. Training aid in the lead elbow hook (see combination of high/low)

Lead arc swing factors that all martial artists should consider

1. The lead arc swing with back of fist or palm (see hook)—high and low as attack to right stancer
   - High—to right stancer
   - Low—to right stancer

2. As attack
   - High—to left stancer
   - Low—to left stancer

3. The lead arc swing as counter
   - High—to right stancer
   - Low—to right stancer
   - High—to left stancer
   - Low—to left stancer

4. The lead arc swing with kicking (or vice versa)
   - As attack to right and left stancers
   - As counter to right and left stancers

5. Counter to arc swing (right stancer)
   - High · Low

6. Counter to lead arc swing (left stancer)

• High • Low

7. Lead arc swing training aid

Reverse arc swing factors that all martial artists should consider

1. The left reverse quarter swing as attack
   • High—to right stancer
   • Low—to right stancer
   • High—to left stancer
   • Low—to left stancer
2. Reverse quarter swing as counter
   • High—to right stancer
   • High—to left stancer
   • Low—to right stancer
   • Low—to left stancer
3. Reverse quarter swing with kicking (or vice versa) as attack
4. Reverse quarter swing with kicking (or vice versa) as counter
5. Counter to reverse quarter swing (right stancer)
   • High • Low
6. Counter to quarter reverse swing (left stancer)
   • High • Low
7. Training aid

LESSONS FROM BOXING AND FENCING

[*Editor's note:* The following annotations were made by Bruce Lee in the margins of books he owned on Western boxing and fencing.]

Annotations on boxing

The advantage of straight hitting

1. Faster—the shortest distance between two points is a straight line
2. More accurate—less chance of missing
3. Greater frequency of hits—more damage can be done
4. Balance is less disturbed
5. Safer, surer, and easier
6. Less injurious to one's hands

Reasons for adding bent-arm blows

1. More angles to punch—flexibility without confinement
2. More combinations possible
3. For opening up an opponent's defense
4. For more powerful countering and finishing blows

The elements of defense

In total fighting, all evasive hits are used to time opponent's:

1. Last extending commitment
2. Gaps between two exertions

All (1) and (2) are means to take the play away from aggressor or to initiate grappling.

Make use of the slipping for scoring and not passive escape all the time.

Leading

Economical, "straight," explosive on advanced targets.

The drop shift

Drop shift to "receive."

The technique of attack
The safety lead—the circling explosion.

Feinting
1. False attack 2. Evasive explosion

Feinting and drawing are united to pressure opponent's commitment or diffuse power.

It is best to practice feinting before a full-length mirror. Practice each method and notice the deception of each as though committing lead for opponent.

The half-effort to surprise opponent for going distance.

The "step-in, step-out" feint
a. Find accurate distance b. Compare with kicks

Set-ups—the sensitive and dominating aura (imposing).

The art of moving
The essence of fighting is the art of moving at the right time.

To maintain balance while constantly shifting the body weight is an art few ever acquire.

To move just enough:
1. Will make an opponent miss
2. Will deliver a counter blow most effectively

Notes on footwork
1. Ability to move the body easily and efficiently,
2. So that balance will not be disturbed,
3. Implies the ability to attack or defend at all time.

The coordination of hands and feet
The forward and backward shuffle using the straight right
1. With other tools
2. With combination of tools
   - Straight
   - Curve
   - Hand and feet

Some boxing combinations
1. Right jab—left cross—1, 2
2. Right jab—right uppercut
3. Right jab—left cross—right hook—1, 2, 3
4. Right jab—right uppercut—right hook
5. Right jab—right hook
6. Right jab—right body hook
7. Left thrust to body—right high hook
8. Left thrust to body—right body hook

Leads and counters

Lead	Counter
1. Jab	1. Snap back, return jab
2. Jab	2. Slip outside, return jab
3. Lead swing	3. Guard with left forearm, return with jab
4. Jab	4. Push aside lead with left, then shovel body hook
5. Rear swing (or hook)	5. Beat opponent to the punch with lead jab
6. Jab	6. Left-hand counter body blow
7. Jab	7. Left cross counter
8. Lead swing	8. Beat opponent to the punch with left cross
9. Rear cross	9. Duck under, return left body shot
10. Rear cross (or swing)	10. Guard with lead forearm and return left cross

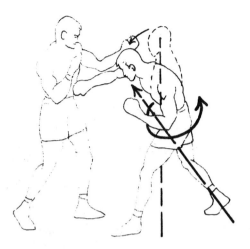

Rocky Marciano's thoughts on boxing

1. The left jab
   - It keeps an adversary off balance and sets him up for such power punches as the right cross and left hook.
2. The right cross
   - Requires perfect timing and coordination
   - Gauge your distance correctly
   - The three "S's" of a correct hand [technique]: straight, snappy, short
3. The left hook
   a. A short, fast hook is best
   b. Starts from the feet up
   - Pivoting on ball of left foot
   - Turn your body toward the right
   - Push your hips up
   - Snap shoulder into punch
   - Left knee goes inside toward right knee, and the left heel goes outward

Pointers on body punching

- Using body punches as a counter-measure is a fairly safe way of delivering them.

- Bend down at the knees and keep your hands well up near your face. Keep your right hand near your chin.
- After throwing body punches, do not bring your head backward, but rather weave to the left with your hands up in defensive position.

A fighter who punches with his hands in front of him is not only better offensively but also defensively.

Jack Dempsey's thoughts on boxing
Exploding body weight is the most important weapon in fist fighting.
a. Falling step b. Leg spring c. Shoulder/waist whirl d. Upward surge

Bobbing and weaving make you difficult to hit at and create more power in your punches.

Personal notes on incorporating boxing hand techniques
1. The straight right
   - High—long, short • Low
2. The right hook
   - High • Low (also upward)
3. The straight left
   - High (also from crouching) • Low

4. The backfist
   - High · Low

Punching right and left

1. Straight punch
   - The three stages
2. Hook (right and left)
   - The three stages
3. Side kick
4. Hook kick

Annotations on fencing

Be aware of your footwork's length and rapidity and you can meet any tactics.

The art of hitting and kicking is the art of correct judging of distance.

The advance

The first requirement in advance is:

1. Psychological moment 2. Hand moves before foot 3. Your body must not be overreached.

The straight thrust

The straight thrust must have the element of surprise:

- When opponent relaxes alertness
- When opponent is about to come out of an instinctive defensive movement (achieved by feinting)

Movements must be executed with calmness (mental) and correct timing (physical).

Speed and precision (constant drill on mechanics).

From prime to seconde = downward curve.

From prime to tierce = upward curve.

Simple parries

The basic rule for all simple parries is to have them all made in a forward direction. This will provide:
• Greater stability • Less exposure • But never be overextended!

Counter parries

The mechanics:
1. Return to starting point
2. Circle around opponent's arm

Functions

1. Against attacks with feints
2. Interrupt and disturb your opponent's feints
3. To add variety

Counter-parries should interject with stop thrust.

A fencer who is in a constant state of physical fitness, as modern fencing requires, is more apt to get off the mark in a fraction of a second and, therefore, to seize an opportunity without warning (basic fitness requirement).

Mobility

Use a medium crouch with slight knee bend.

To find stillness in movement, not stillness in stillness.

On the meaning of defense

In reality, defense is anything which opposes attack. Therefore it can also be considered as preventing attack, or rendering it less effective.

Vary your defensive movements—be versatile.

Once the regular ready position is adopted one is committed, and thus giving kind of a guiding line for opponent. When the hands are nowhere attached, they are ready to intercept from anywhere.

Simplicity

Simplicity is the height of cultivation and partial cultivation runs to ornamentation. Thus, the closer to the true Way of gung fu, the less wastage of movement. Being good in gung fu does not mean adding more but to be able to get off with sophistication and ornamentation and be simply simple—like a sculptor building a statue, not by adding, but by hacking away the unessential so that the truth will be revealed unobstructed—artlessness.

1. More mobility and speed footwork
2. Attacks with a step forward combined with immobilization

The shortening of distance

Play for distance methodically, perhaps hoping to draw a parry by a sudden feint of the straight thrust, which will pave the way for an attack (to draw your opponent to commit—to get a guiding line), having, as object, to cover a gaining of distance and time.

Attack to low line on opponent's step forward.

Accustom the pupil to strike from any angle with accuracy and precision.

The on-guard position

The stance is shorter for greater mobility (quick withdrawal from shin/knee kicks). Body weight should be 40 percent front and 60 percent back leg. Get on the balls of your feet for greater mobility.

The stance is slightly shorter in order to keep the leading leg and foot out of range of a sudden attack. Quick withdrawal from shin/knee kicks. Get on balls of feet for greater mobility.

Incorporating fencing principles
Keep the adversary constantly at a respectful distance by employing a simple angle attack (SAA), stop hit, or time hit.

Different styles demand different methods to cope with them—the five methods.

Always practice absence of touch and definitely involve gaining and breaking ground.

Practice every technique with gaining and breaking down.

The most vulnerable point—the advanced target.

Maintaining the measure (mobility of footwork)
Advancing and retreating to break opponent's rhythm and bridge the gap.

Always combine footwork with techniques being practiced.

Footwork and more footwork. Speed and more speed.

Low-line attack
Attacks to the low line with:
1. Sudden change of level 2. Moving out of line 3. Ducking under attack.

Find truly "neutral" stance.

The smooth progression.

Acquire a development in which the trunk adjusts automatically and lightly.

Develop these qualities
1. Smoothness 2. Ease 3. Accuracy

Work on this!
A great deal of care will have to be taken to cut down to a minimum the amount of time spent on the loss of balance, which is the initial stage in the execution of the movement. This coordinated with the bringing through of the rear leg and hip, makes up that period of fencing time when an adversary can successfully counterattack.

Important
As little opportunity as possible must be given to the adversary to bring off a stop hit at arm, for instance. If that chance is given to him, it is because the take-off of the fleche (running attack) has been too slow in it's first stage—the loss of balance—and, to use a fencing colloquialism, "telegraphed."

When you strike an opponent, it must not be with a dead action, pushed, and remaining on the target, as if the fencer were leaning on his opponent for support. On the contrary, it must have a quality of lightness and spring, as if it were rebounding from the spot which it hit. This spring, which ensures a lightness of hand and flexibility of wrist, will enable the hitter to return quickly to the on-guard position, or continue with some other stroke if need be.

Hand immobilization attack (HIA) moves toward hand; progressive indirect attack (PIA) moves away from hand.

Attacks of an indirect nature should be launched like direct attacks, when the opponent is moving from one position to another.

Another important consideration
The advanced target of shin/knee has its own subdivision.

To minimize the danger of a counter
1. Feints to disturb opponent's rhythm (i.e., cause opponent to lose a period of movement time).
2. Changing of position during attack
   - Slipping—left and right
   - Ducking—sudden change of level
   - Weaving—slip and change
3. Causing opponent to lose a gung fu (or movement) time (the gaining control of opponent's hand before attacking)
   a. PIA
   b. HIA (feet or hand)
   - Draw reaction (for PIA and SAA)
   - Disturb rhythm of attack of opponent (feet)
   - To jam or to check and control
   - To deflect and score
4. False attack
Note: Stop hit to HIA.

5. Attack on opponent's preparation to attack
6. His stepping forward
   - His feints (first feint)
   - His process of trapping the hand
      a. Curving in to intercept
      b. Thrusting through loop holes
   - Finding exact physical (balance) and psychological (psyche out) moment of weakness.
   - Preoccupation with idea of attack
7. Progressive indirect attack
   - Feints
   - False attacks

To disturb an opponent's rhythm
1. Alter the measure to minimize danger of counter
2. Cause opponent to lose a gung fu-time
3. Change head position

Disturb your opponent's rhythm.

Attacks on nearest target
1. To deflect
2. To check
3. To bring about a reaction (for disengage)
4. Stop hit to HIA

Types and reactions of opponents
Before adopting a particular plan of attack, one must find out, for instance, whether the adversary parries, stop hits, or gives ground. Does he parry feints or does he wait for the final of the attack? Does he riposte automatically after each parry? Are his stop hits spontaneous or premeditated? Does he stop hit from any angle or from one position in particular?

The open guard

Object:

1. To draw attacks
2. Parries and riposte
3. Time or stop hit

The three types of opponent

1. Those that parry
   - PIA
   - False attack then HIA
2. Those that stop kick or hit
   - Counter-time
   - Shifting to grappling
3. Those that give ground
   - Sudden passive change of rhythm to jam
   - Preparation (line close) and HIA (occasionally combining PIA, SAA)
   - Speedy simple attack when appropriate distance is secured

Find out

a. His cadence b. His footwork speed c. His preferences

Prepare in progression [forward from] on-guard to be sure second stroke (a timed attack) is well balanced, alive (ready to advance or retreat), and fast and powerful.

Maintain the advantage of moving ahead throughout.

The play on distance/mobility of footwork

a. Advancing and retiring repeatedly to score
b. Small rapid steps to gain ground
c. Up on the balls of feet for distribution of weight

Speed and more speed, greater and greater mobility.

Concerning defense

A semi-restricted defense for:

1. Limited artist 2. Left-hander

Study ripostes direct toward shin/knee

1. In kicking 2. In striking

Constant threat to advanced target—improving respect of distance.

Concerning attacks

Be a careful attacker and regulate one's attack accordingly to opponent's:

1. Reactions 2. Habits 3. Preferences

The three successful factors in a successful attack

1. A fine sense of timing
2. A perfect judgment of distance
3. A correct application of cadence

Simple attack (with minimum initiation) with simple preparation to break opponent's rhythm is the best.

The three basic factors

1. Attack with confidence
2. Attack with accuracy
3. Attack with great speed

Counter-time to draw opponent to react and commit so as to pave path to attack.

Part 4

THE TOOLS
OF COMBAT—
PART TWO:
THE LOWER
LIMBS

THE LEAD SHIN/KNEE KICK

A simple kick this is, but no style thoroughly made use of it quite like jeet kune do, and a lot of scientific study is put into this most efficient and simple kick.

The leading shin kick is a potent weapon both in offense and defense. It is a giant killer. This shin kick is equivalent to a jab in Western boxing except it is longer and much harder to defend against. This kick is the spearhead of your attack and it's effectiveness is simply the adhering to the principle of using the longest against the closest (see the progressive target chart illustrations). And with a pair of shoes on, the effect can be quite devastating. Your opponent will find this simple shin kick a constant threat.

The old slogan of a Chinese fighter is "first kick your opponent in the groin," but in jeet kune do, the practitioner knows better.

- Offense—1. The speed kick 2. The long thrust
- Counter—1. The stop kick 2. The simple thrust
- Obstruction
- Infighting

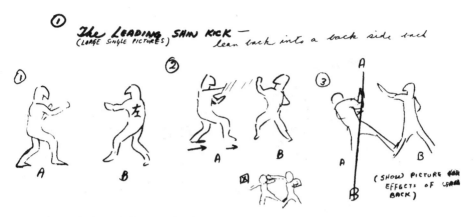

Figure 1. A and B facing each other in ready position.

Figure 2. To make the shin kick more deceptive and at the same time lengthening the opponent's reaction time, A advances with a finger-jab feint to B's eyes. Of course B can stop kick A's advance with a shin kick at this stage, and that is why A's advance has to be sudden (and without any "give-away" motion) to catch B off balance, physically or mentally. Notice A's guarding hand is up.

Figure 3. A perfect shin kick on target. Notice A's body is turned and leaning back for maximum power, reach, and protection. This is actually a low side rear kick.

We know that, apart from Western boxing, all kinds of martial arts, including Chinese boxing, Thai boxing, aikido, judo, and karate, allow attacks to the lower part of the body. Two things are very important in connecting the lower part and upper part of our body; they are our waist and our knees. I will talk about our waist first. The possibility of getting our waist hurt is comparatively small, for in combat, we will not face our opponent with our backs (except in turning our bodies). Moreover, our abdominal muscles are—at least compared to our knees and shins—firm and strong and can therefore endure great pressure. Furthermore, they are concealed behind the protection of the hands and legs. So it is not easy for an opponent to get through to them to hurt us. But our knees are different. In any kind of martial art, especially Chinese boxing, our knees are closest to our opponent when we are preparing for combat. We tend to think of them more as vehicles with which to move our bodies, rather than as a solid target of attack.

However, the structure of our knees is very weak—a few pieces of bone under the skin. There are no real tissues there to develop so we can hardly turn it into an "iron knee." Chinese martial art uses a forward stance whereby the knees are fully exposed to attack. Our supporting leg is also liable to be hurt and, once our knees are hurt, our stance is unbalanced and we cannot support our bodies. We will at once lose our fighting power.

But all kinds of combat, as I have mentioned above, do not forbid attacking the knees. Even in formal matches, there is usually only a groin protective cup, a helmet, and a shin protector.

Another weak point is our shin, especially the middle part. If you are struck there badly, you might not be able to bear the pain. It is because the inner part of that position has a dense group of nerves. Once it is hurt, the pain will be unbearable and you cannot go on fighting.

Thus, a gung fu practitioner must pay special attention to the safety of the shin and train it hard in order to reduce the degree of pain.

Shin/knee side-kick factors that all martial artists should consider
1. The shin/knee side kick as attack
   • To a right stancer • To a left stancer

2. The shin/knee side kick as counter
   - To a right-stancer's right shin/knee kick or other tactics
   - To a left-stancer's low side kick or other tactics
3. The shin/knee side kick combined with hand and other long/close-range tactics as attack
   - To a right stancer
   - To a left stancer
4. The shin/knee side kick combined with hand as counter
   - To a right stancer
   - To a left stancer
5. Countering the leading right shin/knee side kick
   - Right stancer
   - Left stancer
6. Training aid

Other low-kick attacks that all martial artists should consider

1. Other low-kick attacks to shin/knee
   - Front lead leg to right stancer
   - Front lead leg to left stancer
   - Reverse rear leg to right stancer
   - Reverse rear leg to left stancer
2. As counter
   - Lead leg to right stancer
   - Lead leg to left stancer
   - Rear leg to right stancer
   - Rear leg to left stancer
3. Their possible combination with long-range and close-range fighting:
   - The lead leg
4. Combined tactics as attack (the rear leg)
5. Combined tactics—their counters (the lead leg)
6. Combined tactics as counter (the rear leg)
7. Training aid

JKD straight groin toe-kick factors that all martial artists should consider

1. JKD straight groin toe kick—as attack to right stancer
2. JKD straight groin toe kick—as attack to left stancer
3. Counters to the right- and left-stancer's JKD groin toe kick
   - The right stancer
   - Counter to a left-stancer's lead straight groin toe kick
4. The JKD straight groin toe kick combined with long- and close-range tactics as attack to right stancer
5. Combined tactics as attack to a left stancer
6. Combined tactics as counter to a right stancer
7. Combined tactics as counter to left stancer
8. Training aid

Leading straight-kick factors that all martial artists should consider

1. The leading straight kick as attack
   - Parallel (to a right stancer)
   - Parallel (to a left stancer)
   - Upward (to a right stancer)
   - Upward (to a left stancer)
2. As counter to straight lead kick
   - Right upward thrust (right stancer's)
   - Counter: right-hander's right parallel thrust
   - Counter to left-stancer's lead straight kick—upward left lead
   - As counters to left-hander's parallel thrust
3. Leading straight kick with other long- and close-range methods
   - As attack to right stancer
   - Combined tactics as attack to left stancer
4. Leading straight kick with hand
   - As counter to right stancer
5. Combined tactics as counter to left stancer
6. Training aid

THE SIDE KICK

This time I used my longest weapon; my side kick, against the nearest target; your kneecap. This can be compared to your left jab in boxing—except it's much more damaging.

Due to its long reach, a side kick is a very effective weapon in attack and aggressive defense. (It can be aimed at the opponent's solar plexus, ribs, and, sometimes, the face.)

You're letting your foot dangle a little bit instead of an instant direct retraction. The side kick should be brought back a little quicker, especially when you're doing [practicing] free exercises—in other words, when you are not hitting something.

② *The* **BACK** SIDE **KICK** NO PULLING BACK)
(LARGE SINGLE PICTURES - TO ILLUSTRATE

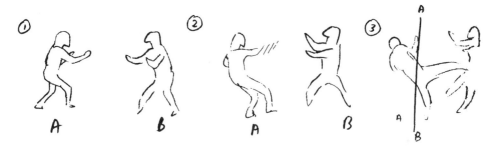

Figure 1. A and B facing each other in ready stance.
Figure 2. With a right-hand feint to the face, A draws the desired reaction from B.
Figure 3. Continuing his forward drive, A thrusts out his back side kick to B's now unprotected ribs (notice the backward lean and the hip extension for maximum reach and power).

Now I want you to see the initial speed and suddenness of your attack of your side kick. Not bad, not bad. Notice your kick when you finish. You just let it drop down. You do not bring it back quick enough. Your initial movement was quick. If you bring it back quick the whole kick will look—*broom!*

Side kick-factors that all martial artists should consider

1. The side kick as attack
   - High upward to right stancer
   - High upward to left stancer
   - Parallel thrust to right stancer
   - Parallel thrust to left stancer
   - Angle-in to left stancer
2. The side kick as counter
3. Counter to side kick—right stancer
   - Upward thrust
4. Counter to right-hander's parallel thrust
5. Counter to right-stancer's angle-in
6. Counter to left-stancer's side kick
   - Upward thrust • Parallel thrust • Angle-in

7. Side kick and hand combinations and other long/close-range tactics as attack
   - To right stancer
   - To left stancer
   - As counter to right stancer
   - As counter (combined tactics) to left stancer
8. Training aid

When you use your leg it is much better to use it to kick at the foam pad or something like that. Watch out with the side kick on air kicking too much because it's bad for the knee joint if you snap it too much without resistance at the end. Just think about economical movement.

Reverse side-kick factors that all martial artists should consider
1. The reverse side kick as attack
   - High to right stancer
   - High to left stancer
   - Parallel to right stancer
   - Parallel to left stancer
   - Low to right stancer
   - Low to left stancer
2. Counters to the right- and left-stancer's reverse side kick: The right-stancer's left reverse thrust
   - High · Parallel · Low
3. Counter to a left-stancer's right reverse side kick
   - Right reverse high
   - Right reverse parallel
   - Right low reverse side kick
4. Reverse side kick combined with other long- or close-range fighting—as attack to a right stancer
5. Combined with four-corner long- or close-range fighting—as attack to a left stancer

6. Reverse side kick combined with other long- or close-range fighting—as counter to a right stancer

7. Reverse side kick combined with other long- or close-range fighting—as counter to a left stancer

8. Training aid

A decisive leap. In your case it was the side kick that caused you to lose your "presence of the primordial state." However, today your side kick became a tool to unlock a spiritual goal. There was spiritual loosening along with physical loosening, a sort of unconcerned immersion in oneself. The original sense of freedom was there. Congratulations! The side kick took the place of the ego.

Your side kick is a very efficient tool as far as the normal function of a tool is concerned. Your side kick has fulfilled magnificently the first function that is to destroy anything or anyone that opposes the will of it's owner; however, the side kick's main function is to be directed toward oneself, to destroy all impulses of the ego, the obstruction of our fluid mind. The latter should control and consecrate the former. Once you understand this, the tool is the embodiment of life and not of death.

Get the power in the momentum rather than in the preparation prior to that. Because you can kick a heavy bag that way but you cannot kick an opponent that way.

Come, let's not treat kicking too seriously, we will turn it into play and we will play seriously, all right!?

THE HOOK KICK

This kick is never a "round-house" as some other styles might call it, but is delivered in a short arc fashion, the tighter and more explosive the better. Remember that the more you open the hook kick (turning it into a swing), the more exposed and vulnerable you become.

With this hook kick, you add variety to your kicking, thus adding more possible combinations. Also, the hook kick can open up the tight and compact defense of some opponents when the straight and side kicks fail to do so.

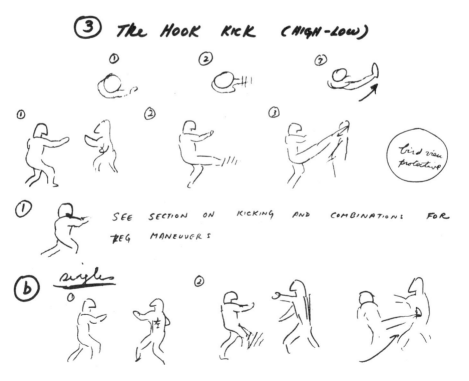

③ The HOOK KICK (HIGH-LOW)

SEE SECTION ON KICKING AND COMBINATIONS FOR LEG MANEUVERS

While it's true that a good man should "be able to kick from all angles," do not go to the extreme and turn the hook kick into a wild swing kick; remember always that the shorter and tighter the kick, the better.

The efficient hook kick

A hook kick is more efficient as a counter than a lead. However, an occasional lead with this kick might surprise your opponent and disrupt his rhythm. This is especially true when preceded by a straight fake kick. Generally, then, a hook kick necessitates some form of feinting first.

Power hook kicking

The power of the hook kick derives from the looseness of the delivery plus correct timing of feet and hip. Do not cock, or "pull back," the foot before delivery. Of course, during the kick you should keep at least one of your hands in front of your body for better defense and quicker follow up.

Note: This is useful when your opponent uses his rear hand to block.

The thing to watch out for is you have to be initially fast and also you've got to bring it back fast. So, you've got to be fast from beginning to end.

Vertical hook-kick factors that all martial artists should consider

1. The vertical hook kick—as attack to a right stancer
2. The vertical hook kick—as attack to a left stancer
3. As counter (vertical hook)—to a left stancer
4. As counter to right- and left-stancer's vertical hook
   • The right vertical hook
5. Counter to a left-stancer's vertical hook

6. The vertical hook combines with hand and other long- or close-range tactics
   • As attack—to a right stancer
   • As attack—to left stancer
7. As counter with other combinations (as counter)—to right stancer
8. Counter—combined tactics to a left stancer
9. Training aid

Leading hook-kick factors that all martial artists should consider

1. The tight and inside hook
2. Hook kick—as attack (high to right stancer)
3. Hook kick—as attack (high to left stancer)
4. Hook kick—as attack (low to right stancer)
5. Hook kick—as attack (low to left stancer)

6. Hook kick—as counter
7. Using right high hook as counter to
   • Right stancer • Left stancer
8. Using right low hook as counter to
   • Right stancer • Left stancer
9. Counter to hook kick—right stancer
   • Counter to high right hook
10. Counter to right-hander's low lead right hook
11. Counter to left-stancer's hook kick
    • High left lead hook
12. Counter to left-hander's low left lead hook
13. Hook kick and hand combinations and other long- or close-range fighting
    • As attack to a right hander
    • As attack (combined long- and close-range) to a left stancer
14. Hook kick with hand combinations and other long- or close-range tactics
    • As counter to right stancer
15. Combined tactics as counter to a left stancer
16. Training aid

Reverse hook-kick factors that all martial artists should consider

1. Reverse hook kick as attack to a right-hander
   - High
2. Reverse hook kick as attack to a left-hander
   - High
3. Reverse hook kick as attack—low to a right stancer
4. Reverse hook kick as attack—low to a left stancer
5. The reverse hook kick as counter—high to right stancer
6. The reverse hook kick as counter—high to left stancer
7. The reverse hook kick as counter—low to a right stancer
8. The reverse hook kick as counter—low to a left stancer
9. Counter to right- and left-stancer's reverse hook kick—left reverse high
10. Counter to right-stancer's left reverse low
11. Counter to left-stancer's reverse right high hook
12. Counter to left-hander's reverse right hook
13. Left reverse hook kick combines with other long- and close-range tactics
    - As attack to right stancer
    - As attack to left stancer
14. Left reverse hook combines with long- and close-range tactics
    - As counter to right stancer
    - As counter to left stancer
15. Training aid for reverse hook kick

How can I be a master of reverse hook kick?

Technique:

1. Training and supplementary exercise

ADDITIONAL STRIKING OPTIONS (LOWER LIMBS)

The sweeping kick

The sweeping kick is equivalent to the backfist, in that it involves the same path, and is delivered mainly with the leading right foot.

Figure 1. A and B facing each other in ready position—A in right stance, B in left stance.

Figure 2. Before the execution of the sweeping kick, A had fired a couple of side kicks to B's ribs to accustom his opponent to the path of his (A's) kicking. Without the slightest movement, A darts in with what appears to be a side kick.

Figure 3. Suddenly with a slight twist, A's right foot passes over B's guard and sweeps around and inward into an explosive seep kick to B's face.

Figure 1. A and B facing each other in right stance.

Figure 2. A had attempted a hook kick preceding by a straight feint with his leading right hand (which naturally obstructs the path of A's hook kick). This time A advanced with a straight feint to draw B's leading right hand block.

The problem with the sweeping kick

Once you get your heel out there and try to spin it around, you're too vulnerable to counterattack. You can start that kick, but then you must be ready to change it as the counterattack comes and base your change on the nature of the counterattack.

The rear spin kick

*mainly as counter more than a lead — due to reach
a timed kick to opponent's advance*

REAR SPIN KICK

Figure 1. A and B facing each other in ready position.

Figure 2. Without telegraphing, A suddenly steps forward with a finger jab to B's eyes. The finger jab here is used as a feint to draw B's reaction and to obstruct his vision.

Figure 3. As soon as B's hand starts to react, A quickly spins into a rear spin kick.

Figure 4. The spin kick scores.

REAR STRAIGHT KICK

Figure 1. A and B facing each other.

Figure 2. Without any giving movement, A darts forward with hands in a threatening manner...

Figure 3. ...while forcefully kicking B on the thigh ("To shoot the general, first shoot his horse").

Note: There is always an opportunity to slap in a finger jab after an attack with a kick or vice versa.

The rear kick

Like the left hand, the rear kick is mainly a counter-weapon, this is especially true with the leg than the hand because kicking is slower than striking. How-

The rear kick

ever, an occasional lead with the rear leg, especially when preceded by feints, tends to disturb the opponent's rhythm (his unfamiliar angles).

The crescent kick

• Landing parts (medium range)

Front leg (inside out)

• Inside angle in side kick
• Reverse hook kick

Straight out

1. Side kick: long, medium, close (downward stomp)

In combat: the side kick is best utilized by directing it downward!

2. Straight toe kick:

• With front leg straight on to destroy vulnerability
• Using rear leg

3. Attacking shin/knee

• Straight downward—to right/left stancer
• Straight on—to right/left stancer
• Cross-stomping—to right/left stancer
• Inward out—to right/left stancer
• Reverse hook—to left stancer
• Reverse hook—to right stancer
• Outside in—to right/left stancer

(*Note:* Look into the ball of foot for attacking shin/knee or instep.)

• Hook kick—to right/left stancer
• Cross stomp—to right/left stancer

Concerning recovery for spin kick

1. As a continuous attack onward
2. As a counter kick and then neutral

Kicking factors that all martial artists should consider

1. Kicking footwork in attack
2. Kicking footwork in defense and counter
3. The importance of combining the hands with feet
4. Training aids: practice your footwork diligently with due attention to details—first practice the right feel in good form—then practice quick recovery—then unite everything as one whole.

Kicking attack principles

1. Make maximum use of knee spring of stationary leg.
2. Withdraw rapidly the kicking foot to avoid being grabbed by the opponent and to be prepared for next movement.
3. Shift the body weight momentarily to another foot.
4. Maintain a strong stance with stationary foot.
5. Decide the kind of kick to be delivered at the selected target and then adjust the body toward it.

The turning kick

This is very convenient when attacking the opponent at the side front and performed with front sole or knee; in both cases turning is executed in two ways: the kick is performed directly from any suitable position, or else move into a suitable position before doing the turning kick.

Jeet Kune Do

Common principles are:

1. Swing the hip forward so that the foot reaches the target in an arc. The foot should be vertical to the target at the moment of impact.

2. When kicking the target at the high section, the foot must pass through its highest point so that the front sole points slightly downward at the moment of impact.

3. The toes of the stationary foot point almost directly forward.

Note: Do not bend the kicking leg more than necessary.

Front sole: This plays a main role in most cases. Solar plexus, temple, and genitals are main targets, but the ribs or neck could be attacked.

Knee: The principle of kicking is basically the same as front sole.

Reverse turning kick (reverse roundhouse kick)

This is a reverse form of the turning kick (tae kwon do's "roundhouse"or "hook" kick). Accordingly it is used in attacking the opponent who is at the side back. The heel is the striking point while the temple and solar plexus are main targets, but also the face, ribs, or neck could be attacked. The kick is executed in two ways: the striking point reaches the target in a straight line or in an arc.

Common principles are:

1. Bring the heel close to the body soon after the kick.

2. Bend the knee of the kicking leg properly during the kick.

3. The heel of the stationary foot points almost directly rear at the moment of impact.

Lateral circular heel kick factors that all martial artists should consider

1. Lateral circular heel kick—as attack (high to right stancer)

2. Lateral circular heel kick—as attack (high to left stancer)

3. Lateral circular heel kick—as attack (low to right stancer)
4. Lateral circular heel kick—as attack (low to left stancer)
5. Lateral circular heel kick—as counter (high)
6. Lateral circular heel kick—as counter (low)
7. Lateral circular heel kick combined with hand and long- and short-range tactics
    • In attack
    • As counter
8. Counter to lateral circular heel kick from right- and left-stancers'
    • Right high heel kick
9. Counter to right low circular heel kick
10. Counter to left-hander's left high circular heel kick
11. Counter to left-hander's left low lateral arc lead
12. Training aid

Reverse straight kick to knee factors that all martial artists should consider

1. The reverse straight kick to knee
    • As attack to a right stancer
    • As attack to a left stancer
    • As counter to the right stancer's attack
    • As counter to the left stancer's attack
2. The reverse straight kick to knee combined with long- and close-range tactics
    • As attack
    • As counter
3. Countering a right-stancer's left reverse straight kick to knee
4. Countering a left-stancer's right reverse straight kick to knee
5. Training aid

Reverse straight kick factors that all martial artists should consider

1. Left reverse straight kick
2. Reverse straight kick

- As attack—high to opponent in right stance
- As attack—high to opponent in left stance
- As attack—low (to groin) to right stance
- As attack—low (to groin) to left stance

3. Reverse straight kick as counter
   - High to right and left stancer
   - Low to right and left stancer
4. Reverse straight kick combined with hand and long- and close-range tactics
   - As attack • As counter
5. For skill development
6. Counter to reverse straight kick
   - Left high reverse straight • Left low reverse straight
7. Counter to left-stancer's reverse straight kick
   - Right high reverse • Right low reverse
8. Training aid

The spinning back kick

In the spin kick you will notice a very good lesson. When you try too much to control the movement, you get too hung up on its execution, and, therefore, you become too tense and your execution is

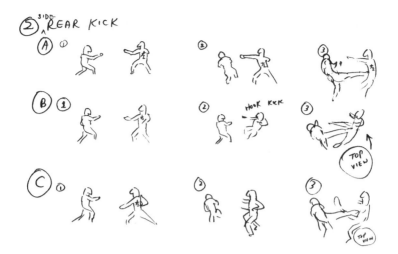

② SIDE REAR KICK

Ⓐ ① ② ③

Ⓑ ① ② HOOK KICK ③ TOP VIEW

Ⓒ ① ② ③ TOP VIEW

poor. However, if you are able to forget about it, to relax—boom!—it will land right on the target! When you ease the burden of your mind, you just do it.

Spinning back kick factors that all martial artists should consider

1. Spinning back kick
   - As attack—high to right stancer
   - As attack—high to left stancer

- As attack—low to right stancer
- As attack—low to left stancer

2. Spinning back kick
   - As counter—high to right stancer
   - As counter—high to left stancer
   - As counter—low to right stancer
   - As counter—low to left stancer

3. Counter to opponent's high left spin kick—right stancer
4. Counter to opponent's parallel left spinning back kick—right stancer
5. Counter left low spinning back kick—right stancer
6. Counter to a left-stancer's spinning back kick—high right stancer
7. Counter to left-hander's right low spinning back kick
8. Spinning back kick combined with hand and other long- and close-range tactics—as attack
9. Spinning back kick combined with hand and other long- an close-range tactics—as counter
10. Training aid

Combination kicking

This is combination kicking. In the beginning you tend to cover too much distance. By moving forward too much the form in kicking is greatly effected.

The pacing kick

The pacing kick: to be done with speed and power in mind.

Additional kicking options that all martial artists should consider

Kicks that can be initiated without changing on-guard positioning too much before and/or after.

Name the kicks that can be initiated without changing on-guard positioning before and/or after
1. Hook kick 2. Side kick
3. Vertical hook 4. Reverse hook
a. Those that go for absolute speed!

Flowing back to neutrality or flow on with attack.

What...

• "Natural" delivery (without disturbing on-guard)
• What parts (*Note*: Enlarge, man!)

Leading upward knee thrust factors that all martial artists should consider

    1. The leading upward knee thrust as attack

    2. The leading upward knee thrust as counter

    3. Counter to a right-stancer's right knee

    4. Counter to left-stancer's lead left knee

5. The leading upward knee combined with long- and close-range tactics—as attack

6. Combined with long- and close-range tactics—as counter

7. Training aid

Reverse upward knee thrust factors that martial artists should consider

1. Reverse upward knee thrust
   • As attack • As counter

2. Combined with long- and close-range tactics
   • As attack • As counter

3. Counter to right-stancer's left upward reverse knee thrust

4. Counter to left-stancer's right upward reverse knee thrust

5. Training aid

Lead hook knee thrust and reverse knee hook factors that all martial artists should consider

1. Lead knee hook—as attack to right stancer

2. Reverse knee hook—to left stancer

3. Lead knee hook—as counter to right stancer

4. Reverse knee hook—as counter to left stancer

5. Combined with long- and close-range tactics—as attack

6. Combined with long- and close-range tactics—as counter

7. Counter to right-stancer's right knee hook

8. Counter to left-stancer's reverse right knee hook

9. Training aid

JKD groin-curve toe-kick factors that all martial artists should consider

1. The JKD groin curve toe kick—as attack

2. The JKD groin curve toe kick—as counter

3. Counter to JKD groin curve toe kick—right- and left-stancers,
   • Right curve toe kick to groin

4. Counter to left-hander's lead curve groin toe kick

5. JKD curve toe groin kick combined with long- and close-range tactics—as attack

6. JKD groin curve toe kick combined with long- and close-range tactics—as counter

7. The JKD groin curve toe kick combined with other long- and close-range fighting—as attack

8. The JKD groin curve toe kick combined with other long- and close-range fighting—as counter

9. Counter to right- and left-stancers, groin curve toe kick—right curve lead

10. The JKD groin curve toe kick combined with hand—as attack

11. The JKD groin curve toe kick combined with hand—as counter

12. Training aid

One idea of the long bag (for kicking) is to make it like the regular punch bag that you made with punched holes on both sides. That way I can lower or make it higher.

The greatest thing in the world to kick is a tree. Not a sapling either, but a large palm tree. When you can kick so you aren't jarred, but the tree is jarred, then you will begin to understand the meaning of a kick.

On using your tools
Use your tools [weapons]:
- To find rhythm
- To attack when opponent is committing
1. Through shifting of balance
   - Leaning or resting back (good for any one-two, one outside range drawing…)
2. Through shifting of footwork
3. The commitment of opponents
   - Attacking
     a. the enemy,
     b. in between two moves
   - Defense
     a. PIA
     b. Awkward position
4. The gap of preparedness
   - Physically
   - Psychologically

A minimum of "fancy stuff"
It has been stripped to a minimum of fancy stuff. Clean and simple destruction. If your opponent is at a distance, kick him in the groin. If he gets close, poke him in the eyes, bring up your knee, pop him with an elbow, dig a corkscrew punch to his stomach.

I've given you the tools—how you use them is up to you
I can give you the tools, but you have to develop your own way of using them.

There should be no method of fighting. There should only be tools to use as effectively as possible.

Learn to move with your tools

Here it is; if you can move with your tools from any angle then you can adapt to whatever the object is in front of you. And the clumsier, the more limited the object, the easier for you to potshot it. That's what it amounts to!

Part 5

ON TRAINING
IN JEET
KUNE DO

AN ORGANIZED LESSON PLAN FOR JEET KUNE DO

Let's get out of the tangled maze

It is proven more efficient and interesting to devote time to only one or two simple techniques at a one-hour session than to have many unrelated and disorganized techniques crammed into it. The simple techniques being taught should be related to the preceding one in a progressive manner, and the instructor should clearly define the technique and manipulate it in different situations with various rhythm, speed, and/or distance, or combine it with other simple techniques.

Students should learn something new in each class period, but one or two new techniques are enough for one session. Until the student begins to spar then he will stop searching for the accumulation of techniques; rather he will devote the needed hours of practice to the simple technique for its right execution. It is not how much one learns but how much one absorbs what he learns. The best techniques are the simple ones executed correctly. When sparring occurs, stress the above thought and the students themselves will realize it is futile to search for more and more new techniques.

Rather, they will devote the needed hours on practicing the correct execution of simple techniques.

Let's be broken rhythm

Like boxing or fencing, jeet kune do is a step-by-step project in which each maneuver must be repeated many times (like practicing throws in judo). First of all, help the student to see what he is trying to achieve; encourage him to see experienced practitioners in sparring sessions. Next, the same drill (take punching practice) should be varied so that it will not become a chore (with paper, with partners, with heavy bag, etc.)

Don't let them be sponges

Give rest periods, but during these short breaks (they are necessary), try to talk and/or demonstrate, but better yet, ask questions. The students will then think for themselves and solve their own problems. They will be involved with the technique rather than merely repeating it, without thought or purpose. They have to be involved.

Come on, pat them on the back

Give recognition where it is due. Compliments definitely stimulate more effort and desire to improve. Recognize and compliment each student accordingly to stimulate his desire to improve. Be generous with honest praising.

True, we are holding the standards of jeet kune do high—but definitely not out of reach. As each new skill is perfected, raise the goal.

Leadership

The success or failure of the training program depends on the quality of its instructors. The best results in any martial art training program can be obtained only if the students are motivated to extend themselves completely in strenuous physical activities and to make every effort to perform all exercises, techniques, and form in the prescribed manner. Only the best leadership can inspire the students to cooperate to this extent.

The instructor

The most essential quality of an instructor is the possession of abounding energy and enthusiasm. Training activities, if they're to be successful, must be carried on in a snappy, vigorous manner. Students invariably reflect the instructor's attitude, whether it be enthusiastic or apathetic. As an instructor, you must have complete mastery of each lesson and subject. Not only must you be able to explain and demonstrate the techniques but you must know the best methods of presenting and conducting them. Mastery of the subject matter is the first step in developing confidence, assurance, and poise. As a well-prepared, confident instructor, you will gain respect and cooperation from your students.

To be a successful leader you, as an instructor, must understand human nature. You must appreciate each student's physical and mental difference and accept it for what it is. The better you understand the students the more successful your instruction will be.

A successful instructor gains the confidence of his students. The method of gaining their confidence is by commanding their respect. You will win your students' respect by your sincerity, integrity, determination, sense of justice, energy, self-confidence, and force of character.

An instructor should exemplify the things he seeks to teach. It will be of great advantage if you yourself can do all you ask of your students and more.

Motivation

A successful training program requires the full cooperation of all the students. Martial art training must be done accurately and intensively if it is to be of value to the students. One of the best incentives to encourage greater effort on the part of the students is participation by the instructor himself. Whenever a student performs with exceptionally good form or results, commend him for his good performance as quickly as you could censor his bad. It is equally important that you praise the less-skillful performers when the occasion merits. As an instructor, you must be able to distinguish between poor performance caused by lack of ability or aptitude on the part of the student and poor performance caused by indifference or lack of effort. You should treat the first with patience and the latter with firmness. You must never apply sarcasm and ridicule.

Formality versus informality

Formality should be stressed but not to extremes. When extreme formalism is insisted upon in martial art training, the chief objective is discipline rather than physical fitness and knowledge The best results are obtained in training when the students participate in the activities with vigor, enthusiasm, and satisfaction. When a class period is conducted in a rigidly formal manner, however, the spirit and enthusiasm of the students is suppressed.

Accuracy and precision of performance should be required unconditionally whenever their attainment is possible. But this insistence upon accuracy and precision of performance should be aimed at giving the students maximum physical benefit and knowledge from the exercises and should not be employed for purely disciplinary purposes. Some degree of discipline must be observed, however, if the instructor is to maintain precision and control.

Training commands

The importance of proper commands in conducting the training program cannot be overestimated. Invariably, the performance directly reflects the command. When the command is given distinctly, concisely, with energy and snap, and with proper regard to rhythm, the performance will reflect the command. A lifeless, slovenly, and disorganized performance results from a careless and indifferent command.

The ways of instruction
1. Bruce Lee's style—private lesson
2. Home private lesson
3. Schools (own or affiliated)
4. Books

The Jun Fan system

1. Sticking to the nucleus
2. Liberation from the nucleus
3. Returning to the original freedom

The ultimate goal of discipline in JKD is where learning gained is learning lost.

Jeet kune do, Jun Fan gung fu (the wrestler example)

1. Nonclassical (solidify one's fluidity)
   No classical postures:
   • Hand position, rigid body position, unrealistic footwork, dissecting a corpse.
   • No rhythmical mess: two-men cooperation; give boxing comparison (form, training, etc.)
2. Directness (respond like an echo, fit in like shadow to object).
   No passive defense: we are offensive.
Everything is stripped to their essential: the satisfaction of one's bare hand.
3. Simplicity (daily minimize instead of daily increase)

The analogies

1. The three stages
2. The sculptor
3. Being wise does not mean add on.
4. The throwing of an object

No sign—door locked—no affiliation—no ties.

Basic fitness program

1. Alternate splits 2. Push-up 3. Run in place 4. Shoulder circling 5. High kicks 6. Deep knee bends 7. Side kick raises 8. Sit-up (twist) 9. Waist twisting 10. Leg raises 11. Forward bends

Lesson one

1. Basic fitness program
2. Salutation
   - Student to student
   - Student to instructor
3. By-jong (ready stance) from natural position:
   - Moving forward to by-jong
   - Dropping back to by-jong
4. Basic footwork (in by-jong position)
   - Step and slide shuffle forward
   - Step and slide shuffle backward
   - Slide and step shuffle forward
   - Slide and step shuffle backward

   Advance and retreat

5. Side kick—right foot only (from natural position, not from by-jong)
   - Synchronization drill (water and whip principle)
   - Kicking to the side from natural position (low first, then according to individual flexibility)
6. Finger jab—good
   - Awareness drill, the centerline (from natural position)
   - Moving forward and/or dropping backward to by-jong from natural stance
     a. Moving into by-jong
     b. Stepping back into by-jong

Lesson two

Salutation to open class

1. Basic fitness program
2. Review lesson one in the following order: nos. 2, 6, 4, 5.
3. Right side kick (warm-up with synchronization) + (rear kick)
   - Side kick (with slide in by-jong stance) with rear foot moving first

- Side kick with step-through (step and slide) with front foot moving first (opposite line retreat in by-jong)
- Side kick with retreat (opponent practices advance)
- Back kick against opponent's lead (left and right)
- Back kick against rear step-through straight kick (use as general review)

4. Basic footwork
   - Curving left (opposite line practice step and slide shuffle forward)
   - Curving right (opposite line practice step and slide shuffle forward)

5. Introduce the four corners (biu jee—practice finger jab from ready stance and use a blackboard to illustrate the four corners).
   - Awareness exercise
   - Inside high
   - Outside high • Inside low • Outside low
     —versus karate thrusts and common street blows

Lesson three

Salutation to open class

1. Basic fitness program
2. Review lesson two: nos. 3, 4, 5
3. The right lead
   - Hammer principle from natural stance (centerline defined)
     —practice with hanging paper
   - With advance—(economy of form, guarding hand); opponent in both left and right stances defends with either one of the upper two gates while retreating
   - With retreat—(opponent practices advancing in both left and right stances with right lead, practitioner retreats just enough, stops and fires own right lead)
   - Right lead to stomach while opponent defends with either one of the two lower gates

4. Pak sao

   • Touching hand • With advance

Lesson four

Salutation to open class

1. Basic fitness program
2. Review lesson three: nos. 3 (drill on paper), 4
3. Introduce right straight kick

   a. With advance (opponent practice retreat)

   b. With right lead

   • To head (opponent practice parry inside or outside)

   • To stomach (opponent practice parry inside or outside)

   c. With pak sao
4. Backfist (the principle of the hinge and whip)

   a. From cross hand

   b. With step and slide

   c. With chop choy and gwa choy (opponent defends accordingly)

   d. (c) with side kick (retreat)
5. Introduce and lecture on the right shin/knee kick and right obstructional kick

Step through side/rear kick with

   a. Right lead to head (or finger jab)

   b. Back fist to head

Lesson five

Salutation to open class

General review

1. Basic fitness program
2. Finger jab

   • Lesson: nos. 6a, b • Lesson two: nos. 5b, c, d, e
3. Right side kick (warm up)

   • Lesson two: no. 3b (get used to right side kick to opponent's
     left stance)

   • Lesson four: no. 5 (get used to right side kick to opponent's left
     stance)

4. Right lead
   - Lesson three: nos. 3a, b, c, d • Lesson three: 4a, b
5. Right straight kick
   - Lesson four: nos. 3a, b, c
6. Right backfist
   - Lesson four: nos. 6a, b, c, d

Lesson six

Salutation to open class

1. Basic fitness program
2. Punching drill (right and left)

Straight punch

   - With paper
   - With partner—lock stance advance and blast (partner first in right stance then in left stance)

3. Kicking drill—side kick (right and left) and rear kick
   - Heavy bag
   - With partner in right and left stance
   - The right stop low kick with partner in right and left stance

4. Introduce the hook kick—to stomach (possibly to head depending on individual's flexibility)
   - Retreat to time opponent's side kick
   - Against right lead
   - Against gwa choy

5. Lop sao
   - Touching (to correct and maintain economy of form)
   - With biu jee (to set up opponent)
   - With side kick (learning to bridge the kicking gap)

Lesson seven

Salutation to open class

1. Basic fitness program
2. Punching drill—backfist
   - With paper
   - With partner

3. Kicking drill—hook kick (left and right)
   - With paper
   - With heavy bag
   - With partner (in both left and right stance)
4. Review lop sao
   - Add double lop sao (opponent blocks inward)
   - Lop sao straight blast (opponent blocks outward)
5. Gwa choy when opponent in left stance
   - Add low obstruction kick to close gap while coming in (bridging gap)

Lesson eight

Salutation to open class

1. Basic fitness program
2. Punching drill—straight blast (right and left)
   - With paper
   - With partner (in both left and right stance)—blast down the line
3. Kicking drill— heavy bag
   - Side kick (left and right)
   - Rear kick (left and right)
4. Review
   - Pak sao—right stance (when opponent is in left stance, just blast with right lead)
   - Lop sao—right stance
   - Chop choy, gua choy (left and right stances)
   - a, b, c with side kick or low stop kick
5. Introduce pak sao lop sao gwa choy

Lesson nine

Salutation to open class

1. Basic fitness program
2. Review lesson eight: no.5

And then add kicking before bridging gap

3. Review four corners
   - With opponent in right stance attacking
   - With opponent in left stance attacking
4. Introduce the kicking set

Teach up to rear kick

Lesson ten

Salutation to open class

1. Basic fitness program

General review

2. Hand technique
   a. Finger jab
   - Opponent in right or left stance
   b. Right lead
   - High—opponent in right or left stance
   - Low—opponent in right or left stance
   c. Right backfist
   - Opponent in right or left stance
3. Foot technique
   a. Side kick—left and right side kick when opponent in left and right stance (especially practice right side kick to opponent's left stance)
   b. Hook kick—same as 3a
   c. Straight kick—same as 3a
   d. Rear kick
4. Kicking set

Continue according to class progress

Lesson eleven

Salutation to open class

1. Basic fitness program

Include jumping rope and isometric program

2. Heavy bag
   - Right lead • Side kick • Hook kick

3. Paper
   - Right lead · Backfist · Hook kick
4. Kicking set (continue)
5. Controlled freestyle sparring

(Limit use of front hand and front leg)

   - Right leg · Pak sao

All in combination:

   - Side kick · Hook kick · Straight kick

Lesson twelve

Salutation to open class

1. Basic fitness program
2. Kicking training (choose one kick and work on speed, power, and agility/flexibility)
3. Punching training (speed and power)
4. Controlled freestyle sparring (limit use of weapon)
5. Kicking set
6. Introduce self-defense (collar grasp)
   - The left-hand grasp · The left-hand shove · The right-hand grasp · The right-hand shove

---

Teaching—the lesson plan

1. Complete use of right hand and right leg are taught before the left hand or leg are developed at all (generally).
2. Use both whole or part method as seen fit—first grasp the idea as a whole, then if it is not clear, divide it into units for learning.
3. Use of commands and formations
4. Students should learn something new each lesson but one or two new actions are enough for one session. Each lesson should reward the students with pleasure, satisfaction of achievement, and the sense of vigorous, joyous movement.
5. Give rest periods, but try to talk and/or demonstrate while the students rest.
6. Remind students that gung fu etiquette descends from knightly manners.

7. Hold the standards of jeet kune do high—but not out of reach. As each skill is perfected raise the goal.

8. Do not force individuals into positions that are "impossible" for them, but find the position as near to ideal as possible.

9. Recognition stimulates effort. Recognize and complement each student's efforts and achievements to stimulate his desire to improve.

10. Give the entire picture. Although gung fu is a step-by-step project, and each maneuver must be repeated many times, help the students to see what they are trying to achieve. Encourage them when possible to observe the sparring of more experienced practitioners.

11. Jeet kune do is fun, and the same drills should be varied so they will not become a bore and a chore. Present them differently and use them often. End each lesson with informal play as soon as possible so that students can practice their newly gained accomplishments.

A few simple techniques, well presented, and an aim clearly seen, are better than a tangled maze of data whirling in disorganized educational chaos.

Motivation (the willingness to learn)

1. A clear understanding of what is to be learned
2. A clear understanding of the reason why the learning of it is important and desirable
3. Praising

Give lessons with absence of touch as often as possible.

Concentration

Dynamic concentration not just mere attention.

Learning accelerates as concentration intensifies.

Reaction

When you wake up, live, and think in a learning situation, that is reaction.

Be involved with, do not be a mere sponge.

Organization

Putting the pieces together into a meaningful mosaic.

Comprehension

The understanding of the application of what is learned, the perception of meanings and implications of techniques studied.

Repetition

The greatest preservative of learning.

In order for it to be effective, it must be thoughtful and purposeful.

The six principal steps

1. Motivation of the trainee
    - Lesson plan · Ranking · Tests · Recognition
2. Maintaining complete attention
    - Command · Awareness · Light and sound
3. Promoting mental activity (thinking)
    - Discussion · Questions · Lecture
4. Creating a clear picture of material to be learned
    - Outline of material
5. Developing comprehension of the significance, the implications, and the practical application of the material being presented
    - Clear goal · Posters
6. Repetition of the five preceding steps until learning has taken place.

BRUCE LEE'S PRIVATE LESSON PLAN

On economy of form

First and foremost, I like to impress a most important rule of teaching in your mind, and that is the economy of form. Follow this rule and you will never feel like you have to add more and more so-called sizzling techniques to keep our students interested. In order to explain economy of form, I'll take a technique to illustrate the theory. Later on, this idea can be applied to any technique, together with the idea of the three stages of a technique [1. synchronization of self, 2. synchronization with opponent, 3. under fighting condition].

This program of teaching not only provides an endless routine of instruction, but a most efficient lesson plan that will bring results to *all* students. I've tested them here in L.A. and regardless of how *little* we show each time, the students interest is kept up because they have to eliminate the extra motions involved and they feel great doing it. All right, back to the idea of economy of form.

To illustrate the idea, I'll take the pak sao (slapping hand)—basically, ecomony of motion means all motions start from the by-jong position; secondly, *hands* are to *move first if it is a hand technique [foot follows], feet first if it is a foot technique.*

So, emphasize the above two truths by practicing pak sao first in the touching hand manner—in other words, students in by-jong position touch each other's hand—though in real combat, one will never start by touching hands; however, this touching hand position will ensure correct form in the beginning stage—economy of form, that is. Each student must attack [in unison] *from the* by-jong without any wasted motion. Now this has been an overlooked basic theory of utmost importance. If any student does his pak sao [or any technique for that matter] with wasted motion, back to the touching hand position he goes to *minimize* his unnecessary motions. So you see that in order to progress to apply pak sao from a distance, this touching hand position has to be mastered. Not only that, the student has to return to the touching hand position to remind him to eliminate unnecessary motion periodically.

From a distance, pak sao is a lot harder—without any given-away motion, one must initiate first hands, then feet, in a progressive, harmonious forward motion—no wonder not too many can hit with a single pak sao! Do you not see now the idea of economy of motion? Just this one theory of economy of motion takes up one heck of a lot of time for perfection, not to mention the three stages of a technique—that is, in terms of pak sao, after learning and mastering pak sao from a distance, one has to bridge the gap between opponent with a kick—to close in safely.

The Three Stages of a technique

STAGE I (synchronization of self)

  (a) correct form
  (b) precision
  (c) synchronization of the whole

} augmenting speed progressively

STAGE II (synchronization with opponent)

  (a) Timing — the ability to seize an opportunity when given
    Distance — correct maintanance of

STAGE III

  Application under fighting condition.

Following the above suggestion will give you endless hours of instruction. Of course, you must use the set system, that is *repetition* of each technique in sets for perfection. Begin now immediately to work on what I mentioned and apply all you've learned with *economy of motion*—you will double your speed and skill doing just that.

I hope I have impressed in your mind a more important rule of our style—stick to the program I've given you, use variety, and do not worry too much that your students need more and more to stay with you—true if they can do perfectly all you've taught them. Remember the idea that one has to come in thousands of times in order to perfect one judo throw. And, of course, use your own experience and imagination. You will do well. I have faith in you.

The ten lessons plan

Lesson one

1. Basic fitness
   - Stomach • Leg loosening–alternate splits • Moderate endurance (involving footwork)
2. Basic footwork (from ready position):
   - Moving forward • Dropping back (from natural position)
   - Sidestep left • Sidestep right
3. Side kick
4. Warm up
   - Deep knee bend • Knee turn • Straight kick
5. Synchronization drill
6. Kicking to the side from natural position
7. Moving in from ready position
   - Teach slide first • Step and slide
8. Finger jab (formation and landing)
   - Awareness drill (sound only)
   - Moving forward to ready position
   - Moving backward to ready position

Equipment needed

1. Air shield
2. Paper
3. Punching pad
4. Body pad
5. Stick

Select test

a. On agility
b. On flexibility

Leg:

• Side • Hook • Up

c. On punching

• Straight hook

d. An explanation of on-guard

Relaxation • Moving forward • Moving backward

e. Footwork

• Stepping forward
• Retreating backward

Lesson two

1. Basic fitness (warm up)
2. Review lesson one: nos. 3 and 4

(Teach retreat from side kick—attacking
with step and slide—attacking with slide.)

3. Show side kick coming in—and retreat
4. Hook kick

a. Synchronization drill—paper
b. Kicking from ready position
c. Moving in from ready position

5. The leading right

a. Synchronization-hammer-foot pivot

• From left stance • Lining up • Right foot forward

b. Moving in—opponent backs up
c. Pak sao

Speed & Cadence

speed must be regulated very carefully to fit in with the speed ~~to correspond~~ of execution of the opponent.

The regulating of one's speed to correspond with that of the adversary is known as Cadence.

with each adversary, the first thing to find out is his cadence, as even a simple attack can fail if that has not been ascertained.

It is a great advantage to be able to impose one's own cadence on the opposition.

man of experience often change their cadence, and effectively hinder the opponent in his effort to regulate his

CERTAIN STYLES & TACTICS

The golden principle : — each movement of yours must correspond to those of the opponent

The more experienced the opponent, the more varied will be his strokes and kicks

sometimes PIA works, sometimes ~~the~~ HIA — in other word, depending on the opponent' tactics and reaction —— IT TAKES TWO TO PLAY

It is impossible to vary one's offensive action if the adversary does not vary his parries.

The stronger man will be he who, if necessary, is able to vary his strokes and kicks.

watch for the opponent's styles, habits, and movements and use them for your advantage.

Tactics against HIA :-

at first sight the answer appears to be to deceive his attempt and stop-hit him, or to attack on his preparation, but it is unlikely that all his attacks on the hand will be deceived, and his feinters, coupled with the numerous hand so deception which have to be made, will finally tire one's hand. It is wiser, against such an adversary, to spar with absence of touch; that is to say, by adopting a low front leading hand, where he will find difficulty in making contact.

Lesson Three

1. Basic fitness
2. Review lesson two's hook kick (no.4)
   - Coming-in hook kick • Retreat • Counter side with hook
3. Review lesson two's leading right (no.5)
   - Snap back with finger jab • Using hook kick • Using side kick
4. Moving back to counter side kick with hook kick
5. Snapping back to counter leading right with finger jab
   - Using hook kick to counter • Using side kick to counter
6. Backfist
   - Hinge principle • Touching hand • Touching hand with footwork (use match)

FIGHTING & LESSON

Instruction should comprise the fighting as well as the technical training. Fighting training should be given for each stroke before going on in the study of a new one.

- HOW ⸺ it is done
- WHY ⸺ it is done
- WHEN ⸺ it is done.

Choice of a stroke

1) should deceive opponent's stroke
2) offensive action move in the same direction as those of the defense. Otherwise the blades are bound to meet while turning ~~in opposite circle~~

To find out REACTION of ~~habit~~ of opponent

① quick simple attack ② feints preceded by attacks on hand
③ false attack with a half lunge.

repetition of a same parry can spell disaster.
observe, deduce and apply.

Lesson four

1. Basic fitness
2. Review backfist (with footwork moving in)
3. Teach the shin/knee kick against attacking opponent (might get a small bag to put in corner)
   • Attack: more water than whip
4. Teach obstructional kick (defense) against opponent's kick (without arching)
5. Introduce spin kick
   a. Lining up b. Leg close
   c. Step and spin attack
   • Attack: more water than whip

Lesson Five

1. Basic fitness
2. Review spin kick
   • As attack
   • Versus side kick (as counter)
   • Versus leg obstruction (as counter)

3. Backfist (attack)
  - With obstructional kick (attack)
  - With low feint (opponent right)
  - With lop sao (opponent left)
4. Obstructional kick (attack)
  - With hook kick
  - With side kick} opponent's fast retreat
  - With spin kick
  - With pak sao} closing kicking distance

Lesson six

General review I

1. Shin/knee obstructional
  a. Attacking (opponent in both right and left stance)
    - Direct kick • As obstruction
    - May be direct
    - May be broken rhythm
  b. Defense (opponent coming in both left and right stance)
    - As stop kick • As an obstructional kick
2. Backfist
  a. After stop-kick attack
  b. Right stance
  c. Left stance
3. Side kick
  a. Right to right
  b. Right to left
  c. After leg obstruction (opponent in • right • left)

Running

Leg flexibility

Sit-up and leg raises

Block for side kick

Block for hook kick
  - Side kick side step • Blocks for spin kick

Block for left thrust kick

Left punch

1. Block for right thrust
2. Block for right hook
3. Block for right backfist
4. Block for left cross
5. Block for left swing

Lesson seven

General review (II)

1. Hook kick
   a. Attack
   b. Versus straight lead
   c. Versus side kick
   d. Versus low obstructional
2. Straight lead
   a. Right-to-right attack
   b. Right-to-left attack
   c. Defense:
      1. Snap back
      2. Slanting right
3. Spin kick
   a. Attack
   b. Counter
   · Side kick · Low obstruction

Lesson eight

Combination kicking

1. Straight, side
2. Straight, rear
3. Hook, spin
4. Side, hook
5. Low side, high side

Lesson nine

Chi sao, plus the basic weapons.

Lesson ten

Chi sao, plus the basic weapons.

Why is it different?

1. The stress of simplicity and directness

2. The stress of nonclassical

3. The stress of health promotion/strength development (isometric)

4. More added values

ONE OF MY PERSONAL WORKOUT PROGRAMS

I did it this way, I trained my hands every Monday, Wednesday, and Friday—and my legs on the alternate days.

Stomach and waist (every day)
• Sit-up • Side bend • Leg raises • Flag • Twist • Back bend

Flexibility (every day)
• Front stretch • Side stretch • Hurdle stretch • Sit stretch • Sliding stretch • Front pulley stretch • Side pulley stretch

Weight training (Tuesday, Thursday, Saturday)
• Clean and press—2 sets of 8
• Squat—2 sets of 12
• Pullover—2 sets of 8
• Bench press—2 sets of 6
• Good morning—2 sets of 8
• Curl—2 sets of 8
   or
• Clean and press—4 sets of 6
• Squat—4 sets of 6
• Good morning—4 sets of 6
• Bench press—4 sets of 5
• Curl—4 sets of 6

Kicking (Tuesday, Thursday, Saturday)
• Side kick—right and left
• Hook kick—right and left

- Spin kick—right and left
- Rear front thrust—right and left
- Heel kick—right and left

Punch (Monday, Wednesday, Friday)

- Jab—speed bag, foam pad, top and bottom bag
- Cross—foam pad, heavy bag, top and bottom bag
- Hook—heavy bag, foam pad, top and bottom bag
- Overhand cross—foam pad, heavy bag
- Combinations—heavy bag, top and bottom speed bag
- Platform speed bag workout
- Top and bottom bag

Endurance (stationary cycling)

- Running (Monday, Wednesday, Friday)
- Cycling (Tuesday, Thursday, Saturday)
- Rope skipping (Tuesday, Thursday, Saturday)

Monday–Saturday (stomach and flexibility

- Bench leg stretch • Sit-up • Side leg stretch • Leg raises • Side bends
- Hurdle stretch • Flag • Sitting stretch
- Twist • Split stretch • Back bends • High kicking

Monday, Wednesday, Friday (hand techniques)

Bean Bag
- Right jab
- Right jab—foam pad
- Left cross

- Right hook—a. tight b. loose c. upward
- Overhand left
- Combination

Top and bottom speed bag
- Right jab • Left cross • Right hook • Overhand left • Combination
  • Platform speed bag—taper off

Tuesday, Thursday, Saturday (leg techniques)
- Right side pulley stretch
- Right side kick
- Left side pulley stretch
- Left side kick
- Right leading hook kick
- Left reverse hook kick
- Right heel kick
- Left spin back kick
- Left reverse front kick

1968 JANUARY	JANUARY 1968
18 11 a.m.–12:40 THUR. — STOMACH 1) SIT UP – 5 SETS 2) SIDE BENDS = 5 SETS 3) LEG RAISES – 5 SETS SKIPPING ROPE – 5 SETS LIGHT BAG — ONE-TWO 3 SETS HEAVY BAG — OVERHAND 3 SETS 3:20 — ONE-LEGGED SQUAT 2 ST. FOREARM/WRIST ISOMETRIC STANCE/SQUAT ISOMETRIC 3:45 – RUNNING (N) (rest knuckles for one day) — 黐手 — 5:30 – DINNER – THE GEE Kung Fu workout.	11:00 – PUNCH – 500 **19** FRI. 12:00 — 2:30 16 黐手 – CHUCK NORRIS 9 P.M — STOMACH : — SIDE BENDS — 5 SETS LEG RAISES — 5 SETS SIT – UP — 5 SETS FOREARM/WRIST ISOMETRIC STANCE / SQUAT – ISOMETRIC ONE-LEGGED SQUAT – 2 SETS LEG STRETCHING : — STAND — 1) straight. 2) side 3) knee out PUNCH SUPPLEMENT — 500 TOTAL — 1000 punch (obstacle on record knuckle

Tuesday, Thursday, Saturday (weight training)

• Clean and press • Squat • Bench press • Curl • Good morning

DAY	ACTIVITY	TIME
Monday	Stomach and Flexibility	7:00 AM–9:00 AM
"	Running	12:00 PM
"	Hand	5:30 PM–6:30 PM and 8:00 PM–9:00 PM
Tuesday	Stomach and Flexibility	7:00 AM–9:00 am
"	Weights	11:00 AM–12:00 PM
"	Leg	5:30 PM–6:30 PM and 8:00 PM–9:00 PM
Wednesday	Stomach and Flexibility	7:00 AM–9:00 AM
"	Running	12:00 PM
"	Hand	5:30 PM–6:30 PM and 8:00 PM–9:00 PM
Thursday	Stomach and Flexibility	7:00 AM–9:00 AM
"	Weights	11:00 AM–12:00 PM
"	Leg	5:30 PM–6:30 PM and 8:00 PM–9:00 PM
Friday	Stomach and Flexibility	7:00 AM–9:00 AM
"	Running	12:00 PM
"	Hand	5:30 PM–6:30 PM and 8:00 PM–9:00 PM
Saturday	Stomach and Flexibility	7:00 AM–9:00 AM
"	Weights	11:00 AM–12:00 PM
"	Leg	5:30 PM–6:30 PM and 8:00 PM–9:00 PM

Random thoughts on training

Exercises for functional power

• Legs
• Hands
• Elbows
• Knees

Basic strength:

• Arm
• Leg
• Big muscle groups

Exercises for speed

Repetition of simple techniques

• Combinations

Exercises for timing and coordination

Sparring

Exercises for flexibility

• Basic flexibility • Leg flexibility

Exercises for endurance

• Cardiovascular endurance (running)

• Punching and kicking (muscular) endurance

Exercises for agility

• Basic agility exercises with light weight

• Jumping with or without kicking

Exercises for basic fitness

a. Stomach

    • Sit-up • Leg raises • Side bend • Twist • Isometric (tensing, suction)

b. Leg

    • Squat • Isometric squat • Jumping squat (with weight)

c. Back

    • Deadlift • Forward three-ways bend

Nutrition and Rest

On leg training

Under normal circumstances, training our legs is more difficult than training our hands. The reason is because we use our hands more frequently in our daily lives. Moreover, when we punch, we can make use of the power of our waist. Thus, it consumes less energy. But footwork is different. A kick uses more energy. Also, the length of the bones of the legs is greater, so we have to bear more difficulties when we train our legs.

So many people concentrate on their hands and neglect the training of their legs. If our footwork and kicks are good, the area of attack will be widened. The attacking power of the legs is greater than fists. You will know it simply when you look at them—the legs are bigger than the arms. Although to train our legs is more difficult, if we train earnestly and patiently, the cartilage will be strengthened and we can use our legs more freely, we can succeed very soon.

I average around two hours a day practicing jeet kune do.

Jogging is not only a form of exercise to me, it is also a form of relaxation. It is my own hour every morning when I can be alone with my own thoughts.

I'm running every day, sometimes up to six miles.

"Sir, how can you be so fast?"
"In what?"
"I mean, how can I get my kick fast?"
"Kick faster."

It is much better to kick at the foam pad or something like that. Watch out with the side kick when air kicking too much because it's bad for the knee joint.

On hitting the heavy bag

The fact that the bag can't strike you back—"perfecting faults."

Always keep well covered and never leave yourself open for one moment.

The power of the punch and kick comes not, as so many people imagine, from the vigor with which the blow is struck, but by correct contact at the right spot at the right moment, and with feet and body correctly in position and balanced.

Move! Move! Move around the whole time, side-stepping, feinting, varying your kicks and blows to the movement.

Remember that the body is an integral part of the kick and punch, it is not only the leg and arm that delivers them.

Carelessness shows after delivering a blow.

A definite routine of kicks and blows—practice first for form, then for power.

The platform speed bag

Many people think of it as training apparatus for timing—it's actually for developing rhythm.

You don't hit like that.

Function: To keep the hands high; accustoming the shoulder muscles to the position and for the eye.

The top and bottom bag

The top and bottom speed bag teaches one to hit straight and fair and square—if hit on the side or top it will be erratic in its movements, and will tell the practitioner that he is not hitting straight.

Treat it like an opponent.

The almost instantaneous return of the bag to the face will soon teach you how, after having delivered the blow, to recover yourself quickly and get out of danger.

It requires more footwork than the platform speed bag; more variety—and one can also hit upward.

Part 6

BEYOND SYSTEM— THE ULTIMATE SOURCE OF JEET KUNE DO

THE ULTIMATE SOURCE
OF JEET KUNE DO

Jungar: From which sect do you come?
Cord: From myself.
Jungar: What is your acknowledged style of fighting?
Cord: My style.

My purpose in creating jeet kune do was not to compare with other branches of martial arts. Anything that becomes a branch would induce bad feeling. Once there is a formation of a branch, then things seem to stop. Students would labor for regulations and rules. Then the meaning of martial art would be lost. Even today, I dare not say that I have reached any state of achievement. I'm still learning, for learning is boundless.

Like a man's body, you would not say that your hand was better than your leg or vice versa; you have to coordinate the two, to use them both skillfully in order to produce a satisfactory result.

It is not a shame to be knocked down by other people. The important thing is to ask when you're being knocked down, "Why am I being knocked down?" If a person can reflect in this way, then there is hope for this person.

If you have mastered a system of gung fu, after you have mastered it, you have to let go of it and head for a higher level. Do not hold to what you have. It is like a ferry boat for people who want to get across waters. Once you have got across, never bear it on your back. You should head forward.

INTERCHANGABILITY
TOTALITY ———————> ~~CHANGE~~ EMPTINESS

SELF-KNOWLEDGE ——> TRUTH

ULTIMATE FREEDOM ——> TOTALITY

FLUIDITY ———————> INTERCHANGABILITY
SELF-KNOWLEDGE ——> AWARENESS
TOTALITY ——— ULTIMATE FREEDOM

I don't believe in system, nor in method. And without system, without method, what's to teach?

There must be emotional expression or emotional content in your technique.

Knowledge is of the past; learning is in the present, a constant movement, in relationship with the outward things, without the past.

The classical style moves and expresses in fragments. Be totally sensitive to arrive at "total movement."

When real feeling occurs, like anger, fear, etc., can one "express" himself with the classical method, or is he merely listening to his own screams and yells and mechanically performing his routine?

Is he a dead entity? Is he a living, expressive human being or merely a patternized mechanical robot?

Are you a flowing entity, able to flow with external circumstances, or are you resisting with your set choice pattern?

One can function freely and totally if he is "beyond system."

The man who is really serious, with the urge to find out what truth is, has no style at all. He lives only in what is.

Is your choice pattern forming a screen between you and the opponent and presenting you a "total" and "fresh" relationship with him?

When there is no center and no circumference then there is truth. When you freely express you are the total style.

Constant drilling on classical blocks and thrusts insensitizes oneself, making one's creativity duller and duller.

The unconventional attack is met in terms of one's chosen pattern of rhythmical classical block—the attack being broken rhythm—our defense or counterattack will always be lacking pliability and aliveness.

If any style teaches you a method of fighting, then you might be able to fight according to the limit of that method, and really that is not fighting as is.

NOTES

There must be emotional expression or emotional content in your technique

The classical man is just a bundle of routines, ideas, and express tradition. When he acts, he is translating every living moment in terms of the old.

It is indeed to see the situation simply. Our minds are very complex.

Knowledge is of the past; learning is in the present, a constant movement, in relation with the outward thing, without the past.

The classical man style moves and express in fragments. ——— Be totally sensitive to arrive at "total movement"

To express yourself in freedom, you must die to everything of tradition yesterday.

There is no such thing as doing right or wrong when there is freedom

∧

NOTES

When real feeling occurs, like anger, fear, etc. Can one "express" himself with the classical method, or is he merely listening to his own screams and yells, and mechanically performing his routine?

Is he a dead entity? Is he a living, expressive human being, or merely a patternized mechanical robot?

Are you a flowing entity capable to flow with external circumstance, or are you resisting with your set choiced pattern.

One can function freely and totally if he is "beyond system"

The man who is really serious, with the urge to find out what truth is, has no style at all. He lives only in what is.

Is your choice pattern forming a screen between you and the opponent and preventing you a "total" and "fresh" relationship with him.

When you aware completely there is no space for a conception, a scheme, an "I" and the "opponent", with complete abandonment.

When there is no center and no circumference then there is truth. When you freely express you ARE the total style

Constant drilling on classical block and thrusts insensitized oneself, making one's creativity duller and duller.

Fighting is not something dictated by your conditioning as a gung fu man, a karate man, a judo man, or whatnot.

Seeking the opposite of a system is to enter another conditioning.

At this moment stop inwardly—when you do stop inwardly, psychologically, your mind becomes very peaceful, very clear. Then you can really look at "this."

From the partial pattern we react and this reaction is mainly dead routine.

If you follow the classical pattern, you're understanding the routine, the tradition, the shadow—you are not understanding yourself.

How can one respond to the totality with partial, fragmentary pattern?

Classical forms dull your creativity, condition and render frozen your sense of freedom. You no longer "be" but merely "do."

Classical concentration is exclusion, whereas awareness is total and excludes nothing.

That state of mind can be understood by watching it but never trying to shake it, never taking sides, never justifying, condemning, or judging—which means watching it without any choice.

Physical and psychological totality. The classical man functions within the pattern of a style.

Jeet Kune Do 截拳道

Jun Fan Gung Fu

THE WRESTLER EXAMPLE

1) Non-Classical —— no classical postures
   SOLIDFY ONE'S FLUIDITY
   hand position, rigid body position, unrealistic footwork DISSECTING A CORPSE
   no rhythmical mess
   # two men co-operation
   # give boxing comparison (form, training etc.)
   # runner

2) Directness ——
   RESPOND LIKE AN ECHO
   FIT IN LIKE SHADOW TO OBJECT
   no passive defense
   we are offensive
   Everything is stripped to their essential
   #攻擊　　# the satisfaction of one's bare hand

3) Simplicity ——
   DAILY MINIMIZE INSTEAD
   OF DAILY INCREASE
   The three stages
   # the sculptor —— BEING WISE DOES NOT MEAN ADD ON
   # the throwing of an object

NO SIGN — DOOR LOCK — NO AFFILIATION WITH, NO TIDE —

The one unitary process, the total movement.

In the greater, the lesser is, but in the lesser, the greater is not.

When there is no thought derived from memory, experience, or knowledge, which are all of the past, there is no thinker at all.

It is when you are uninfluenced and die to your conditioning of the classical response that you can be aware of something totally fresh, totally new.

Classical drills deaden!

Understand this freedom, the freedom from the conformity of styles.

To free yourself, observe closely what you normally practice. Do not condemn or approve; merely observe.

Learning to exist in the now
Education: To discover, but not merely to imitate.

Living generally means living in imitation and therefore in fear.

Create immediately an atmosphere of freedom so that you can live and find out for yourselves what is true, so that you are able to face the world with the ability to understand it, not just conform to it.

Life itself is your teacher, and you are in a state of constant learning.

Freedom lies in understanding yourself from moment to moment.

An intelligent mind is one that is constantly learning, never concluding—styles and patterns have come to conclusion, therefore they ceased to be intelligent.

An intelligent mind is an inquiring mind. It is not satisfied with explanation, with conclusions; nor is it a mind that believes, because belief is again another form of conclusion.

Additional Notes on Jeet Kune Do

Jeet Kune Do is not a "method of concentration or meditation". It is "being", it is an "experience", a "way" that is "not a way"

Jeet Kune Do seeks "Enlightenment" which results from resolution of all subject-object relationships and oppositions in a pure void (that is not void) "ENLIGHTENMENT" is not an experience or activity of a thinking and self-conscious subject.

PURE BEING { Jeet Kune Do is the AWARENESS OF "PURE BEING" (beyond subject and object), an immediate grasp of being in its "THUSNESS" and "SUCHNESS" [Not "PARTICULARIZED REALITY"]

MIND is an ultimate reality which is aware of itself and is not the seat of our empirical consciousness —— by "being" mind instead of "having" mind. "NO MIND AND 'NO-MIND'" "NO FORM AND 'NO-FORM'"

convergence with all that IS

To think that this INSIGHT as a subjective experience "attainable" by some kind of process of mental purification is to doom oneself to error and absurdity —— "mirror-wiping zen"

Intelligence is the understanding of self.

Truth comes when your mind and heart are purged of all sense of striving and you are no longer trying to become somebody; it is there when the mind is very quiet, listening timelessly to everything.

The individual is of first importance, not the system. Manmade system.

Be "self-aware" rather than a repetitious robot.

Inward freedom, rather than mechanical efficiency.

To present a possible direction, nothing more.

The futility of maintaining a facade. To act in one way on the surface when actually experiencing something quite different.

Being oneself leads to real relationships.

Acceptance of feeling as is.

Since understanding is rewarding, it is most enriching to open channels for mutual communication.

Accept the other person's feeling.

The allowance of differences.

Priceless potentialities.

Don't be in a hurry to "fix things." Enrich your understanding in the process of discovery.

A good martial artist, not a "master."

A maturing martial artist, not a matured artist.

An actualizing artist, rather than an actualized master.

The function of jeet kune do is to liberate, not to bind.

Learning techniques without inward experiencing can only lead to superficiality.

What *is* is more important than what *should* be.

Forms are "protective isolation," where frozen movements are fixed—a solace for the fearful.

Self-expression is important.

Only the self-sufficient stand alone—most people follow the crowd and imitate.

"Being," giving expression, inwardly rich.

When one understands totality and fluidity, he does not search for partialized movements to create artificial flow.

Style is an isolating, self-enclosing activity.

To view totality one has to be a total outsider.

His technique is one entanglement of past conditioning.

Is his action the action of experience? Time-bound? Conditioned? Repetitious past?

Creative action, with sensitivity—that positive state of innocence.

The ultimate has no symbol, no style, no superhuman.

What is the point of education if you in yourself are not intelligent? If you are not creative? So education consists in cultivation of intelligence (not cunning, passing exams, etc.).

There is intelligence when you are not afraid. There can be no initiative if one has fear. And fear compels us to cling to tradition, gurus, etc.

The important thing for you is to be alert, to question, to find out, so that your own initiative may be awakened. Understanding.

The poorer we are inwardly, the more we try to enrich ourselves outwardly.

One must not merely copy but try to convey the significance of what you see.

Tradition = the habit-forming mechanism of the mind.

Sensitivity is not possible if you are afraid of this, that, etc.—the inner-authority game. Authority destroys intelligence.

To think about oneself all the time is to be insensitive, for then the mind and heart are enclosed and lose all appreciation of beauty.

Great freedom = great sensitivity.

There is no freedom if you are enclosed by:
1. Self-interest 2. Walls of discipline

Books, teachers, parents, the society around us, all tell us *what* to think, but not *how* to think.

What is the point of being educated, of learning to read and write, if you are just going to carry on like a machine? After all, it is merely the root to function from.

Real freedom is the outcome of intelligence (understanding).

The more we understand, the greater and deeper will be our contact with all that is around us.

The ultimate source of jeet kune do
The enlightenment

It is being itself, in becoming itself. Reality in its *isness*, the *isness* of a thing. Thus *isness* is the meaning—having freedom in its primary sense—not limited by attachments, confinements, partialization, complexities.

Morally
Teaches us not to look backward once the course is decided upon.

Philosophically
Treats life and death indifferently.

The abiding stage (letting go itself from itself)
The point where the mind stops to abide—the attachment to an object—the stop of the flow—not to get your attention arrested. To transcend the dualistic comprehension of the situation.

Prajna immovable
Prajna immovable is the destroyer of delusion. Not to move means not to "stop" with an object that is seen. "The one mind." "Nonassertiveness."

Any space between two objects where something else can enter.

The delusive mind is the mind intellectually and effectively burdened. It thus cannot move on from one move to another without stopping and reflecting on itself, and this obstructs its native fluidity—creating.

Fluidity is nonhindrance to follow its course like water.

Jeet kune do's aggressive mental training is not a mere philosophical contemplation on the effervescence of life or a frozen type of mold, but an entrance into the realm of nonrelativity and it is real.

The point is to utilize the art as a means to advance in the study of the Way.

To be on the alert means to be deadly serious, to be deadly serious means to be sincere to oneself, and it is sincerity that finally leads to the Way.

A struggle of any nature can never be settled satisfactorily until the absolute fact is touched—where neither opponent can affect the other. Not neutrality, not indifference, but *transcendence* is the thing needed.

Learning gained is learning lost.

The undifferentiated center of a circle that has no circumference: The jeet kune do man should be on the alert to meet the interchangeability of the opposites. But as soon as his mind "stops" with either of them, it loses its own fluidity. A jeet kune do man should keep his mind always in the state of emptiness so that his freedom in action will never be obstructed.

While walking or resting, sitting or lying, while talking or remaining quiet, while eating or drinking, do not allow yourself to be indolent, but be most arduous in search of "this."

Instead of looking directly into the fact, cling to forms (theories) and go on entangling oneself further and further, finally putting oneself into an inextricable snare.

We do not see *it* in its suchness because of our indoctrination, crooked and twisted.

Discipline in conformity with the nature.

The process of maturing does not mean to become a captive of conceptualization. It is to come to the realization of what lies in our innermost selves.

The great mistake is to anticipate the outcome of the engagement; you ought not to be thinking of whether it ends in victory or in defeat. Just let nature take its course, and your tools will strike at the right moment.

Jeet kune do
1. The absence of a system of stereotyped techniques.
2. The "fitting-in" spirit.

Technical skill is to be subordinate to the psychic training, which will finally raise the practitioner even to the level of high spirituality.

He is no more himself. He moves as a kind of automaton. He has given himself up to an influence outside his everyday consciousness, which is no other than his own deeply buried unconscious, whose presence he was never hitherto aware of.

To bring the mind into sharp focus and to make it alert so that it can immediately intuit truth, which is everywhere, the mind must be emancipated from old habits, prejudices, restrictive thought process, and even ordinary thought itself.

Three components

1. Absence of thought is the doctrine: and it means not to be carried away by thought in the process of thought—not to be defiled by external objects—to be in thought yet devoid of thought.
2. "Absence of stereotyped technique" as the substance in order to be total and free.
3. Nonattachment as the foundation.

All lines and movements are the function.

It is man's original nature—in its ordinary process, thought moves forward without a halt; past, present, and future thoughts continue as an unbroken stream.

"Absence" means freedom from duality and all defilements.

"Thought" means thought of thusness and self nature.

True thusness is the substance of thought and thought is the function of true thusness.

To meditate means to realize the imperturbability of one's original nature. Meditation means to be free from all phenomena and calmness means to be internally unperturbed. There will be calmness when one is free from external objects and is not perturbed.

True thusness is without defiling thought; it cannot be known through conception and thought.

There is no thought except that of the true thusness. Thusness does not move, but its motion and function are inexhaustible.

The mind is originally without activity; the Way is always without thought.

By knowledge is meant knowing the emptiness and tranquillity of the mind. Insight means realizing that one's original nature is not created.

Being empty means having no appearance, having no style or form to let opponent work on.

Being tranquil means not having been created in its thusness—not being created means not having any illusions or delusions.

Separation

It is inexpressible because as soon as one tries to express it, what one expresses is itself a thing, which means that by so doing one remains in the state of being linked with things.

Have no mind that selects or rejects. To be without deliberate mind is to have no thoughts.

There is no need to exert oneself in special cultivation outside the daily round of living. There is no difference between such enlightenment and what is ordinarily termed knowledge, for in the latter a contrast exists between the knower and the known, whereas in the former there can be no such contrast.

We are always in a process of becoming and nothing is fixed. Have no rigid system in you and you'll be flexible to change with the ever-changing. Open yourself and flow at once with the total flowing now.

The two diseases
1. One is riding an ass to search for an ass
2. One is riding an ass and being unwilling to dismount

It is basically a practice of resistance. Such practice leads to clogginess, and understanding is not possible, and its adherents are never free because the Way of combat is not based on personal choice and fancies. The truth of the Way of combat is perceived from moment

Jeet Kune Do

to moment, and only when there is awareness without condemnation, justification, or any form of indentification.

In this art, efficiency is anything that scores.

Many a martial artist likes "more," likes "different," not knowing that truth and the Way exhibit in the simple everyday movements. It is here they miss it. (If there is any secret, it is missed by seeking.) The physical bound goes for puffing and straining and misses the delicate way (the fan and the plug); the intellectual bound goes for idealism and the exotic and lacks the efficiency and actual seeing into realities.

The immovable mind

Do not be overconscious in sparring, or else you will be tied down—would rather teach them to advance one step rather than to think of retreating one step.

The five main points
1. The highest truth is inexpressible.
2. Spiritual cultivation cannot be cultivated.
3. In the last resort nothing is gained.
4. There is nothing much in the teaching.
5. In throwing punches and moving therein lies the wonderful Tao.

I wish neither to possess nor to be possessed.
I no longer covet paradise.
More important, I no longer fear hell...
The medicine for my suffering
I had within me from the very beginning,
But I did not take it.
My ailment came from within myself,
But I did not observe it.
Until this moment.
Now I see that I will never find the light
Unless, like the candle, I am my own fuel,
Consuming myself.

Express your self—not someone else

I mean, at least you can think there are different approaches [within martial art]. But each person must not limit himself to one approach. We must approach it with our *own* self, you know? Art is the expression of our own, unique *self*, whereas if you go to a Japanese style, for example, then you are expressing the Japanese style—you are not expressing yourself.

Martial art as self-expression

To me, ultimately, martial art means honestly expressing yourself. Now it is very difficult to do. I mean it is easy for me to put on a show and be cocky and be flooded with a cocky feeling and then feel, like, pretty cool and all that. Or I can make all kinds of phony things, you see what I mean? And be blinded by it. Or I can show you some really fancy movement—but, to express oneself honestly, not lying to oneself—and to express myself honestly—that, my friend, is very hard to do. And you have to train. You have to keep your reflexes so that when you want it—it's there! When you want to move, you are moving, and when you move you are determined to move. Not taking one inch, not anything less than that! It has to be that if I want to punch, I'm going to do it, man. And I'm *going to do it*! So that is the type of thing you have to train yourself into it, to become one with it. You think—it is.

An artist's expression is his soul made apparent, his schooling, as well as his "cool" being exhibited. Eliminate "not clear" thinking and function from your root.

"How can I be me?"

When I first arrived, I did "The Green Hornet" television series back in 1965 and as I looked around, man, I saw a lot of human beings. And as I looked at myself, I was the only robot there. I was not being myself. I was trying to accumulate external security; external technique, the way to move my arm, and so on. But I was never asking *what would Bruce Lee have done if*—the word "if"—*such a thing had happened to me*? When I look around, I always learn something, and that is: to always be yourself. And to express yourself, to have faith in yourself. Do not go out and look for a successful personality and duplicate him. That seems to me to be the prevalent thing happening in Hong Kong. They always copy mannerism, they never start from the very root of their being: that is, *how can I be me?*

We can see through others, only when we see through ourselves.

Don't court the flattery or approval of others

You see, I've never believed in the word *star*. That's an illusion, man, something the public calls you, you see. When you become successful, when you become famous, it's very very easy to be blinded by all these happenings. Everybody comes up to you and it's *Mister Lee*. When you have long hair they'll say "Hey, man, that's "in," that's the "in" thing. "But if you have no name, they all say "Boy, look at the disgusting juvenile delinquent!" I mean, too many people are "yes, yes, yes" to you all the time; so unless you realize what life is all about and that right now some game is happening, and realize that it is a game, fine and dandy, that's alright. But most people tend to be blinded by it, because if things are repeated too many times, you believe them. And that can become a habit.

Not every man can take lessons to be a good fighter. He must be a person who is able to relate his training to the circumstances he encounters. Self-actualization is the important thing. And my personal message to people is that I hope they will go toward self-actualization rather than self-image actualization. I hope that they will search within themselves for honest self-expression.

Daily thoughts to aid in self-actualization

At once absorbingly open
And rootily relaying one's

Captivating total presence
With appropriate inward time.
Be aware of aura of living: the well-balanced posture and hara.

Flow in the total openness of the living moment.

"Quality" of physical and movement reaction: sensitivity, flexibility, accuracy, power, smoothness, speed, agility—over all, dynamic!

Daily discovery and understanding is the process of growth and learning.

We live and not live for.

Be aware of illusion

Be flexible so you can change with change.

My only sure reward is *in* my actions and not *from* them. The quality of my reward is in the depth of my response—the centralness of the part of me I act from.

A goal is implied but the need seems to be for direction—to feel in the process of becoming.

When I listened to my mistakes I have grown.

There will never be means to ends, only means. And I am means. I am what I started with, and when it is all over I will be all that is left of me.

On cultivating the spirit

The cultivation of the spirit is elusive and difficult, and the tendency toward it is rarely spontaneous. When the opportunties for action are many, cultural creativeness is likely to be neglected. The cultural flowering of New England came to an almost abrupt end with the opening of the West. The relative cultural sterility of the Romans might perhaps be explained by their Empire rather than by an innate lack of genius. The best talents were attracted by the rewards of administrative posts just as the best talents in America are attracted by the rewards of a business career.

When man comes to a conscious vital realization of those great spiritual forces within himself and begins to use those forces in science, in business, and in life, his progress in the future will be unparalleled.

I feel I have this great creative and spiritual force within me that is greater than faith, greater than ambition, greater than confidence, greater than determination, greater than vision. It is all of these combined. My brain becomes magnetized with this dominating force which I hold in my hand.

Whether it is the godhead or not, I feel this great force, this untapped power, this dynamic something within me. This feeling defies description, and there is no experience with which this feeling may be compared. It is something like a strong emotion mixed with faith, but a lot stronger.

All in all, the goal of my planning and doing is to find the true meaning in life—peace of mind. I know that the sum of all the possessions I mentioned does not necessarily add up to peace of mind; however, it can be if I devote to real accomplishment of self rather than neurotic combat. In order to achieve this peace of mind, the teaching of detachment of Taoism and Zen proved to be valuable.

To think that this insight is a subjective experience "attainable" by some kind of process of mental purification is to doom oneself to error and absurdity—"mirror-wiping Zen."

It is not a technique of introversion by which one seeks to exclude matter and the external world, to eliminate distracting thoughts, to sit in silence emptying the mind of images, and to concentrate on the purity of one's own spiritual essence. Zen is not a mysticism of "introversion" and "withdrawal." It is not "acquired contemplation."

Do not separate meditation as a means (dhyana) from enlightenment as an end (prajna)—the two were really inseparable, and the Zen discipline consisted in seeking to realize this wholeness and unity of prajna and dhyana in all one's acts.

The three faults
1. The invention of an empirical self that observes itself
2. Viewing one's thought as a kind of object or possession, situating it in a separate, isolated "part of itself"—"I have" a mind.
3. The striving to wipe the mirror

This clinging and possessive ego-consciousness, seeking to affirm itself in "liberation," craftily tries to outwit reality by rejecting the thoughts it "possesses" and emptying the mirror of the mind, which it also "possesses"—emptiness itself is regarded as a possession and an "attainment."

There is no enlightenment to be attained and no subject to attain it.

Zen is not "attained" by mirror-wiping meditation, but by "self-forgetfulness in the existential 'present' of life here and now." We do not "come," we "are." Don't strive to become, but be.

The void (or the unconscious) may be said to have two aspects:
1. It simply is what it is.
2. It is realized, it is aware of itself, and to speak improperly, this awareness is "in us," or better, we are "in it."

It is to see things as they are and not to become attached to anything—to be unconscious means to be innocent of the working of a relative (empirical) mind—when there is no abiding of thought anywhere on anything—this is being unbound. This not abiding anywhere is the root of our life.

Prajna is not self-realization, but realization pure and simple, beyond subject and object.

To see where there is no something (object)—this is true seeing; the seeing is the result of having nothing to stand on. It is simply "pure seeing," beyond subject and object, and therefore "no-seeing."

Zen liberates the mind from servitude to imagined spiritual states as "objects," which too easily become hypostatized and turn into idols that obsess and delude the seeker.

Pure seeing

"Non-seeing" and "no-mind" are not renunciations but fulfillment. The seeing that is without subject or object is "pure seeing."

The direct awareness in which is formed "truth that makes us free"—not the truth as an object of knowledge only, but the truth lived and experienced in concrete and existential awareness.

There exists, in the martial art world, systems that are mechanical, classical, "no-soul." The intelligent people feel that such systems . . . are "frames" that can kill the life of freedom of expression by their too rigid limitation. They feel that such practices are merely "doing" and not "being." Instead of promoting inward experience, the routines and workouts are imitative repetition, a mere product. Furthermore, these people feel that an ideology is a mere projection of hope. If one loves, one need not have an ideology of love.

Freedom cannot be preconceived

Freedom is something that cannot be preconcieved. To realize freedom requires an alert mind, a mind that is deep with energy, a mind that is capable of immediate perception without the process of graduation, without the idea of an end to be slowly achieved.

The margin of freedom for the classical practitioner is getting narrower all the time.

There is no condemnation, no demand for a pattern of action in understanding. You are merely observing—just look at it and watch it. The perceiving mind is living, moving, full of energy, and only such a mind can understand what truth is.

Classical methods and tradition make the mind a slave—you are no longer an individual, but merely a product. Your mind is the result of a thousand yesterdays.

Life is wide, limitless—there is no border, no frontier.

Not conviction, not method, but perception is the way of truth. It is a slate of effortless awareness, pliable awareness, choiceless awareness.

The moment you have a center, there must also be a circumference; and to function from a center, within a circumference, is slavery.

It is an "altogether" feeling, without a center.

Wipe away and dissolve all its experience and be "born afresh."

It is not how he dresses—that's his own personal taste anyway—but what really counts is what is behind those clothes of the martial artist, don't you think?

Life is something for which there is no answer; it must be understood from moment to moment—the answer we find inevitably conforms to the pattern of what we think we know.

Simplicity is an inward state of being in which there is no contradiction, no comparison; it is the quality of perception in approaching any problem—it is not simply when the mind approaches any problem with a fixed idea of belief, or with a particular pattern of thought.

On meditation

A simple mind, surely, is one that functions, that thinks and feels without a motive. Where there is a motive, there must be a way, a method, a system of discipline. The motive is brought about by the desire for an end, for a goal, and to achieve that goal there must be a way, etc. Meditation is a freeing of the mind from all motives.

Acceptance, denial, and conviction prevent understanding—let your mind and the speaker's mind move together in understanding, with sensitivity, then there is a possibility of real communion with each other. To understand, surely, there must be a state of choiceless awareness in which there is no sense of comparison or condemnation, no waiting for a further development of the thing we are talking about in order to agree or disagree—don't start from a conclusion above all.

Require not just a moment of perception, but a continuous awareness, a continuous state of inquiry in which there is no conclusion.

A state of perception and nothing else—that is, a state of being.

Action is our relationship to everything.

Action is not a matter of right and wrong. It is only when action is partial, not total, that there is right and wrong.

Awareness works only if it is allowed free play without interference.

True art cannot be handed out

Time-wise, I wouldn't have time to teach, but I'm willing—when time permits—to honestly express or to "open myself" to you; to act as sort of a signpost for a traveler. My experience will help, but I insist and maintain that art—true art that is—cannot be handed out. Furthermore, art is never decoration or embellishment. Instead, it is a constant process of maturing (in the sense of not having arrived!). When we have the opportunity of working out, you'll see that your way of thinking is definitely not the same as mine.

Art, after all, is a means of acquiring "personal" liberty. Your way is not my way, nor mine yours.

So whether or not we can get together, remember well that art "lives" where absolute freedom is. With all the training thrown to nowhere, with a mind (if there is such a verbal substance) perfectly unaware of its own working, with the "self" vanishing nowhere, the art of JKD attains its perfection. This is just a short note to a fellow martial artist. "The process of becoming."

My followers in jeet kune do, do listen to this: All fixed set patterns are incapable of adaptability or pliability. The truth is outside of all fixed patterns.

Accumulation is self-enclosing resistance, and flowery techniques strengthen the resistance.

But can you neither condemn nor justify and yet be extraordinarily alive as you walk on? You can never invite the wind, but you must leave the window open.

Intensity and/or enthusiasm is this god within us—one that instinctively becomes the art of the physical "becoming" and within this transition we no longer care to know what life means. We are indeed furnishing the "what is" by simply being.

Intelligence is sometimes defined as the capacity of the individual to adjust himself successfully to his environment, or to adjust the environment to his needs.

Simplicity is the end of art, and the beginning of nature.

THINK ON THESE THINGS

Daily affirmations

Willpower

Recognizing that the power of will is the supreme court over all other departments of my mind. I will exercise it daily when I need the urge to action for any purpose; and I will form habits designed to bring the power of my will into action at least once daily.

Emotion

Realizing that my emotions are both positive and negative, I will form daily habits which will encourage the development of the positive emotions and aid me in converting the negative emotions into some form of useful action.

Reason

Recognizing that both my positive and negative emotions may be dangerous if they are not controlled and guided to desirable ends, I will submit all my desires, aims, and purposes to my faculty of reason, and I will be guided by it in giving expression to these.

Imagination
Recognizing the need for sound plans and ideas for the attainment of my desires, I will develop my imagination by calling upon it daily for help in the formation of my plans.

MEMORY
    Recognizing the value of an alert memory, I will encourage mine to become alert by taking care to impress it clearly with all thoughts I wish to recall; and by associating those thoughts with related subjects which I may call to mind frequently.

SUBCONSCIOUS MIND
    Recognizing the influence of my subconscious mind over my power of will, I shall take care to SUBMIT to it a clear and definite PICTURE OF MY MAJOR PURPOSE in life and all minor purposes leading to my major purpose, and I shall keep this PICTURE CONSTANTLY BEFORE MY SUBCONSCIOUS MIND BY REPEATING IT DAILY

CONSCIENCE
    Recognizing that my emotions often err in their over-enthusiasm, and my faculty of reason often is without the warmth of feeling that is necessary to enable me to combine justice with mercy in my judgments, I will encourage my conscience to guide me as to what is right or wrong, but I will never set aside the verdicts it renders, no matter what may be the cost of carrying them out.

Memory

Recognizing the value of an alert mind and an alert memory, I will encourage mine to become alert by taking care to impress it clearly with all thoughts I wish to recall and by associating those thoughts with related subjects which I may call to mind frequently.

Subconscious mind

Recognizing the influence of my subconscious mind over my power of will, I shall take care to submit to it a clear and definite picture of my major purpose in life and all minor purposes leading to my major purpose, and I shall keep this picture constantly before my subconscious mind by repeating it daily!

Conscience

Recognizing that my emotions often err in their overenthusiasm, and my faculty of reason often is without the warmth of feeling that is necessary to enable me to combine justice with mercy in my judgments, I will encourage my conscience to guide me as to what is right and what is wrong, but I will never set aside the verdicts it renders, no matter what may be the cost of carrying them out.

Things live by moving, and gain strength as they go.

> I have clearly written down a description of my DEFINITE CHIEF AIM in life, and I will never stop trying until I shall have developed sufficient self-confidence for its attainmen
>
> Bruce Lee

You will never get any more out of this life than you expect.

Keep your mind on the things you want and off those you don't.

Be a calm beholder of what's happening around you.

There is a difference—a. the world; b. our vision of or reaction to it.

Be aware of our conditioning; drop and dissolve our inner blockage.

Inwardly, psychologically, be a nobody.

We start by dissolving our attitude, not by trying to alter outer conditions.

No one can hurt you unless you allow him to.

See that there is no one to fight, only an illusion to see through.

On the need for a positive mental attitude

The aphorism "as a man thinketh in his heart, so is he" contains the secret of life. James Allen further added, "A man is literally what he thinks." This might be a shocking statement, but everything is a state of mind. I ran across some very interesting passages in a magazine and I'm writing them down to let you read it.

I am the captain of my mind

I've always been buffeted by circumstances because I thought of myself as a human being of outside condition. Now I realize that I am the power that commands the feeling of my mind and from which circumstances grow.

On joy and suffering

Joy and suffering are the fruit of right and wrong thinking. Suffering, especially, is mostly self-manufactured; we are never so happy or so unhappy as we suppose. To go one step beyond, according to Taosim, suffering and joy are one!

Defeat is a state of mind

Defeat is also a state of mind; no one is ever defeated until defeat has been accepted as a reality. To me, defeat in anything is merely temporary, and its punishment is but an urge for me to greater effort to achieve my goal. Defeat simply tells me that something is wrong in my doing; it is a path leading to success and truth.

Adversity as a bridge to self-knowledge

Since I'm talking on defeat and sorrow, I might mention the saying which states that "happiness is good for the body, but sorrow strengthens the spirit." In a time when everything goes well, my mind is pampered with enjoyment, possessiveness, etc. Only in times of adversity, privation, or mishap does my mind function and think properly of my state. This close examination of self strengthens my mind and leads me to understand and be understood.

On cultivating faith in oneself

Faith, too, is a state of mind. It can be induced or created by affirmation or repeated instructions to the subconscious mind through the principle of autosuggestion. This is the only known method of voluntary development of the emotion of faith. It is a well-known

fact that one comes, finally, to believe whatever one repeats to one's self, whether the statement be true or false. If a man repeats a lie over and over, he will eventually accept the lie as truth. More-over, he'll believe it to be the truth. Every man is what he is because of the dominating thoughts which he permits to occupy his mind.

I can if I think I can

Thus thoughts are things, in a sense that thought can be translated into its physical equivalent. I begin to appreciate now the old saying "he can because he thinks he can." I believe that anybody can think himself into his goal if he mixes thought with definiteness of pur-pose, persistence, and a burning desire for its translation into reality.

The garden of the mind

The mind is like a fertile garden, it will grow anything you wish to plant—beautiful flowers or weeds. And so it is with successful, healthy thoughts or with negative ones that will, like weeds, stran-gle and crowd the others. Do not allow negative thoughts to enter your mind for they are the weeds that strangle confidence.

Using visualization to rid your mind of negative thoughts

I'll give you my secret for ridding my mind of negative thoughts. When such a thought enters my mind, I visualize it as being written on a piece of paper. Then I mentally light it on fire and visualize it burning to a crisp. The negative thought is destroyed, never to enter my mind again.

Visualize success

Visualize success rather than failure, by believing "I can do it" rather than "I can't." Negative thoughts are overpowering only if you encourage them and allow yourself to be overpowered by them.

Intense desire creates opportunities

We are told that talent creates its own opportunities. But it sometimes seems that intense desire creates not only its own opportunities, but its own talents.

Don't become discouraged

Here I ask you, are you going to make your obstacles stepping stones to your dream, or stumbling blocks—because unknowingly you let negativeness, worries, fear, etc. take over?

It's not the obstacle—but your reaction to it!

Believe me that in every big thing or achievement there are always obstacles, big or small, and the reaction one shows to such obstacles is what counts, not the obstacle itself. There is no such thing as defeat until you admit so yourself—but not until then!

How to think of past, present, and future

My friend, do think of the past in terms of those memories of events and accomplishments which were pleasant, rewarding, and satisfying. The present? Well, think of it in terms of challenges and opportunities, and the rewards available for the application of your talents and energies. As for the future, that is a time and a place where every worthy ambition you possess is within your grasp.

Worrying is a waste of energy

Don't waste a lot of your energy in worry and anticipation. Remember my friend to enjoy your planning as well as your accomplishment, for life is too short for negative energy.

Sometimes a shock can serve as a motivational spur

So, action! Action! Never wasting energy on worries and negative thoughts. I mean who has the most insecure job as I have? What do I live on? My faith in my ability that I'll make it. Sure my back screwed me up good for a year but with every adversity comes a blessing because a shock acts as a reminder to oneself that we must not get stale in routine. Look at a rainstorm; after it's departure, everything grows!

Remember that one who is possessed by worry not only lacks the poise to solve his own problems, but by his nervousness and irritability creates additional problems for those around him. Well, what more can I say but *damn that torpedo, full speed ahead!!*

The four idea principles

1. Find a human need, an unsolved problem.

2. Master all of the essentials of the problem.

3. Give a new twist to an old principle.

4. Believe in your idea—and act!

Five-step idea-getting process

1. Gather materials.

2. Masticate the facts.

3. Relax and drop the whole subject.

4. Be ready to recognize and welcome the idea when it comes.

5. Shape and develop your idea into usefulness.

The power of ideas

There are two ways of making a good living. One is the result of hard work, and the other, the result of the imagination (requires work, too, of course). It is a fact that labor and thrift produce a competence, but fortune, in the sense of wealth, is the reward of the man who can think of something that hasn't been thought of before. In every industry, in every profession, ideas are what America is looking for. Ideas have made America what she is, and one good idea will make a man what he wants to be.

I know my idea is right, and, therefore, the results would be satisfactory. I don't really worry about the reward, but to set in motion the machinery to achieve it. My contribution will be the measure of my reward and success.

When you drop a pebble into a pool of water, the pebble starts a series of ripples that expand until they encompass the whole pool. This is exactly what will happen when I give my ideas a definite plan of action.

Probably, people will say I'm too conscious of success. Well, I am not. You see, my will to do springs from the knowledge that I *can* do. I'm only being natural, for there is no fear or doubt inside my mind.

Success comes to those who become success-conscious.

If you don't aim at an object, how the heck on earth do you think you can get it?

You learn a lot during teaching; however, seeing is not enough, you must do; knowing is not enough, you must apply.

All riches begin as a state of mind. And you have complete control of your mind.

To get one must give—there is never a something for nothing.

Form the habit of affirming one's definiteness of purpose in meditation at least once daily.

What you are is because of your habits of thought.

Your thought habits are subject to your control!

A dominating purpose—a definite plan.

Repetition of thought—emotionalized with burning desire.

Daily habitual practice—backed by faith.

Backed by persistence—guided by going the extra mile.

Ideas are the beginning of all achievement.

Any idea that is constantly held in the mind and emotionalized begins at once to clothe itself in the most convenient and appropriate physical form that is available.

A positive mental attitude attracts wealth.

Thoughts backed by faith will overcome all problems.

The dominating success-conscious has no time for thoughts of failure.

Recognize and use the spiritual power of the infinite.

Every circumstance of every man's life is the result of a definite cause—mode and control are yours.

Know where you are heading and prepare yourself as thoroughly and accurately by refining what is available.

The spiritual power of man's will removes all obstacles.

Something for something—never something for nothing.

Be proficient in your field as well as in harmony among fellow men.

Self-reliance—find your own need, your own qualification.

Defeat is not defeat unless accepted as a reality—in your own mind.

Regardless! Get what you want and no less! Go an extra mile and another extra mile.

Be a practical dreamer backed by action.

Action—silence is golden.

The law of averages—put in more, come out with more.

Going the extra mile is the stepping-stone for greater compensation.

The man who won't be licked, can't be licked.

From going the extra mile, one not only gains but also improves himself.

Put "going the extra mile" to work as part of one's daily habit.

The spirit of harmony. The oneness of the whole.

The power can be created and maintained through daily practice—continuous effort.

Take inventory of everyone with whom you have contact.

You can catch more flies with honey than with salt.

Reading—the mental food (specialized reading).

No one ever does anything with enthusiasm unless he benefits thereby—reward proportionately.

Enthusiasm attracts enthusiasm.

Faith is a state of mind that can be conditioned through self-discipline. Faith will accomplish.

Faith is the maintaining of the soul through which one's aims may be translated into their physical equivalent.

Faith makes it possible to achieve that which man's mind can conceive and believe.

The possession of anything begins in the mind.

Thoughts are things.

Your state of mind is everything.

Make at least one definite move daily toward your goal.

Build yourself around an atmosphere of prosperity and achievement.

Persistence—persistence—and persistence.

Every man today is the result of his thoughts of yesterday.

Faith backed by action—applied faith.

Your mental attitude is what counts.

What you *are* is because of established habits of thoughts and deeds.

Form the kind of habits that will lead to the major purpose.

The *intangible* represents the real power of the universe. It is the seed of the tangible.

He *is* because he *thinks* he is—positive or negative.

The spirit of the individual is determined by his dominating thought habits.

When you look after your thoughts, your thoughts will look after you—magnetize them with positiveness.

Habits are due to repetition.

Success is where aimless drifting ceases.

As the inner, so the outer.

The ego is fixed entirely by the application of self-suggestion.

The subconscious mind favors thoughts inspired by emotional feelings. It also gives preference to dominating thoughts.

The six-step creative method

1. Develop the creative *attitude*.
2. Analyze, to focus on the wanted *solution*.
3. Seek out and fill your mind with the *facts*.
4. Write down *ideas*, sensible and seemingly wild.
5. Let facts and ideas *simmer* in your mind.
6. Evaluate, recheck, settle on the *creative ideas*.

As the twig is bent, the tree's inclined

It cannot be that, when the root is neglected, what should spring from it will be well ordered.

Our doubts are traitors and make us lose the good we oft might win by fearing to attempt.

On obtaining happiness in work

In order that people may be happy in their work these three things are needed:

- They must be for it
- They must not do too much of it, and
- They must have a sense of success in it.

It is later than you think! Know yourself!!

Faith without work is death.

Stand not upon the order of going, but go at once.

A gentle answer can turn away wrath.

I respect faith, but doubt is what gets you an education.

Patience and gentleness is power.

Keep quiet and people will think you a philosopher.

Be slow of tongue and quick of eye.

Despair is the conclusion of fools.

Do you wish men to speak well of you? Then never speak well of yourself.

Self-conquest is the greatest of victories.

Without respect, love cannot go long.

The three most difficult things in life
The three things most difficult are
- To keep a secret
- To forget an injury
- To make good use of leisure

Never trouble trouble till trouble troubles you.

He who knows himself best, esteems himself least.

I'll not willingly offend, nor be easily offended.

What's amiss I'll stop to mend, and endure what can't be mended.

Endure and keep yourself days of happiness.

What is defeat? Nothing but education, nothing but the first step to something better.

Knowing is not enough; we must apply. Willing is not enough; we must do.

To tolerate is to insult.

The whole: unity is formless. Formless is unity.

Fluidity and emptiness are convertible forms.

The nature of water

Water is an example of wholeness without form; it can fill any container and yet it is substance without shape. Because it is formless, it permeates all.

To the "masters" and "experts" in America

1. If you would pass for more than your value, say little—it is easier to look wise than to talk wisely (acting wisely is, of course, even harder).
2. The unknown is always wonderful! These "masters" gather around them a mysterious veil of unknown sanctity, and men honor them as great masters!

3. Silence is indeed the ornament and safeguard of the ignorant.

4. The more he wants to pass at a value above his worth, the more he will keep his mouth shut; for once he talks or moves, people can judge him by the standard.

Damn the "15th degree" red-belt holders," the "honorary super-masters" and those "experts" that graduated from the advanced-super-three-easy-lessons courses!

Firmness/gentleness

What is gentleness? It is a pliable reed in the wind . . . it neither opposes nor gives way.

What is the highest state of yielding? It is like clutching water.

What is true stillness? Stillness in movement.

What is adaptation? It is like the immediacy of the shadow adjusting itself to the moving body.

You wish to know what is internal school and external school? Not two!

One should forget oneself and learn from others. One's attention is on the mind (imagination), not on the breath—not I'm doing, but *it's* doing. The body is following its own wisdom and is completely free from mental driving or direction.

To change with change is the changeless state.

The stillness in stillness is not the real stillness, only when there is stillness in movement does the universal rhythm manifest.

The flow of movements is in their interchangeability.

Nothingness cannot be confined; Gentleness cannot be snapped.

The nature of simplicity

A profound simplicity of common sense; the straightest, most logical Way.

A simpleton

Lays down no first law, takes everything that happens as it comes.

False teachers of the Way of life use flowery words.

The really great Zen artist states the utmost in the minimum of lines or effort. The closer to the source, the less waste there is.

Genius

The capacity to see and to express what is simple, simply!

> Not being tense but ready,
> Not thinking but not dreaming,
> Not being set but flexible
> Liberation from the uneasy sense of confinement

It is being wholly and quietly alive, aware and alert, ready for whatever may come.

Your mental attitude determines what you make of it, as stepping-stone or stumbling block.

Remember no man is really defeated unless he is discouraged.

It is not what happens that is success or failure, but what it does to the heart of man.

I want you to know that when the mean is in order, the end is ultimately inevitable.

Remember, success is a journey, not a destination.

Remember my friend, everything goes to those who aim to get. Low aim is the biggest crime a man has.

One will never get any more than he thinks he can get. You have what it takes. Look back and see your progress—damn the torpedo, full speed ahead!

I have found, after much soul-searching, that deep down what I honestly value more than anything else is quality: doing one's best in the manner of the responsibility and craftsmanship of a number 1.

Being yielding and devoted must not exclude strength, for strength is necessary to the softness if it is to be the helper of firmness.

If the receptive were to push ahead on its own initiative, it would deviate from its natural character and miss the way. By submitting to and following the creative, it attains its appropriate permanent place.

Caution in crediting, and reserve in speaking, and in revealing one's self to but a very few, are the best securities both of a good understanding with the world, and of the inward peace of our own minds.

Parting and forgetting? What faithful heart can do these? Never part without remembering and thinking of during one's absence. It may be that you will never meet again in life.

The string is broken and time passes on. Meet again we may, but will it be in the same way? With the same sentiments? With the same feelings? Rarely.

Remembrance is the only paradise out of which we cannot be driven away. Pleasure is the flower that fades, remembrance is the lasting perfume. Remembrances last longer than present realities; I have preserved blossoms for many years, but never fruits.

Don't regret the past, but make the most of the hours that last and don't worry over the day that is well on its way.

Don't gamble over a hard time, but know that the worst is the best in its prime.

Don't weaken in trouble, but lift up your spirits and efforts redouble.

Life is only a fleeting moment, if a dreamless day.

So while we may, let's snatch this moment and make it stay in the memory of a future day.

The good life is a process, not a state of being. It is a direction, not a destination.

The good life constitutes a direction, selected by the total organism, when there is psychological freedom to move in *any* direction.

Evaluation by others is not a guide for me.

A stunt man by day and a mechanic at night.

Notes on self-will
Self-will seems to be the only virtue that takes no account of man-made laws.

A self-willed man obeys a different law, the one law to hold absolutely sacred—the human law in himself, his own individual will. What does self-willed mean? Hell, isn't it the exact meaning of "having his own will?" Well, that's a start, knowing, above all, that indeed he is the captain of his soul, the master of his life. Now what causes such realization and, consequently, brings about a change in one's behavior is, "To be real, to accept responsibility for one's self." Realizing the fact that you simply "live" and not "live for."

We must accept the other person's feeling.

It becomes easier to accept the other person's feelings if one can first learn to accept one's own feelings.

Thus, being one's true, open self leads to true relationships—minus bullshit.

Random notes

It need not be an immediate reaction to what you have heard that requires an immediate evaluation or judgment, rather shouldn't an understanding of it, of the whole situation totally, suffice?

Do your best to understand the root in life and realize that the *direct* and the *indirect* are, in fact, a complementary *whole*.

Growth is the constant discovery and understanding in one's *process* of living.

Be flexible so you can change with change. Empty yourself! Open up! After all, the usefulness of a cup is in its emptiness.

Flow, my friend; flow in the *total openness* of the *living moment*.

So don't be in a hurry to "fix" things; rather, enrich your understanding in the ever-going process of discovery and finding more the cause of your ignorance.

> The sun sets low in the west; the farewell song is over,
> We are separating.
> Leaning on the sandalwood oar I gaze at the water,
> Far away, the sky. Far away, the loved one far away.
>
> Since you left, I know not whether you are far or near,
> I only know the colors of nature have paled
> And my heart is pent-up with infinite yearnings.

Leaning upon the single pillow,
I try to conjure up the Land of Dreams
where I may seek for you.
Alas! No dreams come, only the dim
lamplight fuses with the shadows.

My boat glides down the tranquil river,
Beyond the orchard which borders the
bank.
I leave you my poems.
Read them.
When the silence of the world possesses you,
Or when you are fretted with disquiet.

In order to go rowing in our boat we have waited
For the setting of the sun.

A slight breeze ripples the blue surface
And stirs the water lilies.
Along the banks,
Where the cherry blossoms fall like rain,
We watch a glimpse of strolling lovers.

Fierce desire pulls me
I yearn to tell them of passion.
Alas, my boat floats away
At the mercy of the moving current
My heart looks back in sadness.

Two swallows, and two swallows,
Always the swallows fly in couples.
When they see a tower of jade
Or a lacquered Pavilion,
One never perches there without the other.

When they find a balustrade of marble
Or a gilded window,
They never separate.

Rapidly my boat is gliding down the river,
Under a cloud-strewn sky.
I look into the water;
It is clear as the night.

When the clouds float past the moon,
I see them floating in the river,
And I feel as though I were rowing in the sky.
I think of my beloved
Mirrored so in my heart.

If I knew the cause of my ignorance, I would be a sage.

The usefulness of a cup is in its emptiness and the same can be said of a martial artist that has no form, and is therefore devoid of "style" because he has no preconceived prejudices with regard to combat, no likes or dislikes. As a result, he is fluid, adaptable and capable of transcending duality into one ultimate totality.

Like any art, martial art is ultimately self-knowledge. A punch or a kick is not to knock the hell out of the guy in front, but to knock the hell out of your ego, your fear, or your hang-ups. Once that is clear, then you can express yourself clearly.

Economical expressing—a way of liberation

A choice method is the cultivation of resistance, and where there is resistance there is no understanding. A well-disciplined mind is not a free mind.

"Fixed" forms can never bring freedom (fluidity). This type of "dead" training is not an adequate response to the ever-changing moment in combat. This ever-changing moment must be met newly, freshly, for the moment is always new.

Cultivation in classical forms is an impediment to truth, for forms are something that has not yet happened. How can a mind which is the result of partialized mechanical form understand the formless?

Self-knowledge (we give to student) does not leave a cumulative residue as memory. Self-knowledge is the discovery from moment to moment of the ways of the self in relationship to one's opponent.

As most people avoid facing what is in combat, there is built up an organization with rituals and stunts—as more and more of this "mess" accumulates, one is drifting further and further away from combat.

An established set style. Chained down. In bondage. Bound. It can never comprehend the new, the fresh, the uncreated. The means destroys the freshness, the newness, the spontaneous discovery.

If there is any secret, one must have lost it by striving for it. The truth is here but men want to decorate the simple truth—the snake with feet.

Ways to raise the pupil's mind above duality, to the absolute awareness which transcends it.

The root of jeet kune do

What we are after in JKD is the *root* and not the branches. The root is the real knowledge; the branches are surface knowledge. Real knowledge breeds "body feel" and personal expression. Surface knowledge breeds mechanical conditioning, imposes limitations, and squelches creativity.

The root is the fulcrum on which will rest the expression of your soul; the root is the "starting point" of all natural manifestation. If the root is right, so, too, will be all of its manifestations.

The roots are:
1. Physical ingredients
   - On-guard positioning
   - Footwork and movement
   - Postures in relaying force
2. Underlying ingredients
   - Balance
   - Economy of form
   - Intuitive expression of self in applying force and releasing speed
   - Organic quiet awareness—continuity of being
   - Totality in structure and consciousness of the *whole*

- Efficient mechanics
- Capability to regulate one's rhythm as with the opponent's, plus the ability to disturb same
- Strong, dominating aura to flow with or against the "harmonious unit"
- Having no public
- Sincerity and honesty
- To function from the root

Random thoughts

Gap of awareness—not introspection.

Choiceless awareness—do not condemn, do not justify.

Just watch choicelessly and in the watching lies the wonder. It is not an ideal, an end to be desired. The watching is a state of "being" already, not a state of "becoming."

What is art?

Art is communication of feelings.

Art must originate with an experience or feeling of the artist.

Adequate form requires individuality rather than imitative repetitiousness, brevity rather than bulkiness, clarity rather than obscurity, simplicity of expression rather than complexity of form.

Many of you know that I am a martial artist by choice, an actor by profession and, toward daily actualizing my potentiality through soulful discoveries and daily exercising (in my case), to become also an artist of life.

I regard acting as an art, much like my practice in martial art, because it is an expression of the self. Acting, like any profession, demands your wholehearted devotion, no ifs, ands, or buts about it.

As in the combative arts, to train a deliverer and make him ready, mentally and physically, is difficult enough, and to find one with just that right appropriateness and that rare quality of a dedicated artist can happen once in a blue moon.

Just what is an actor? Is he not the sum total of all that he is—his level of understanding, his capability to captivate the audience because he is real in the expression of his personal feelings toward what was required by the scene? You can spot such artists from ordinary ones like that. The American has a word for it, it's called charisma. What you see on the screen is the sum total of his level of understanding, his taste, his educational background, his intensity, etc.

Having gone through a lot of these ups and downs, I realize that there is no help but self-help. Self-help comes in many forms: daily discoveries through choiceless observation, honesty, as we always wholeheartedly do our best, a sort of indomitable, obsessive dedication and, above all, to realize that there is no end or limit to this, because life is simply an ever-going process.

The duty of a human being—in my personal opinion—is one who is transparently real, to simply be. In this world there are a lot of people who cannot touch the heart of the matter but talk merely intellectually (not emotionally) about how they would do this or do that; talk about it, but yet nothing is ever actualized or accomplished. Of course we have many others and we can go into a few.

Notes on self-expression

Among people, a great majority don't feel comfortable at all with the unknown—that is, anything foreign that threatens their protected daily mold. So, for their sake of security, they construct chosen patterns to justify.

To be a martial artist means and demands absence of prejudice, superstition, ignorance, and all that—the primary, essential ingredient of what a quality fighter is and leave the circus acts to the circus performers. Mentally, it means a burning enthusiasm with neutrality to choose to be.

Martial art, acting, and life in general

I am sure most people dislike the unknown and will think that, unlike the lower animals, we are indeed intelligent beings. However, the problem is one where some people have a self, most people have a void, because they are too busy in wasting their vital creative energy to project themselves as this or that—dedicating their lives to actualize a concept of what they should be like rather than to actualize their ever-growing potentiality as human beings; a sort of "being" versus having—that is we do not "have" mind, we are simply mind. We are what we are.

Once the intelligence issue is established, I wonder how many of us have really gone through the trouble of reexamining all these so-called ready-made intelligent answers that are constantly crammed down our throat ever since heaven knows how long. Maybe starting from our first sign of capacity to learn. Yes, we possess a pair of eyes, the function of which is to observe, to discover, etc. Yet many of us simply do not really see in the true sense of the word. I must say that when the eyes are used externally to observe the inevitable faults of other beings, most of us are rather quick with readily equipped condemnation. For it is easy to criticize and break down the spirit of others, but to know yourself takes maybe a lifetime. To take responsibility of one's actions, good and bad, is something else. After all, all knowledge simply means self-knowledge.

Forces (when viewed from totality)
a. Fitting in with crispy force—with uncrispiness.
b. Fitting in with uncrispy force—with crispiness.

Obstacles in the way of knowledge
In the long history of martial art, the instinct to follow and imitate seems to be inherent in most martial artists, instructor and student

alike. This can be due partly to being human, and partly because of the patterns of styles (consequently to find a refreshing, original master teacher is a rarity nowadays). Ever since the establishment of institutes, academies, schools, kwoons, and their stylized instructors, the need for a "pointer of the Way" is echoed.

In conclusion

Each man belongs to a style which claims to possess truth to the exclusion of all other styles, and these styles become institutes with their explanations of the Way, dissecting and isolating the harmony of firmness and gentleness, establishing rhythmic forms as the encyclopedia of particular techniques. All goals, apart from the means, are therefore an illusion, and becoming is a denial of being. By an error repeated throughout the ages, truth, becoming a law or a faith, places obstacles in the way of knowledge. Method, which is in its very substance ignorance, encloses it within a vicious circle. We should break such circles not by seeking knowledge, but by discovering the cause of ignorance.

A PARTING THOUGHT—IN MY OWN PROCESS

Any attempt to write a "meaning-ful" article on how I, Bruce Lee, feel and think or express myself, is first of all a very difficult task, because I am still in my own process of learning, constantly discovering and constantly growing.

As though this assignment is not tough enough, I am in the midst of preparing my next movie, *Enter the Dragon*, a coproduction between Concord and Warner Bros., plus another Concord production, *The Game of Death*, which is only halfway done. I have been busy and occupied with mixed emotions as of late.

Of course, this writing can be made less demanding should I allow myself to indulge in the usual manipulating game of role cre-ation. Fortunately for me, my self-knowledge has transcended that, and I've come to understand that life is best to be lived—not to be conceptualized. I am happy because I am growing daily and hon-estly don't know where my ultimate limit lies.

To be certain, every day there can be a revelation or a new discovery that I can obtain. However, the most gratification is yet to come: to hear another human being say "Hey, now here is some-thing real!" Oh I know, I am not called in to write any true confession, but I do want to be honest, that is the least a human being can do.

Basically, I have always been a martial artist by choice, and an actor by profession. But, above all, I am hoping to actualize myself to be an artist of life along the way. By martial art, I mean like any art, it is an unrestricted athletic expression of an individual soul. Oh yes, martial art also means daily hermitlike physical training to upgrade or maintain one's quality. However, martial art is also about unfolding the bare human soul, that is what interests me.

Yes, I have grown quite a bit since the day when I first became a martial artist and am still growing along the process. To live is to express oneself freely in creation. Creation I must say is not a fixed something, a solidification.

So I hope my fellow martial artists would open up and be transparently real, and I wish them well in their own process of finding their cause.

—Bruce Lee

Walk On

INDEX

ABC (attack by combination), 119
ABD (attack by drawing), 123
abiding stage, 340
adjustment, close-range and long
    range, 144
advance, in fencing, 253
aikido, 20, 44, 264
all-infighting, 139
Allen, James, 362
arm(s): aggressive actions on, 108, 172;
    importance of, 182; in simple
    attack, 104
arrogance, 22, 32
Art of War (Sun Tzu), 32
attack(s): components of successful, 95–
    97, 107–108, 109, 141; defense
    and, 140; dynamic, 65–66; factors
    in, 100, 261; function of, 102–103;
    as gamble, 68; opponent and, 66,
    330; simplicity in, 106
    techniques of: covering, 116; 143;
        footwork in, 189–90; on oppo-
        nent's preparation, 100–102, 105,
        107; preparation of, 96, 125–26;
        technique of (boxing), 249; timing
        of, 66, 154, 187; varying, 89–90
    types of: broken-time, 107; by com-
        bination (ABC), 119, 120–22;
        compound, 96; direct, 127–28; by
        disengagement, 105, by drawing
        (ABD), 123; the five ways of, in
        JKD, 103–25; hand, 123–26;
        hand-immobilization, 111; indirect,
        68; leg, 126–27; low-line, 257, 266;
        progressive indirect, 114–18; re-
        newed, 181; running, 257; from
        stance, 186; in tempo, 178; two-
        feint, 103
attention, distracting, 30
attitude, use of, 157, 362
authority, 339; in boxing, 209
autosuggestion, 363
awareness: in attack, 101; choiceless, 58,
    333, 357, 386; continuous, 357,

385; defensive, 173–74; gap of,
386; of pure being, 62; of self, 336;
of the now, 64, 334; unconscious,
36, 355; visual, 30, 364

back, in sparring, 25
back elbow, 243
backfist, 229–32; extended, 241
Baker, Robert, 49
balance, 87, 99, 125, 135, 193, 195, 201,
    385
Black Belt Hall of Fame, 47
Blake, William, 15
block, 115–16
blows: avoiding, 69; basic, 157–58; bent-
    arm, 248; triple, 160
bluff, 23, 106
bob, 165; and weave, 166, 197. See
    also body sway
body, use of, 63, 64, 182, 251–52, 324
body feel, 146, 149, 154, 156, 172, 174,
    182, 385
body harmony, in sparring, 25
body power, full, 211
body sway, 119, 166. See *also* bob and
    weave
boxing: 28, 47; attack in, 119; Chinese,
    20, 37, 264; counters, 250; essence
    of, 45; hand techniques, 252–53; in
    JKD, 56; leads, 250; lessons from,
    247–53; rules of, 37; Thai, 39, 40,
    51–54; Western, 37, 40, 44,
    120–22, 208
broken rhythm, 25, 57, 107, 125, 143
by-jong position, 309–10

cadence, 88–89, 99, 100, 105, 107, 143,
    164
Cadwell, Linda Lee, 8–9, 12, 16
challenges, function of, 32–33
change beat, 126
chi sao, 115
chin, 184
Chinese Connection, The, 49
circular parry, 172–73
clans, 21
clawing, 156
close guard, 184
close-range factors, 141

nonclassical emphasis of, 61, 317; origin and development of, 47–64, 56; power of, 31; principles of, 160, 317, 347, 343–45; schools of, 59; stages of, 160; strategies of, 65–181; and Thai boxing, 51–54; title of, 49–51, 54; ultimate source of, 327–58, 385

jogging, 323

joint locks, 37, 80, 137

judo, 20, 28, 39, 40, 41, 264, 295, 332

Jun Fan Gung Fu Institute, 298

Jun Fan method, 51, 299

karate: 20, 36, 40–41, 264, 332; Korean, 20

katas, 27

kendo, 44

kick and hand combinations, 149, 240

kick(ing)
    aspects of: body in, 324; combinations, 149, 240, 287; factors, 282; in jeet kune do, 26, 70–72, 158; meaning of, 290–91; from on-guard position, 185, 287–88; power of, 324; training, 290, 318–19
    types of: back, 74; crescent, 281; direct-to-the-path, 150; groin, JKD, 71, 263, 267, 290; groin hook, direct-speed, 150; heel, 72; high hook, 150; high reverse hook, 150; hook, 68, 71, 149, 273–77; lateral circular heel, 283–84; lead shin/knee, 263–67; leading hook, 275–76; leading straight, 71, 267; parallel side, 70; rear, 280; rear spin, 280; reverse hook, 277; reverse straight, 72, 284–85; reverse turning, 283; shin/knee counter stop, 150; side, 56, 68, 70, 268–72; spinning back, 71, 285–87; sweeping, 278–80; turning, 282–83; upward side, 70–71; vertical hook, 275

Kimura, Taky, 52

knee: in forward stance, 265; in gung fu, 37; as striking weapon, 74, 75, 142, 154; thrust, 288–90; vulnerability of, 264–65, 323

Krishnamurti, 143

lateral circular heel kick, 283–84

lead arc swing, 245–46

lead elbow hook, 243

lead left: 218–21; to body, 210–20; factors, 221; straight, 219

lead punch: 210–21; advantages of, 212–13; as defensive weapon, 210; essentials of, 213–14; initiating, 213; as offensive weapon, 210; speed and deception in, 211

lead right: 214–18; to body, 215–16, 217–28; counters to, 216–17; factors, 215; high/low, 218

lead shin/knee kick, 263–67

leading finger fan, 239

leading right finger jab, 238–39

leading straight, 144

leading straight kick, 267

leading upward knee thrust, 288–89

leads, boxing, 250

Lee, Brandon, 12

Lee, Bruce: ability of, 33; as actor, 8, 52, 349–50, 387, 391; character of, 10; death of, 8; first mass fight of, 80–85; illness of, 8, 11, 15–16; and JKD, 47; as martial artist, 391–92; private lesson plan of, 309–17; as teacher, 20–21, 47, 298; workout programs of, 318–25; as writer, 15, 16–17, 247

Lee, James, 52

Lee, Shannon, 12

left cross, 151–52, 233–34

left reverse spin blow, 242

left-stancer parrying, 171, 173

leg-immobilization attack, (LIA), 111, 112

leg: in attack, 68, 126–27; and hand, co-ordination of, 327; importance of, 182; movements, speed of, 156; obstructing, 126; in PIA, 117; technique, training in, 320, 322–23; throw, 76, 79

Leonard, Benny, 196

lesson plans (JKD), 300–306

Lewis, Joe, 53

Little, John, 11–12

long bag, 290

long-range combat techniques, 136–37, 152

Jeet Kune Do

TO THE READER

A portion of the proceeds derived from the sale of this book will go to benefit both the Bruce Lee & Brandon Lee Medical Scholarship Endowment at the University of Arkansas and the Brandon Bruce Lee Drama Scholarship at Whitman College in Walla Walla, Washington. If you would like to make your own contribution to these two very worthy causes, we encourage you to write or call:

University of Arkansas

4301 West Markham #716
Little Rock, AK 72205–7199
(501) 686–7950

Whitman College

Development Office
Walla Walla, WA 99362
(509) 527–5165

For further authentic information on Bruce Lee or the art and philosophy of Jun Fan jeet kune do, please write to:

The Jun Fan Jeet Kune Do Nucleus

967 E. Parkcenter Boulevard
Box 177
Boise, Idaho 83706

For information on other titles in the Bruce Lee Library, please write to:

TUTTLE PUBLISHING
364 Innovation Drive
North Clarendon, VT 05759-9436
(802) 773-8930